JUL -- 2002

The Recruitment of Political Leaders:
A Study of Citizen-Politicians

The Urban Governors Series

The Recruitment of Political Leaders: A Study of Citizen-Politicians

Kenneth Prewitt
University of Chicago

The Bobbs-Merrill Company, Inc.
Indianapolis
New York

Heinz Eulau, Stanford University
Kenneth Prewitt, University of Chicago
Coeditors, The Urban Governors Series

Copyright © 1970 by The Bobbs-Merrill Co., Inc.
Printed in the United States of America
Library of Congress Catalog Card Number 72–99162
First Printing

To My Parents

Preface

This study, like the others in *The Urban Governors* series, is based on data collected by the City Council Research Project, Institute of Political Studies, Stanford University. The CCRP was a collaborative research and research-training program made possible by grants from the National Science Foundation. Members of the project, all at one time or another doctoral candidates in political science at Stanford, were Betty H. Zisk, Boston University; Ronald Loveridge, University of California; Robert Eyestone, University of Minnesota; Peter A. Lupsha, Yale University; Thomas E. Cronin, University of North Carolina; Gordon Black, University of Rochester; Katherine Hinckley, Rice University; Stephen Ziony, City University of New York; Charles F. Levine, University of Illinois at Chicago Circle; and Helmut Kramer, Institute for Advanced Studies, Vienna. Heinz Eulau, Stanford University, served as principal investigator and Kenneth Prewitt, University of Chicago, served as associate investigator.

Although the CCRP was centrally directed, each investigator contributed to the design of the research and was free to utilize the commonly collected data as he saw fit. Each monograph in this series, therefore, reflects the writer's own theoretical and substantive interests, and each writer is alone responsible for what he has written. Yet, the series as a whole constitutes more than the sum of its parts. At the heart of the project was a concern with decision-making in small, natural-state legislative groups. Decisions coming out of city councils have far-ranging consequences for the lives of residents in a metropolitan region. While the project's central focus was on legislative behavior within the city council, topics as diverse as problems of metropolitan integration or the socialization and recruitment experiences of individual councilmen became matters of inquiry. As a result, the individual monographs in this series are variously linked not only to the literature on legislatures and representation, but also to the literature on urban government, policy outputs, elections, interest group politics, and other aspects of political life.

The "web of government" is complex, and its complexity makes for complex analysis. We solved the problem of complexity in the real world of politics by dividing the analytic labor among the project's members, and it is for this reason that each volume in this series must stand on its own feet. But we would also insist that each volume contribute to the common enterprise of managing the intricacy of political life without imposing on it any fashionably simple model of what politics is all about. In general, the units of analysis used in the different monographs are individual councilmen. A comprehensive study based on councils rather than on councilmen as units of analysis is also in preparation.

The major source of data was interviews conducted with 435 city councilmen in eighty-seven cities of the greater San Francisco Bay region during 1966 and 1967. A description of the research site, research design, interview success, and related matters can be found in the Appendix. Some of the interviews were conducted by the members of the research team, but the bulk were undertaken by a group of professional interviewers including Jean J. Andrews, Sheryl Brown, Marion N. Fay, Helen M. Smelser, Sofia K. Thornburg, Mary E. Warren, and Betty E. Urquhart. Peter Lupsha served as field coordinator, Jean Stanislaw as research aide, and Virginia Anderson as project secretary. During the analytical phase of the project, we have had the help of Sally Ferejohn as research assistant, Tex Hull as computer adviser, and Lois Renner as secretary.

The author of this volume would like to express his appreciation as well to Robert Peabody, who critically read an earlier version of the manuscript.

Heinz Eulau
Kenneth Prewitt

Contents

List of Tables

List of Figures

Chapter 1

From the Many Are
Chosen the Few

In political life, some men lead and other men follow. There can be no organized community life without hierarchy and no hierarchy without ranking. Ranking, in turn, implies that some lead and others are led; or, in language more appropriate to this study, some men govern and other men are governed. Thus, all communities having an organized social life by definition have governors. Whatever the community's wealth, size, permanence, or purpose, a few of its citizens are always called upon to govern the remainder.

This axiom figures prominently in social theories as divergent as those of Marx and Mosca, Pareto and Plato, Madison and Machiavelli. Actually, two axioms are involved, the second implicit in the first. One axiom states that members of the political society possess unequal amounts of political power. With Pareto, we say, "Every people is governed by an elite, by a chosen element in the population."[1] The second axiom is that the few control (or govern) the many. With Laski, we say, "What, as a matter of history, can alone be predicted of the state is that it has always presented the striking phenomenon of a vast multitude owing allegiance to a comparatively small number of men."[2] The struggle of some democratic theorists to keep these axioms separate in the hope of showing that political society is possible without political elites has been put to rest (several times) by both the inescapable facts of

---

[1] V. Pareto, *Mind and Society* (New York: Harcourt, Brace & Co., 1935), p. 246.
[2] Harold Laski, *Grammar of Politics* (London: G. Allen & Unwin, 1925), p. 21.

1

history and the persuasive logic of such theorists as Michels and
Mosca. As Mosca writes in a famous passage:

> In all societies—from societies that are very meagerly developed and have
> barely attained the dawnings of civilization, down to the most advanced
> and powerful societies—two classes of people appear—a class that rules and
> a class that is ruled. The first class, always the less numerous, performs all
> political functions, monopolizes power and enjoys the advantages that
> power brings, whereas the second, the more numerous class, is directed and
> controlled by the first. . . .[3]

Scholars have posed many questions about the historical fact so
aptly summarized by Mosca. We find, for instance, some scholars
wanting to know *why* there are governing elites. What social and
psychological and economic conditions of human life account for
the inevitability of the few governing the many? Marx in part
formulates the "why" question in his inquiry into understanding
whether history might eventually lead to the withering away of the
state, and thus of a ruling class. Most scholars, however, take the
existence of governing elites for granted and ask how the few are
selected, on whose behalf they rule, and what social functions they
perform. The rich literature in political sociology of the late nineteenth and early twentieth century is largely concerned with these
questions: Weber, Mosca, Pareto, Michels, and, for American political science, Lasswell, ask not why there are political elites, but
what are the consequences of how they are selected and how they
rule. A third set of questions reflects normative concerns: What is
the best way to select the few and to organize the relationship between ruled and ruler?

Of these three types of questions about governing elites—causal,
functional, and normative—the second set guides my efforts in this
study. The causal question is bypassed by accepting as axiomatic
that the few will govern the many. The normative question is not
completely ignored, but no systematic attempt is made to assess
whether the public officeholders studied here are the best qualified
of all possible officeholders in their communities. Dismissing the
causal and the normative issues does not, however, narrow the
topic enough. Within the range of questions remaining, I concentrate on leadership selection. I examine the social and political
processes through which eighty-seven political communities select
from among large populations the few citizens who occupy the
important public offices.

---

[3] Gaetano Mosca, *The Ruling Class*, translated by Hannah D. Kahn (New York:
McGraw-Hill Book Co., 1939), p. 50.

In the vocabulary of elite analysis, this is known as the question of political recruitment. As will shortly be apparent, however, I broaden this into the more comprehensive topic of *leadership selection*. At the same time, the study is narrowed, since the research site is limited to democracies—that is, to political communities where the vote is critical in selecting from among the many the few who are to rule.

Governing bodies flourish in the United States. There are legislative, executive, judicial, and hybrid types. They operate at the federal, state, regional, district, and local levels. The Bureau of the Census reported 91,236 separate governmental units at the beginning of 1962. California alone, the site of the present study, has 57 county governments, 373 municipal governments, more than 15,000 school districts and nearly 2,000 other special districts. The thousands of governing units in the United States are filled with thousands upon thousands of persons who annually make millions of decisions affecting the lives of all community members.

The nearly 100,000 governing units in the United States share two common features. First, they must be constituted. That is, constitutionally defined offices have to be filled, else the operations of government would cease. It is the selection of the particular persons to fill elective political posts that transforms a government unit from a set of specifications embedded in a legal code into a governing body. Some of these governing units are large and complex, others small and simple; some have a wide range of powers, others only a few; some operate with nearly unlimited resources, others with very restrictive budgets; some are relatively autonomous authorities, others dependent and constrained. They hold in common, however, responsibilities for regulating the behavior and committing the resources of some population. We say they govern.

The second feature common to all these governing bodies is that they comprise but a tiny fraction of the total population. All forms of government have this attribute. Whether governors hold power by virtue of the consent of the many, through arbitrary usurpation, or owing to long established tradition, and whether the governed look upon their governors with pride, indifference, or hostility, the governors are few in comparison with the populations they govern. From a national population of nearly 200 million in the United States, several hundred occupy the important government posts at the national level; from a state population of 10 million, about 180 men hold the important state level elective posts in Ohio; from a city population of 3.5 million, 50 Chicago aldermen are selected; from a village population of 7,500, 5 men serve on the Jerseyville village board. Whatever else government may mean, it certainly demonstrates that the available political offices number some small fraction of the population of the community being governed. Bryce writes:

> In all assemblies and groups and organized bodies of men, from a nation down to a committee of a club, direction and decisions rest in the hands of a small percentage, less and less in proportion to larger size of the body, till in a great population it becomes an infinitesimally small proportion of the whole number. This is and always has been true of all forms of government, though in different degrees.[4]

Leadership Selection Processes

Let us assume the following situation. A community of fifty thousand citizens—call it a city, a district, a state, a nation or whatever—is to be governed by a group of fifty of its members. By some process, one person out of a thousand citizens will be selected to governing office. It is this process that interests us here. We examine the process empirically with data collected from 435 councilmen in eighty-seven nonpartisan cities of the San Francisco Bay Area. (These data, and some of their limitations, are more fully discussed in the Appendix. Readers unfamiliar with nonpartisan city councils are urged to read the Appendix before continuing with the book.)

Selecting the few who will govern from the many who are governed is a generic political process. It has repeated itself in hundreds of thousands of communities countless times throughout history. All we need do is supply the name of a political community—the city of Istanbul, the district of Bukedie, the state of California, the nation of Sweden—and provide actual population figures, as well as identify the legally defined government posts to be filled, and we will have discovered the setting for leadership selection.

The hypothetical situation reveals more clearly the axiom of this research. Large collections of individuals select smaller groups to act on their behalf. When the larger group, the population, expects the smaller group, the authorities, to regulate behavior and commit resources we say that government is established.

It is no accident that the classical definitions of government stress the processes by which the smaller group of leaders are con-

---

[4] J. Bryce, *Modern Democracies* (New York: Macmillan Co., 1924), p. 542.

stituted from the larger group of citizens. For example, we are told that democracy differs from monarchy in its method of "leadership selection." The same measuring rod is used to distinguish the aristocracy from the meritocracy or to differentiate other forms of government. For political theorists, often the characteristic most central to typing forms of government is the mode by which a relatively small group of persons comes to hold positions of political authority.[5] History provides various examples of leadership selection processes. We can borrow from the list found in Keller's *Beyond the Ruling Class* to suggest the more frequently encountered types of leadership selection.[6] Of course, these are theoretically "pure" types; empirical cases will be certain combinations of several types.

(a) Biological reproduction: most dramatically witnessed in forms of hereditary monarchies. The scepter is handed down through the family lines, usually following the principle of primogeniture. (b) Co-optation and appointment: an elite group designates its own successors. The elite group often exercises considerable latitude in sponsoring careers and controlling entry points into political office. (c) Selection by rote or lot: a deliberately random method for selecting leaders from among a group of presumed peers. In a rote system, each member of the collectivity takes a turn; in a lot system, some random device is employed to designate the leaders. (d) Purchase of office: seldom a consciously chosen system but, with some modification, it is an aspect of leadership selection which probably appears more frequently than we care to admit. In the United States, the combination of heavy campaign contributions and subsequent patronage positions in machine politics is a clear case. (e) Forcible appropriation: best evidenced in succession to leadership following a *coup d'état*. An unstable but certainly not unusual pattern of elite selection. (f) Apprenticeship and examination: there is a heavy emphasis on achievement criteria. The incumbent undergoes a generally extensive training

---

5 Lasswell and Kaplan write, "What is important, and what varies from one body politic to another, is the set of principles according to which the elite is recruited." They go on to note that a political system can be said to be egalitarian or inegalitarian depending on recruitment criteria. "A rule is defined to be egalitarian, not in the degree to which *power* is equally distributed, but rather *access* to power. Power is never equally distributed; there is always an elite. . . ." Harold Lasswell and Abraham Kaplan, *Power and Society* (New Haven: Yale University Press, 1950), p. 226.

6 Suzanne Keller, *Beyond the Ruling Class* (New York: Random House, 1963), p. 179, is the source from which the list is taken.

period and finally earns his position of responsibility in a competitive examination. Civil service positions in many countries are filled with such selection mechanisms. (g) Election: from a large and usually heterogeneous population a few members earn their right to govern by defeating other would-be leaders in a competitive election. There is a variation on this pattern which interests us indirectly; an already constituted group selects a particular member to be chairman or "most equal," such as a city council electing its own mayor.

The common element in each of these selection processes is that a few come to rule the many. We will not be interested in whether the many want to be ruled by the few. Rather we will explore the processes by which leaders are selected.

A Framework for Studying Leadership Selection

The axiom with which we begin—from among the many are selected the few who govern—can be represented by a very simple diagram. We draw a big box and let it represent the governed population; we then draw a much smaller box within the larger one and let it represent the governing few (Figure 1–1).

Figure 1–1

The Governed and the Governors

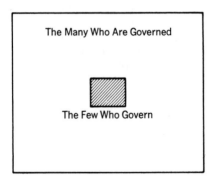

Such a representation is exceedingly simple, however. A more complex representation is suggested by the ancient Chinese Box Puzzle. In this puzzle, a series of different size boxes are so designed that the smallest box fits into the next larger one, that one into the next larger one, and so forth. The thought which interests me here is that the smallest box, the core, is contained in all of the larger boxes. In the puzzle, however, we do not reach this smaller box until we have uncovered, so to speak, all the intermediate boxes between the largest all-inclusive box and the smallest most exclusive box.

The Chinese Box Puzzle suggests an approach to studying the selection of political leaders. There occurs a gradual but continuous process of selection and elimination which narrows the entire population to the few who hold office. Every political community has a comparatively large number of citizens who meet the minimal legal requirements for holding political office. From these citizens come some persons who are attuned to political matters—the politically attentive public. From this public comes another and yet smaller group which is politically active. And from this group comes an even fewer number of citizens who are actually recruited into the channels which can lead to public office. From these are chosen the candidates and from the candidates are chosen the few who will hold office.

Each stage in this narrowing process can be represented by a "box" in the Chinese Box Puzzle. The smallest box, the governing few, is contained in each of the larger boxes. An intermediate box, the politically active for instance, simultaneously is contained in the larger box and provides the persons, smaller in number, who constitute the next smallest units. As the few approach leadership posts, they are successively part of a smaller and smaller pool.

Leadership selection processes, then, refer to those institutional and individual factors which establish each successively smaller pool. For it is the shaping of these smaller and smaller groups of citizens that eventually determines which few come to govern the many. We will empirically construct a Chinese Box Puzzle by tracing the collective careers of the citizens who govern eighty-seven cities in the San Francisco Bay Area. Diagram 1 is both a schematic presentation of our framework and an outline of much of our study.

In Figure 1–2 four boxes intervene between the largest box representing the "many" or the total population and the smallest box representing the "few" or the elected officials. These intervening boxes illustrate distinct social processes that select and train citizens for political leadership posts. In so doing, these processes shape the pool from which leaders are drawn. Four theories are germane to the processes through which leaders are selected: (1)

Figure 1–2

Chinese Box Puzzle

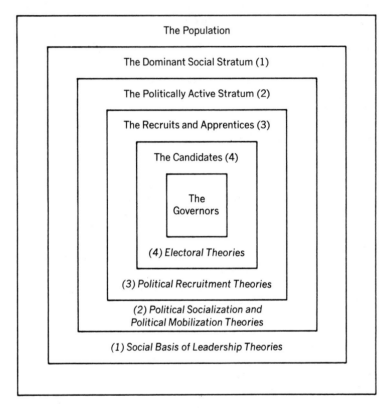

the social basis of leadership theories; (2) political socialization and political mobilization theories; (3) political recruitment theories; and (4) electoral theories. Brief explications will indicate the way in which the framework will be used to examine leadership selection.

Social Basis of Leadership

A history of the inquiry into elite recruitment would largely be a review of studies of the way in which social stratification systems intersect with political hierarchies. The basic hypothesis, as one student states it, is: "Stratification analysis suggests the probability that the political life-chances of those with high social status will be considerably better than those with average or low prestige."[7]

To determine whether the leadership group mirrors or distorts the population from which it is selected, students have compared a demographic profile of the political leaders with the demography of the population as a whole. Not unexpectedly, throughout history and across cultures a close link has been found between the stratification system of a nation and its political leadership. Officeholders tend to be drawn not equally from all groups but in disproportionate amounts from the dominant socioeconomic strata.

We employ a similar strategy, but will attempt to take the analysis one step further. Our intent is to use stratification hypotheses to help understand the shape of the pool from which political leaders are drawn. We will concentrate not only on the presence of the demographic distortion, but attempt as well to establish the degree of the distortion and to account for the factors which affect just how much distortion there is in a given community.

We recognize, of course, that the social basis approach to leadership can only determine who is "eligible" for positions in the government hierarchy. It cannot tell us who will actually become leaders. This is so for two reasons. First, not all the social and economic notables become political officeholders. By knowing a person's status we know something about his chances of success *if* he seeks office, but we have no way of knowing whether he will choose a political vocation. Second, though upper-status groups contribute disproportionately to the political leadership class, they are not necessarily the exclusive contributors. A theory of leadership selection must provide an explanation of those, however few, who overcome class disadvantages to become public leaders. Nevertheless, the initial step in describing leadership selection is to discover from what segment of the population leaders are likely to be drawn.

Political Socialization and Mobilization

From the eligibles come a much smaller group of citizens who belong to the politically active stratum. These citizens are "abnormally" active in public affairs. They run the political parties; serve on local commissions; dominate community activities; know

---

[7] Donald Matthews, *The Social Background of Political Decision-Makers* (Garden City, N.Y.: Doubleday & Co., 1954), p. 9.

the ins and outs of the political game; are called upon, or nominate themselves, for numerous public tasks; and are more likely than most citizens to select themselves or to be selected for public office. Some, though not all, will at one time or another hold elective office. If these are the people who dominate public affairs and who contribute overwhelmingly to leadership positions, it is important to understand the social and institutional processes which produce them.

Clues about the processes shaping the politically active stratum are found in political socialization and political mobilization theory. In particular, we will work with an "exposure hypothesis." It is an individual's location in a network of social-political relationships that determines whether family background, educational experiences, occupational choices, leisure time activities, or community conditions "expose" him to political stimuli in very unequal amounts. Obviously, whether socialized or mobilized into politics, persons entering the active stratum are influenced by an identifiable and differentiating set of social experiences. By establishing what these social experiences are, we can take a step in explaining the process which narrows the entire citizenry to the few who govern.

The initial section of the book is devoted to two topics: the social basis of leadership and the processes which shape the politically active stratum. These issues are the foundation stones of any theory of leadership selection. To return to the analogy of the Chinese Box Puzzle, the socially eligible and the politically active represent two groups smaller than the larger group—the population—in which they are contained but larger than the smaller group—those who actually hold office—which is contained within them.

Identifying the political stratum in the community does not inform us who will hold elective posts. The next two boxes in Figure 1–2—"The Recruits and Apprentices" and "The Candidates"—refer to the selection processes which intervene between entry into the active stratum and officeholding. Theories of recruitment and electoral behavior point to the social processes and the individual characteristics relevant to this stage of shaping the leadership class.

Recruitment and Apprenticeship

One approach to studying leadership selection seeks to identify the processes channeling political aspirations. A second and, as it turns out, closely related approach is to identify the processes mobilizing talent and resources to public office. Very frequently these two approaches overlap in the social processes identified. Both research questions—how the politically ambitious focus on particular offices and how political institutions fill the many posts that keep the institutions operating—are embedded in recruitment theory. The difference in the two approaches lies in whether the observer views recruitment from the vantage point of the individual or from that of the political institution.

Governments, including city councils, mobilize talent. Somehow the 488 city council positions in the eight-county Bay Area must be filled. The "must" here is intended in the legal, not functional sense. City charters (constitutions) specify the number of council seats and the legal criteria for filling them. This is but the beginning, however. Once the legal posts are defined, certain processes, initiated by any of dozens of community agencies, are used to find persons who will fill them. At the national level, the screening-selecting-mobilizing task is carried out by the political parties. In local, nonpartisan communities, less is known about how offices are filled. A major task of leadership selection theory is to establish what the processes are that recruit persons into elective office (from those persons already identified by their presence in the political stratum) and to explain how those processes operate.

In addition, political recruitment is concerned with the way in which individuals focus and channel their political ambitions. A useful guide in exploring this topic is to think of recruitment as a process that legitimates claims to political office. The individual with political aspirations knows that his claim on office will rest on his having been selected according to generally accepted procedures. There are two aspects of legitimacy involved here. In the first place, there are certain constitutionally defined criteria for holding public office. If the City Charter stipulates that a candidate must have received a plurality of votes, then no man expects to be seated unless he has attracted this amount of public support. Men have political legitimacy ascribed to them by virtue of being selected according to the set of rules previously legitimated.[8] Men who wish to wield political authority will be sensitive to the formal

---

[8] The notion of how the legitimacy of the officeholder is dependent upon the legitimacy of the selection procedures is taken from Mosca, when he writes, "And since it is in the nature of the human being that many men should love to command and that almost all men can be brought to obey, an institution that gives those who are at the top a way of justifying their authority and at the same time helps to persuade those who are at the bottom to submit is likely to be a useful institution." *The Ruling Class*, p. 397.

requirements and will perforce use the prescribed channels to legitimize their claim on the office. In this sense a person's political ambitions will be expressed and realized within some generally recognized constraints.

In addition, there are less formal and less obvious ways in which recruitment processes might legitimate political ambitions. At the national level, for instance, no man expects to gain office without receiving the support of one of the major parties. Certainly, there is nothing in the Constitution that decrees that this be so, but the very elaborate set of norms which have grown up around the political parties in the United States make it so. These norms help the politically ambitious channel and focus their aspirations. Similar "informal" mechanisms work at the local level as well. One of these, apprenticeship, is discussed below. Others, such as belonging to the "right" club or having the support of the local paper, can be identified as well. These nonprescribed but more or less institutionalized features of the recruitment process force a certain order to leadership selection practices. Not just any route will take one to public office.

By jointly examining the processes which mobilize talent and the processes which legitimate political ambitions, we will be using political recruitment theory to show how the politically active are narrowed to the few who actually become candidates for public office. Before moving to the question of candidacy and electoral theory, however, we can add a few remarks about the place of apprenticeship in leadership selection.

Apprenticeship is closely connected with recruitment. Like recruitment, apprenticeship serves two functions, one for the individual and one for the institutional order. Viewed from the perspective of the individual, apprenticeship is his gateway to political office. He proves his worth, as it were, to hold the more elevated elective offices. In partisan politics, apprenticeships generally are served out in the party structures, doing the chores, raising the money, and forever supporting other people's candidacies. In the nonpartisan community, apprenticeships probably will be served in community affairs, running a Little League, serving on the planning commission, and similar activities. Whatever we discover the apprentice positions to be, chances are that the individual looks upon them as training ground for a more prestigious position. However, this is an empirical problem and cannot be answered until the data have been examined.

From the viewpoint of the political institution, apprenticeships are important aspects of leadership selection. First, the practice of apprenticeship further reduces the population from which leaders will be chosen. If serving an apprenticeship is an institutionalized part of becoming an elected leader, then those responsible for final selection of candidates (whether the "those" is an incumbent elite, community influentials, or the voters) are provided with a useful criterion for helping them choose between contenders. Or, as often is the case, apprenticeship is a useful criterion for locating persons who can be urged to serve in the elected posts. Second, the institution of apprenticeship reduces the training burden on the government. With a rapid turnover of officeholders and a consequent influx of freshmen officeholders after each election, the task of instructing the new in the ways of the group can be burdensome. If many of the chores of governing have already been learned in an apprentice position, the task of in-role socialization is considerably reduced.

Recruitment along with apprenticeship training further narrows the pool from which political leaders are selected. Not all the politically active serve in elected posts; in fact, very few of them do. Thus, we turn to recruitment and apprenticeship as those processes which screen and sort within the politically active stratum. We now have narrowed the pool considerably: Any person who has been recruited into the channels leading to office and who is serving an apprenticeship has strong chances of seeking candidacy or of being asked to run for office.

The Candidates and Elections

Candidacy, campaigns, and elections finally combine to reduce the population to the very small minority who hold formal positions of political authority. Our model of leadership selection is the gradual reduction of the many to the few, of the many citizens who satisfy the legal requirements of officeholding to the very few citizens who actually occupy those offices. Elections and the activities surrounding them operate as the final screening-sorting device. Through elections, personal ambitions are translated into victories or disappointments. Elections determine who will occupy and who vacate the chairs of government. In democratic politics, from both an individual and institutional viewpoint, an election identifies the "few."

Research resources have been heavily committed to the study of elections. During the initial decades of systematic political inquiry, particularly in the United States, voter choice and candidate election dominated empirical research. To a lesser degree, they still do. Elections are dramatic political events; they are comparatively easy to study; and unlike other aspects of leadership selection, elections are public and are fixed in time and place. But such methodological advantages aside, there are other reasons why elections have been so much studied.

In a representative democracy, it is thought to be more important to control *who* is to gain office than to try and control the behavior of the incumbent. Theorists, politicians, and citizens alike recognize that effective, day-to-day control by the people of their governors is exceedingly difficult. Instead, competitive elections are assumed to be the mechanism that makes a democracy democratic. Men will compete for office; the voters will choose; and democratic government will be assured.

Apologists for the representative form of democratic government place much confidence in elections. Those more skeptical express doubts about whether elective competition can guarantee a competent, let alone a representative, government. Their doubts take many forms: For complicated psychological reasons, the voter will shy away from selecting men of superior qualities. Men of talent and virtue will find their social (and economic) rewards in nonpolitical careers. Structural arrangements, since they can be manipulated by clever men for personal gain, can never guarantee anything. Even if men of excellence achieve public office, the act of exercising power is corrupting.

Aspects of this debate between advocates and skeptics will be examined in greater detail in Chapters 6 and 8. For now, we simply note that whatever the rationale behind or promise of electoral competition, elections do select leaders. When contestants number more than available offices, as they do in the overwhelming number of cases, the counting of the vote separates the also-rans from the victors. As such, elections narrow the pool of candidates to the governing few.

This is the case whether voter turnout is high or low, whether elections are fixed or honest, whether the candidates are numerous or scarce, whether the contest is close or lopsided. Although these are important problems, they are not relevant to the framework proposed for this study. Elections have many attributes and many consequences. The consequence of primary interest to us here is that campaigns and elections become part of the selection processes that narrow the many to the few at a critical juncture, and mark the final entry into positions of authority.

The Strategy of Analysis

The analytic framework proposed leads to two strategies of inquiry: First, it is necessary to consider both institutional and individual aspects of leadership selection; second, it is necessary to concentrate more on the central tendencies in the data than to explore the variations.

Institutional and Individual Analysis

Political recruitment theory often suffers from being either too institutional or too individual. The institutional approach is perhaps best illustrated by studies of political parties in their nominating and campaigning functions. The individual approach is perhaps best illustrated by the "sociology of the political career" studies. Though either approach can be useful, explanations of leadership selection using only one of them suffer from many instances of misplaced inference. The social observer either studies institutions and deduces the attributes of the individuals in them, or he studies individuals and attempts to induce the characteristics of the institutional order.

Lasswell's pioneering work on political careers is an example of deducing the individual from the institutional phenomenon. Lasswell, in his early writing, stressed that politics had to do with influence and power. From a model of these institutional realities of politics he made inferences about the individual. Since the political role entails an exaggerated involvement with power, those who aspire to political roles must be driven by a need for power.[9] Mills' famous *The Power Elite* is an example in political recruitment analysis of inferring the institutional from the individual attribute.[10] Mills noted that the top political leadership of the United States shared certain background experiences, especially wealth, religion, and an Eastern school education. From this ob-

---

[9] See, for instance, Harold Lasswell, *Power and Personality* (New York: W.W. Norton & Co., 1948), p. 22, where he writes, "If there is a political type . . . the basic characteristic will be the accentuation of power in relation to other values within the personality when compared with other persons." In a subsequent essay, Lasswell somewhat reformulated his argument. See his "The Selective Effect of Personality on Political Participation," in Richard Christie and Marie Jahoda (eds.), *Studies in the Scope and Method of "The Authoritarian Personality"* (Glencoe, Ill.: The Free Press, 1954), pp. 197–225.

[10] C. Wright Mills, *The Power Elite* (New York: Oxford University Press, 1957).

servation he concluded that those social and economic groups over-represented in leadership circles receive a disproportionate share of the benefits of society.

At issue here is not the correctness or incorrectness of specific inferences made by scholars studying political recruitment. We simply point out that an analysis which incorporates both insti-tutional and individual variables can more easily avoid the errors of misplaced inference. The institutional variables with which we will be working include (1) the legal parameters which affect move-ment into and out of political office and (2) the more or less insti-tutionalized agencies, and the criteria they employ, which screen and select from among the possible officeholders. The individual variables to be used in the analysis include those normally asso-ciated with political career analysis: social background, socializa-tion and recruitment experiences, career expectations, and so forth.

Institutional Variables. 1. The Legal Code. Laws prescribe many features of the political community and consequently help deter-mine who is likely to become an officeholder. Laws specify the actual number of offices to be filled, and they outline in some rough form the responsibilities of those positions. Laws establish minimum requirements for officeholding. These may be ascrip-tive, such as age or race, or they may be achieved, such as educa-tional level or skills. Laws make clear the criteria by which to determine when an incumbent has a legitimate claim on his office.

We tend to take the legal code for granted and probably devote less time to examining its effects on leadership selection than we should. Or at least we take it for granted until some changes are suggested. As soon as one set of authorities, or challengers, at-tempts some structural engineering, we are sharply reminded that the legal code is a critical attribute of the structure by which pub-lic leaders come to hold office. Such simple matters as expanding or contracting the number of elective offices, or dropping or add-ing a seemingly harmless eligibility criterion for office, have far-reaching consequences for leadership selection, some intentional and some probably not.

The legal condition most important to leadership selection in the communities studied here is nonpartisanship. Nonpartisan-ship coupled with at-large elections affects the circumstances under which citizens are likely to become politically active, the routes taken into office, and the use (or nonuse) of the council as a step-ping stone to higher office.

Nonpartisanship means, among other things, that the agencies which recruit and screen will be more numerous and varied than is often the case in partisan communities. When a few political parties have enough electoral strength to compete for political positions, most, if not all, contenders for those positions will be nominated through the party machinery. This reduces the number of effective nominating agencies to the number of parties. In the absence of parties, however, the task of recruiting and nominating will be more dispersed. Relatively small groups of citizens can gain access by supporting a particular candidate.

The absence of political parties affects voter behavior as well. We know from a large number of studies that voters in the United States (and elsewhere) vote the party label more often than the man. Habitual Democrats or Republicans respond to personalities, issues, and policies in terms of their association with a particular party. If there are no party labels, as there are not in the elections we study, voters will be deprived of this acceptable and accessible shortcut for making political choices. It is less clear, then, just how the campaign activity affects the makeup of the governing unit. If city councilmen cannot run on a party ticket and if voters have no reliable guide to the policy views of the candidates, factors other than the partisan composition of the community will affect the political coloring of the council.

Nonpartisanship is also a way of looking at politics and, as a norm, affects political recruitment. Many candidates for council office will prefer to think of their activity as having little to do with politics. They confuse the rhetoric of nonpartisanship with being "nonpolitical," a status which they often esteem. The stigma attached to politics in many communities is a stigma attached to party politics, not to council activity. The latter is thought of as community service in much the same way as the Chamber of Commerce or a local charity drive is. This image of the council will have a significant impact on the self-selective tendencies of certain groupings in the community. A man who might never consider party activity has no difficulty picturing himself as a councilman. The norms of nonpartisanship can also lead to self-elimination by certain groups.

There are, of course, numerous other features of nonpartisan city council politics which distinguish them from partisan municipalities and from other levels of government. Some of these impinge on our theory and others do not. Constituencies which select councilmen are relatively small, sometimes as small as a few hundred voters. This increases the opportunities of exposure for the would-be leader. In council elections, there are usually two or three seats available, and the candidates do not directly compete with each other. It is less an "I win, you lose" and more a "some win and some lose" situation.

2. Institutionalized Selection Agencies and Criteria. Political communities have relatively institutionalized, though not necessarily legally prescribed, processes affecting who is likely to become a political leader. There will be distributed throughout the community screening-sponsoring groups, each observing some selection criteria. A variety of public and semipublic groups can sponsor candidates, and these also can veto candidates and block political careers. Incumbent elites, exercising the prerogatives of co-optation and appointment, might act as screening-sponsoring groups as well.

To identify the community groups that control the routes to political leadership is to describe a very important feature of the polity. This is just the initial step, however. After identifying the critical groups, it is necessary to discover what criteria they use for preventing some citizens, allowing others, and urging yet others to become political leaders. Groups with different political persuasions, of course, apply different criteria. We would not expect the Chamber of Commerce to seek out and support the same candidates as the local Italian-American Club. The screening-selecting groups and the criteria they use in exercising their influence are major elements in how the many are narrowed to the few in any polity.

The presence of the electorate is another factor taken into consideration. In democracies, control over leadership selection is shared between those who are already leaders and those who will never be. Eligibility criteria are determined in part by voters who have only vague ideas about what officeholding entails and only tenuous contacts with the world of politics. How interested the public is in politics, how citizens decide to vote, how attentive they are to candidate selection, how predisposed they are to punish incumbents by removing them from office, these and other facets of citizens' voting help determine who will choose, or be chosen, to run for office.

Of particular relevance are the cultural stereotypes about who should be political leaders. Such views affect leadership selection in two ways. Stereotypes about politics and politicians will condition self-selective tendencies. When political positions are viewed as low prestige posts, men with more attractive career alternatives will avoid politics. The image of politics in a community affects who even considers a political career.

In addition, cultural stereotypes affect voter decisions. For example, it is assumed that the American electorate considers a divorcé inappropriate as a President. Such views have considerable impact on both nomination and election processes. The way in which public stereotypes affect leadership selection is not well understood, but there is no doubt that the images of politics held by the public have a definite, if unknown, connection with the processes by which the governors are chosen.

The impact of sponsoring-screening agencies and the selection criteria which they apply can hardly be overestimated in a theory of leadership selection. Informal in the sense that they are not embedded in the legal code, the agencies, criteria, and processes of selection are nevertheless institutionalized aspects of any political scene.

Individual Variables. Of the many individual characteristics relevant to leadership selection patterns, the personal trait most central is political ambition. Political observers frequently assume that there is an unending supply of candidates for office, and, further, that men once in office are determined to stay there and when possible to seek a more exalted position.

These assumptions can be shown to be false. Most citizens do not want political careers, and many of those who at one time or another hold public offices are only too glad to give them up. If we take into account all levels of officialdom, it is clear that there is a shortage of citizens willing to serve. From school boards to Presidential cabinets, men have to be urged, cajoled, and sometimes even threatened into serving. It is equally clear that large numbers of incumbents retire voluntarily. As is reported later, significant proportions of city and state legislators choose their own time for departing office; they decide not to run again. An even larger proportion evince no interest in seeking a higher office.

The desire to hold office affects leadership selection differently, depending on how many citizens have such a desire. Most citizens are reluctant to assume any public chores; these, the politically indifferent, comprise by far the largest share of any community. Other citizens will suffer a term or two of office, but then withdraw. Others will be willing to keep a particular office over a considerable period of time. Finally, a very small minority of citizens in any community will be eager to work themselves up the political career ladder. Every community has some of all types but it is

probable that the size of each group is inversely related, sharply
so, to the commitment in resources and time demanded. The in-
differents will number many times more than those interested in
political office. Those willing to serve at the local level will be a
larger group than those with ambitions to advance.

Political ambition, or lack thereof, is only one of many individual characteristics included in a theory of leadership selection.
Much of what has traditionally been covered under the label of
"career analysis" is relevant. If political recruitment refers to the
processes by which institutions fill political offices, the political
career is the pattern of movement through those offices. As such,
the career is a distinctly "individual" variable; it is studied by
examining the movement of an incumbent into and through the
political jobs that accompany his movement through the life-
cycle.

The political career has an objective and a subjective dimension. There is the sequence of positions held and the rate of
mobility through them—what we can call the objective career. Sub-
jectively, the political career is how the individual uses his recol-
lections of past events, orientations toward present experiences,
and expectations about future happenings. To borrow from
Everett Hughes, the career is a "moving perceptual screen" through
which a politician views and interprets his political life.[11]

Incorporated in the notion of career is information about (a)
initial political interest, the events associated with and conditions
under which the individual is first introduced to the world of politics; (b) recruitment, the contacts, experiences, and predispositions
that specifically place a person in the channels leading to elected
office; (c) in-role socialization, the seasoning process, that is, learning the behavior appropriate for carrying out his duties; and (d)
career expectations, the intensity of career commitment and the
future political plans of the incumbent.

In addition to ambition data and career data, an exhaustive
treatment of individual characteristics pertinent to leadership
selection should include attention to the relevant personality attributes of the political man. Psychological propositions about political leaders have been of two types. First, it has been argued that

---

11 Everett C. Hughes, "Institutional Office and the Person," in *Men and Their
Work* (Glencoe, Ill.: The Free Press, 1958), p. 63. Empirical analysis of the polit-
ical career along the lines suggested here can be found in John Wahlke, Heinz
Eulau, William Buchanan, and LeRoy Ferguson, *The Legislative System* (New
York: John Wiley & Sons, 1962), especially Chapters 4–6.

the probability of becoming a politician is better than average for certain personality types. Personality needs such as "power accentuation" or "affiliation drives" presumably operate as self-selective factors in determining those who choose to make a career in political life. A second set of propositions is less about self-selection tendencies and more about successful incumbencies. Personality attributes such as "ego strength" or "adaptive facilities" determine who will be successful in political life. "Inappropriate" personality types, though sometimes drawn to political jobs, will be found wanting and will either eliminate themselves or be eliminated.

In general, it is difficult to work with personality theory and leadership selection. In a few instances, carefully constructed psychoanalytic political biographies have suggested rich insights. Beyond these, however, matters of methodology and of theory have prevented the few empirical studies from having much to conclude. Given the theoretical aims of this study and the type of survey data available, we devote little attention to personality variables.

Modalities in the Data

If the initial decision about the analysis was to incorporate both institutional and individual variables, the subsequent decision turned on how the variables were to be handled. It quickly became clear that a choice would have to be made between two writing strategies. One approach would be to study variations in the leadership selection process from city to city, for instance, the differences in large and small communities, the differences in cities where the political parties are active in nonpartisan politics and where they remain inactive, the differences in politically competitive and noncompetitive cities, and so forth. The second would be to restrict analysis to the central tendencies in the data and to seek out the implications of the modalities rather than the dispersion around the central tendencies.

The second approach was chosen. A word of explanation is probably in order. We eliminated the first approach for three reasons: First, city-by-city analysis of some of these data is being prepared for another volume; second, we did not want to write a book about city size and electoral competition, or partisanship in nonpartisan cities, or any one of a dozen topics which would have moved to the fore as soon as the variances in the data were explored; third, the analytic framework of the Chinese Box Puzzle is best investigated through the analysis of the central patterns.

The approach of this study, then, is to trace the collective movement of more than four hundred citizens through the stages which begin with their initial political awareness and end with their holding public office. A councilman governing in any of the eighty-seven cities studied did not just "appear in office." He has a political history, a series of experiences which make him very atypical when measured against the average citizen. By simultaneously investigating a large number of such political histories, we move toward an understanding of how political leaders are chosen in American communities. At the same time, we move theoretically toward an understanding of generic processes which, we might suppose, affect selection into leadership positions at other levels of government and indeed in spheres other than politics.

Empirically describing the successive stages of leadership selection is not the only goal, however. There are political and normative implications of the central tendencies in the data. The writing strategy adopted for this book helps us separate two important questions in political recruitment analysis and to relate each of these questions to other issues of political life. The Chinese Box Puzzle informs us who from among all the citizens stands a good chance of holding public office. That "who governs the people" is related to "how the people are governed" hardly needs discussion. The second question, and one frequently confused with the first, has to do with the manner in which the governors are chosen. Irrespective of who they are, the pathways taken to office by political leaders certainly affect the way in which they will govern. Thus, we will be relating two issues in leadership selection to questions about public rule: How does who governs affect the political order? How does the choosing of governors affect the political order?[12]

---

12 Attention to these questions using the city council data but employing a city-by-city analysis can be found in Kenneth Prewitt and Heinz Eulau, "Political Matrix and Political Representation: Prolegomenon to a New Departure From an Old Problem," *American Political Science Review* 63, No. 2 (June 1969):427–41.

Chapter 2

The Social Bias in
Leadership Selection

Every citizen, the democratic creed holds, has an equal chance of winning political office. The creed is embedded as a principle in the legal code of the nation: Elective posts are there for the taking to any who muster sufficient electoral support. Excepting minimal citizenship, age, and residence requirements, no other selective criteria hold the status of law. Regulations establishing an open recruitment system are, in turn, buttressed by political folklore—the widely believed log-cabin-to-white-house myth expresses the idea that the talented, whatever their starting point, can gain the rewards of political office.

But, in spite of creed, code, and folklore, all citizens do not have equal chances to join the governing few. Persons in some social groups are heavily favored over persons in other social groups. Sex, color, religion, social status, wealth, and occupation are criteria which, from the beginning of the nation's experiment in democracy to the present day, selectively determine who will occupy political office. The political leaders of the country have never been and probably never will be a random sample of the population. Instead, officeholders are disproportionately selected from socially more favored groups.

Both ascriptive statuses and achievement traits significantly weight a citizen's chances in the competition for political resources and, consequently, for political office. On balance, it is advantageous to be white, male, Protestant, college-educated, in a prestige occupation, above average in income, and native stock, preferably of Anglo-Saxon descent.[1] Of the selective criteria influencing lead-

---

[1] These of course are the modal characteristics. In large urban centers, candidates for office will often be Catholic and of ethnic background. Indeed, in some

ership recruitment in the United States, race, religion, birthplace, and sex are the most obvious. Nonwhites are highly underrepresented in public office. Although comprising 11 percent of the population, only 429 blacks (as of August 1967) held elective office of any kind at any level.[2] Similar constraints often affect the foreign-born. Persons pursuing a political career are usually second-generation American, and, in many parts of the country, of much older native stock than that.[3] Religion as an entry criterion to public leadership positions is diminishing in significance, dramatized by the Kennedy election and related to the gradual secularization of American life. Historically, however, Protestants and specifically those of the prestige churches dominated public leadership. Jews, Catholics, and the fundamentalist Protestant sects are still consistently underrepresented in political office.[4] Finally, sex is the most consistently pervasive ascriptive criterion

---

constituencies the traits listed above could be a disadvantage. That they are, however, the modal characteristics selectively affecting who will hold office is demonstrated by many studies. For useful summary statements see Wendell Bell, Richard J. Hill, and Charles R. Wright, *Public Leadership* (San Francisco: Chandler Publishing Co., 1961), especially Chapters 5, 6, and 9; Donald R. Matthews, *The Social Background of Political Decision-Makers* (Garden City, N.Y.: Doubleday & Co., 1954), Chapter 3; Suzanne Keller, *Beyond the Ruling Class* (New York: Random House, 1963), Appendices III, IV, and V; C. Wright Mills, *The Power Elite* (New York: Oxford University Press, 1957).

2 This figure is taken from the New York *Times*, August 8, 1967, p. 28. The figure of 429 includes "Every Negro elected to local, county, state, or Federal office."

3 Keller summarizes the evidence on the social backgrounds of various elites, including political. She estimates that two percent of the political leadership is foreign-born and 15 percent is second-generation. Keller, *Beyond the Ruling Class*, p. 310. Matthews compares the percentage of Senators who were foreign-born with the percentage of the total population and finds, "the proportion of United States Senators who were foreign-born has fluctuated considerably since 1789. Beginning at the rather high figure of 15 percent, it has declined to a mere two percent at present (1949–51), while always paralleling the rise and fall in the numbers of the foreign-born in the population at large. But regardless of the times there consistently has been a smaller proportion of immigrants among Senators than among the population as a whole." *Social Background*, p. 25. Data presented by Keller, Matthews, and others suggest that though foreign birth is not an absolute barrier to public office, it is a handicap to an aspirant seeking a political career.

4 Keller estimates 81 percent of the political elite to be Protestant. *Beyond the Ruling Class*, p. 311. Matthews writes, "Congress is far from an accurate reflection of the religious composition of the American people, and the distortion is in favor of the religious views of the upper and upper-middle classes." *Social Background*, p. 26.

determining who becomes a political leader: Politics is a man's world.[5]

It is not always easy to distinguish ascriptive from achieved traits. A value which, in theory, is available to those who strive for it is, in practice, semi-inheritable. For instance, although the son cannot claim as his birthright a prestige occupation or a college degree, parental possession of these values improves his chances of achieving them. Ambiguities notwithstanding, we adopt conventional usage and label income, occupation, and education as achievement traits.

A man's occupation, wealth, and education affect whether he becomes a member of the politically active stratum and whether he is likely to hold political office. However emphatically the democratic creed is asserted, class distinctions are relevant to the formation of the leadership cadre. Social strata overlap political strata. Officeholders are more likely to be selected from groups located toward the upper end of the status hierarchy than from groups socially or economically disadvantaged. Of course, the closeness of fit between social status and political participation varies from community to community and from office to office, but the pattern wherein social advantage is converted to political resource is never entirely absent.[6]

Table 2–1 presents information about the councilmen in our study. Clearly, the councillors are not chosen in proportionate numbers from every population grouping. For instance, although fewer than a third of the Bay Area families have incomes over $10,000, more than four out of five of the councilmen are selected from that income group. Whereas the median education for the population is a high school diploma, the median education for councilmen is a college degree. As is the case at other levels of

5 Bell, Hill, and Wright review relevant data on sex as a selective criteria and conclude, "the over-all picture remains one of severe underrepresentation of women in public offices in general and in the upper levels in particular." *Public Leadership*, p. 35.
6 Evidence supporting observations in this paragraph is to be found in every study of political recruitment conducted in the United States. Keller, for instance, reports that 91 percent of the political elite are college graduates, that 24 percent come from families where the father was a professional, and another 35 percent where he was an official or proprietor. *Beyond the Ruling Class*, pp. 311–12. Matthews reviews the occupations of Presidents, Vice-Presidents, Cabinet members, Senators, Representatives, Governors, State Legislators, and reports, "about 90 percent of each group . . . is drawn from the top 15 percent or so of the labor force." *Social Background*, p. 28.

Table 2–1

Comparison of the Councilmen and the Population from Which
They Are Selected with Respect to Demographic Characteristics

	Population	Councilmen
SEX		
% Male	49	95
RACE		
% Nonwhite	4	*
BIRTHPLACE		
% Foreign-born	8	5
RELIGION		
% Catholic	‡	34
% Jewish	‡	2
% Protestant	‡	64
OCCUPATIONAL STATUS		
% White collar	52	80
EDUCATION		
% More than high school degree	57	95
Median school years completed	12†	16
INCOME		
% Less than $3,000	11	0
% Between $3,000 and $10,000	39	19
% More than $10,000	28	81
Median Income	$7,920†	$14,907

* Less than 1 percent.
† This is the mean of the median for all cities.
‡ Data not available.

American government, socioeconomic characteristics exercise a
selective effect on leadership selection. That we find national and
state patterns repeated on the local level is to be expected. If anything, the lower salience of local politics for all but the most attentive should exaggerate the gap between the profile of the population and the profile of the leadership; lower socioeconomic strata
disenfranchise themselves in municipal elections at a greater rate
than do the better educated and well-to-do voters.

Several Approaches to an Explanation of Differential Recruitment

Socioeconomic characteristics partly determine the reservoir
from which officeholders are selected. However, to assert that

socioeconomic considerations help form the leadership reservoir is something very different from understanding how this happens or understanding how selection from within the reservoir takes place. Descriptions of the leadership pool should not be confused with analysis of selection processes.[7] To understand the influence of social stratification on political recruitment, we must distinguish between a demographic profile and the actual selection of office-holders. All that Table 2–1, and the many prototypes of this table found in the literature, tell us is that elected officials do not mirror the class composition of the population they govern.

Selection Agencies and Socioeconomic Bias

Patterns of recruitment presumably reflect the social values of those who control recruitment channels, as well as reflecting individual aspirations and self-images. In politics, the application of discriminatory criteria may be carried out by nominating committees or other recruitment agencies. In other words, social prejudice may operate from the top down.

Persons who control the pathways to public office tend to perpetuate their own kind. Various possibilities are available and the particular technique used will differ from one office to the next. When the office is strictly appointive, as are, for instance, most judicial positions, it is easy for those already established to select new appointees with the appropriate social, religious, or racial traits. When the office requires professional training, as is, again, the case in the judicial branch as well as in many executive positions, persons who control training programs can apply discriminatory criteria.

For elective offices, class distinctions can be perpetuated by controlling the nomination processes or the apprenticeship positions (the latter frequently being appointive). The desire for group solidarity leads to selection, consciously or not, of new recruits who in their attributes are similar to those doing the selecting. No conspiracy theory need be implied in order to explain this process. As will be shown in later chapters, citizens are attracted

---

7 Keller writes, "Most discussions of ruling castes, ruling classes, and elites fail to distinguish between two dimensions: the processes leading to the development of a core group responsible for performing the leading social functions, and the reservoir from which this core group is recruited. These two dimensions are often used interchangeably because it is difficult to separate them historically. . . ." *Beyond the Ruling Class*, p. 32.

into political careers by friends and associates. Since the people
with whom one associates possess similar social characteristics,
there is a subtle social process perpetuating selective criteria quite
independent of any self-conscious attempt to exclude persons in
the lower echelons of the stratification system.[8]

Those already involved in the political process who search for
new talent and who help aspirants move toward public office are
sensitive to demonstrated accomplishment. Nominating or search
committees understandably are impressed with past performance
of potential recruits. Nothing more effectively demonstrates performance than advanced education or high social status or a
prestige occupation. What has been observed about political recruitment in Germany is equally applicable in the United States.
"Socioeconomic selectivity became more pronounced the higher
the party office. . . . This was the result (in part) of the tendency
among many party members to defer to influential people and to
presume that, simply because they have higher occupational and
educational status, they have leadership ability and should, therefore, be elected."[9]

---

[8] A very instructive discussion of the tension between selective recruitment and
open recruitment can be found in Samuel J. Eldersveld, *Political Parties: A
Behavioral Analysis* (Chicago: Rand McNally & Co., 1964), Chapter 3. He finds
that both the Democratic and Republican parties in Detroit practice "social
counterinfiltration," that is, they systematically recruit party workers and party
officials from social strata not normally represented in the party. A demographic
profile of the parties does reveal that recruitment selectivity operates, but it also
shows the balancing tendency—the need for broad social representation in order
to insure electoral success.

[9] Renate Mayntz, "Oligarchic Problems in a German Party District," in Dwaine
Marvick (ed.), *Political Decision-Makers* (New York: The Free Press of Glencoe,
1961), p. 180. James David Barber argues a somewhat contrary position. In a
section called "The Recruiter's Own Preferences," Barber writes, "it is probably true that the party boss's personality enters into the recruiter-candidate-
community equation. . . . He is . . . continually backstage while the performer
he has selected receives the applause. In a good many cases this dimension of the
relationship no doubt gives rise to feelings of jealousy and a certain secret dis-
dain for the candidate who thinks he knows so much and owes so little. Generally
the recruiter probably seeks the best man he can get. But the temptation to
choose nominees who are not glaringly superior to him may also be a strong
one." Barber continues this argument at some length and adds as well that incumbents in a position to choose their successor may push "the nomination of a
person who will not do quite so good a job" so that any comparison between
predecessor and successor will reflect favorably on the former. The difficulty
with Barber's thesis is that, if carried to its logical conclusion, each generation
of leadership would be less talented than the one preceding it. It is difficult to
imagine historical evidence for such a conclusion. Barber's argument can be

The corollary argument about skills and talents also helps explain why selection agencies might apply discriminatory criteria in helping some reach office and excluding others. Finding persons with expertise and organizational skills is a constant problem for citizens who have the responsibility of filling the many appointive and elective posts in the community. The citizens' committee charged to nominate candidates for the school board or the library commission or the planning committee goes about its duties under a considerable handicap. The list of qualified candidates is limited, information about candidates is in short supply, and committee members usually must work against time pressures. They necessarily use shortcuts. A fallible but easily accessible shortcut for estimating talent is to presume that occupational status is equal to accomplishment, which in turn is assumed to be equal to skills. Under pressure to find "qualified" nominees, it is not surprising that the committee will turn to the well-known lawyer or the successful businessman. Another shortcut, already mentioned, is for the nominating committee to choose candidates similar in status to themselves. These two shortcuts for locating talent in a community combine to disproportionately reward members of high-status groups with leadership positions.

In many ways, then, socioeconomic bias is part of the nominating and selecting procedures. The bias is perpetuated from one generation of municipal leaders to the next. Reasons for the bias are to be found more in the natural processes at work in the community than in elitist motivations by manipulators intent on excluding the "wrong kind" from office. The social prejudice is buttressed as well by self-selective tendencies.

Self-Selection and Socioeconomic Bias

Self-selection and the seeking of political office is a difficult topic for analysis. Self-selective tendencies are not easily distinguished from those selection processes that are less a part of individual psychology and more a part of community processes. For instance, there is no satisfactory method for distinguishing individual aspirations from political opportunities. Is it self-selectivity or political opportunity which explains why the mayor of a large city thinks in terms of a congressional seat, whereas the mayor of a

found in *The Lawmakers: Recruitment and Adaptation to Legislative Life* (New Haven: Yale University Press, paperback edition, 1965), pp. 239–40.

smaller city thinks, at best, in terms of a countywide office?[10] Similarly, it is difficult to distinguish between a self-generated political career and one chosen because friends and associates urge it. Are we to call a man who quickly, even eagerly, responds to the suggestion that he seek political office a self-starter or is his political involvement in response to mobilization efforts by others?

The difficulties of separating self-selection from other recruitment processes are particularly troublesome in the effort to understand socioeconomic bias. Many persons behave as if they were taking themselves out of the competition for political office. And self-elimination appears much more often in some social groups than others. Consider, for instance, the ghetto resident. He has no reason to view himself as a potential recruit for political office. There are no models for him to emulate. His sense of what life holds simply precludes attention to a political career. It may be logically correct to say that he is self-eliminated from the competition for political positions. But it is even more correct to say that his self-image is realistic. The historical advantage of one social group becomes part of the political folklore and members of other social groups do not seek careers in those areas of life presumed to "belong" to, in this case, the middle class.

The mutual reinforcement of public stereotypes and self-elimination can be seen operating in an entirely different social stratum as well. The stigma attached to politics frequently keeps upper-class persons out of political life, especially out of party organization activity. The rich in the United States, as Mosca writes, "feel a certain aversion to entering public life."[11] In a public opinion survey of twenty years ago it was found that the better-off and more highly educated citizens in America were those least likely to see politics as a desirable occupation for their sons.[12]

The burden of responsibility for socioeconomic bias in the se-

10 In the most sophisticated study available on questions of individual aspirations and political opportunities, the author concedes defeat on the issue of separating the two variables. Joseph A. Schlesinger first argues, "A man in an office which may lead somewhere is more likely to have office ambitions than a man in an office which leads nowhere." Then he adds, "It makes little difference to the theory of ambition whether men adopt the ambitions suitable to the office or attain the office because of their ambitions." See his *Ambition and Politics* (Chicago: Rand McNally & Co., 1966), pp. 8–9.
11 Gaetano Mosca, *The Ruling Class,* translated by Hannah D. Kahn (New York: McGraw-Hill Book Co., 1939), p. 58.
12 Albert J. Reiss, Jr., *Occupations and Social Status* (New York: The Free Press of Glencoe, 1961). See the discussion in William Mitchell, "The Ambivalent Social Status of the American Politician," *Western Political Quarterly* 12 (September 1959):689; and the discussion in Barber, *The Lawmakers,* pp. 5–6.

lection of political leaders cannot be entirely placed on the nominating and selective agencies. Persons who bear responsibility for finding political candidates must pick and choose from those citizens who present themselves, that is, from those willing to become politically active. The underrepresentation or overrepresentation of any given social group is partly the result of self-elimination and self-selection.

The Voters and Socioeconomic Bias

There is a third hypothesis sometimes advanced to account for the persistent social bias in leadership selection, an hypothesis which makes assumptions about voter preferences. Briefly stated, the voter views citizens whom he respects for nonpolitical accomplishments as candidates for his respect in the political sphere. The political aspirant's success in business, military, civic, or academic endeavors is relevant to his political image, since the voter uses the candidate's past accomplishments as an indicator of his future performance. Achievement in business or military affairs is assumed to indicate general leadership ability. Since, by definition, the well-educated, the better-off, or the holder of a prestige occupation is someone who has "achieved," who has accomplishments, his chances of gaining respect from the voter are increased.

A variant of this hypothesis, more complicated and psychological, has been advanced by Verba. He writes that the average citizen is not comfortable elevating others to positions of authority.[13] The very act of choosing someone to govern implies an inequality between voter and leader. However, if political leaders also possess some other trait highly valued in society—wealth, status, intellect, skill, age, or whatever is valued—the exercise of their power is less challenging to the persons who elect them. Thus, in American society where "getting ahead" is highly valued and is measured socioeconomically, the voter tends to estimate the political aspirant's "right to rule" in terms of his social status. In this sense, social prestige legitimates political authority.

The three approaches to analyzing social bias in political recruitment are not mutually exclusive. Class criteria may simultaneously be applied by functionaries who control nomination

---

[13] Verba's point appears in an unpublished paper; it is reviewed in Kenneth Prewitt, "Political Socialization and Leadership Selection," *The Annals of the American Academy of Political and Social Science* 361 (September 1965):99.

procedures, by citizens as they select or eliminate themselves, and by the voters in casting their ballots.

Councilmen and the Middle Class

We have seen that in their socioeconomic traits the councilmen imperfectly mirror the communities they govern. But to learn that councilmen are atypical in this regard does not specify the degree of distortion between the governed and their governors. For instance, although the median income of councilmen is nearly double that of the population in general, we cannot tell from this figure what stratum of the population is most overrepresented. It is clear that councilmen are disproportionately drawn from groups above average in income, but it is not clear whether they are drawn from the most wealthy groups.

A large number of studies both in the United States and other industrialized nations have found that it is the middle class which supplies the recruits for political positions.[14] De Tocqueville observed this to be the case in American democracy in the early nineteenth century. He felt that American voters support candidacies of persons superior in status to themselves, but not too superior. Other commentators have expanded on the theme. Not only the working class but the upper class is generally excluded from political leadership in the United States. It is members of the middle class who embody American values; they are the achievers. Civic consciousness and community responsibility are prevalent values among the middle class. Its members see themselves and are seen by others as the legitimate bearers of American culture. They believe themselves to have the skills and perspectives most appropriate for running American society. They select themselves and are selected to govern the ninety thousand political units of the country.[15]

---

[14] For a review of relevant findings, see Keller, *Beyond the Ruling Class*, pp. 206–7, 215–16, and 292–93.

[15] Harold D. Lasswell was one of the initial commentators to discuss the implications of the "eclipse of the aristocracy" and the consequent rise of the middle class in political life. See, for example, his discussion in *Politics: Who Gets What, When, How* (Glencoe, Ill.: The Free Press, 1951), pp. 299–310. Dahl's analysis of changing political recruitment patterns in New Haven is an empirical examination of the process by which the middle class supplants the upper class as the supplier of political leadership. Robert A. Dahl, *Who Governs?* (New Haven: Yale University Press, 1961), Chapters 1–7.

Although there is some agreement that middle-class individuals are predominant among members of the political elite, there is less agreement about why this is so. Keller, after reviewing the pertinent literature, remarks, "Whether middle-class predominance is because voters show a tendency to prefer candidates of higher level than themselves, or because middle-class parents are more likely than parents in other classes to encourage political aspirations in their children, or because nominating committees prefer middle-class candidates, is still an open question."[16] Our data permit no clear answer to Keller's question, but they do suggest tentative conclusions.

First, however, we must determine whether indeed it is the middle class which is disproportionately represented among the municipal officeholders. To answer this question it is necessary to find out from which strata in the status hierarchy councilmen most often are chosen. To do so, we first computed the median income and median education of each council, and then calculated the income and education percentiles of the general population equivalent to the council medians. If a council's median income is $12,000 and if 10 percent of the citizens over twenty-five years of age make in excess of that amount, then the council median is equal to the ninetieth percentile. In other words, the percentile informs us what proportion of the community is wealthier and what proportion less wealthy than the council median. This is a rough estimate of the socioeconomic strata from which councilmen are selected. Figure 2–1 shows how many councils are located at various percentile levels.

Figure 2–1 suggests two things about the class composition of the municipal leadership in the Bay Area.

1. Councilmen are not selected in proportionate amounts from all groups in the community. Confirming what we saw in Table 2–1, it is the better educated and wealthier citizen who is likely to hold office. In addition, the data identify the lower limit of the socioeconomic hierarchy which supplies political leadership. Councilmen come from the upper two-fifths of their communities.

2. Our expectation that the middle class supplies the majority of councilmen is supported by the evidence in Figure 2–1. It is not the very best educated and the wealthiest who predominate in public office. If few councillors are recruited from the work-

---

16 Keller, *Beyond the Ruling Class*, p. 292.

Figure 2–1

Percentile of the Population Represented by the
Median Income Level and the Median Educational
Level of the Council

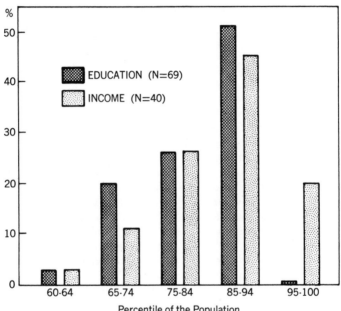

Percentile of the Population

* Loss of cases in the income figure is because census bureau provides the distribution
of income only to $10,000 for small cities. Communities in which the council median
was greater than $10,000, or greater than the upper limit set by the available data, have
been left out of the analysis.

ing classes, a large group of them do come from social strata less
prestigious than the very top.[17]

Figure 2–2 illustrates this more clearly. Although no council education score represents the less educated 60 percent of its community, more than a third of the councils fall between the sixtieth

_____

[17] Dahl writes, "The monopoly enjoyed by the middling white-collar strata
over public life in New Haven is sufficiently explained, then, by the fact that
while low standing and occupation are disadvantages to the wage earner, the
high standing and occupation of the Social Notables do not confer corresponding
advantages." *Who Governs?*, p. 238.

and the eightieth percentile. Nearly one-half fall within the next highest decile. Only one-fifth of the council medians are scores equivalent to the best educated 10 percent of their community; none are drawn from the highest 5 percent.

Figure 2–2

Contribution to the City Councils from
Different Strata in the Population as
Measured by Education

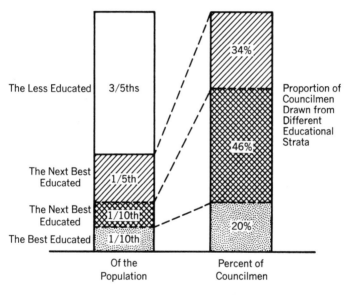

Ratio of Over-Contribution from
the Different Educational Strata:
Citizens between the 60th and   80th Percentile — 2.00
80th and   90th Percentile — 4.60
90th and 100th Percentile — 1.70

Clearly, leadership selection is affected by socioeconomic considerations; the social composition of municipal leadership is a systematic distortion of the communities they govern. The aspirant for
public office will find the going difficult if he is not among the
upper two-fifths of the population in education and income. On
the other hand, persons at the apex of the social stratification
hierarchy do not command all the public offices. It is not the case

that the higher up the status ladder the political aspirant is, the better his chances of holding elective office. In the competition for public office, the most advantaged group in our cities is the one having 80 to 85 percent of the population below it on the status scale but 5 to 10 percent above it.

Socioeconomic considerations significantly affect the processes by which the many are narrowed to the few. The top two-fifths of the population constitutes the reservoir from which municipal leadership is drawn; members of the middle and upper-middle class supply the vast majority of officeholders. With respect to the Chinese Box model of political recruitment, then, we suggest an initial finding. The processes by which the governing units are constituted begin long before political nomination and election processes take place. Potential leaders are initially selected by being differentially allocated to social status positions. City councilmen are selected not from the entire population but from a social stratum with a clear lower limit and a less definite though real upper limit.

There remain several other observations to make about the evidence comparing status measures of the councilmen with the social composition of the communities they govern. We have ignored, for instance, the issue of whether the social and economic characteristics of leaders differ from community to community. Data as presented in Table 2–1 and Figure 2–1 take no account of whether a community is rich or poor, well educated or not. Some comparative analysis is in order.

Social Bias Compared Across Communities

In its social composition, the officeholding group is atypical. It is possible, however, that this very atypicalness is subject to constraints, is itself patterned in some important way. At issue is whether the class composition of the community limits the degree to which its leaders are a biased sample. We expect this to be the case and hypothesize that the more uneducated the population, the less well-educated the councilmen; the poorer the community, the less wealthy its leaders; the more working-class the city, the fewer white collar councillors. Figure 2–3 confirms this. The socioeconomic differences between councilmen parallel the socioeconomic differences between the communities in which they are elected. Although never proportionately drawn from the various social categories, municipal leadership is relatively representative.

Figure 2–3

Relationship Between Status Characteristics
of the Councilmen and the Socioeconomic Composition
of the Cities

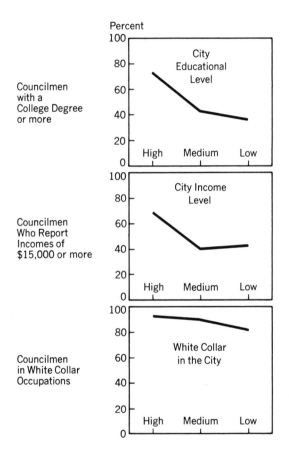

The class composition of the community does indeed restrain the
degree of social bias between leaders and led.

Investigations of leadership selection in two other metropolitan
regions, Philadelphia and St. Louis, report similar findings. In the
Philadelphia area, "Metropolitan political leadership is representative of its constituency in terms of both occupation and education." And in the greater St. Louis area, it was found that

"Councilmen do tend to have *similar* socioeconomic status as the individuals in the municipalities which they represent."[18] The Philadelphia and St. Louis findings corroborate those reported in Figure 2–3. It is probable that the pattern repeats itself throughout the nation: The social bias in political recruitment is systematically affected by the class composition of the political community from which the leaders are selected. What might explain this pattern?

A Statistical Explanation

To find a consistent relationship between the class composition of the community and the socioeconomic traits of the leadership may be nothing more than a statistical artifact. As shown earlier (Figure 2–1), councilmen tend to be selected from socioeconomic strata somewhere in the upper two-fifths but below the highest echelons in their community. It is this finding which permits a statistical explanation of the relative bias in the socioeconomic gap between leaders and led (Figure 2–3).

In order to explain why this is so, we must consider the community data. We are using census statistics to describe the class composition of the communities. The coding conventions adopted by the Census Bureau have certain consequences. For instance, in census statistics the wealthiest 5 percent of the low-income city look like the wealthiest 5 percent of the high-income city, whatever may be the actual differences between the incomes of the persons in these respective groups. This is because the highest income category used in census statistics is $25,000 and over.[19] Thus, the wealthiest person in the poorer community reports an income

18 Oliver P. Williams, Harold Herman, Charles S. Liebman, and Thomas R. Dye, *Suburban Differences and Metropolitan Policies: The Philadelphia Story* (Philadelphia: University of Pennsylvania Press, 1965), p. 228. Bryan T. Downes, "Municipal Social Rank and the Characteristics of Local Political Leaders," *Midwest Journal of Political Science* 12, No. 4 (November 1968):519. Both Williams and his associates and Downes advance their findings as *counter* to well-established findings at the national and state levels showing that with respect to social and economic traits the leadership is a biased sample. However, in neither the Philadelphia nor the St. Louis study do the authors compare councillors with a demographic profile of the community as a whole. That is, they fail to do what Matthews, Keller, and others have done at the national level or what we have done at the municipal level.

19 In urban places with populations in excess of 10,000. In smaller communities, the highest income category is only $10,000, making our analysis even more difficult.

which exceeds the census categories just as does the wealthiest person in the upper-income city. For example, one of our cities has a median income of $11,000 and another city has a median income of $8,000, yet both have between 4 and 5 percent of their citizens who report incomes in excess of the highest census category.[20] The case is similar with regard to educational comparisons. Irrespective of the median education in their city, the best educated 5 percent in one city look just like the best educated in the next; the highest group in any city tends to have college degrees. But the median education for the total population may be anywhere from twelfth grade to the bachelor degree. For example, two cities in which identical proportions of the population (.084 percent) have a college degree or better differ by two years in their median education levels.[21]

Now, if councilmen were recruited only from the highest status groups, the distance between leaders and led would increase as the population is poorer and less educated. This does not happen precisely because officeholders are drawn from throughout the upper two-fifths of the population. Although the upper 5 percent of the wealthy suburb may look like the upper 5 percent of the working-class city, the upper two-fifths of these cities will differ considerably.

This variability is reflected in Figure 2–3. Since in absolute terms the education, occupation, and income of groups supplying leaders vary from community to community, the socioeconomic traits of elected leadership vary.

However, this is only part of the explanation. The relationship between the class makeup of the community and the class makeup of the council is a result of recruitment processes as well as the distribution of different socioeconomic groupings in the community.

Social Bias Patterns and Interpersonal Recruitment

Recruitment patterns in elective politics are strongly influenced by interpersonal relationships; this is especially the case when political organizations are middle class and when they depend heavily on

---

[20] In Los Altos, where in 1960 the median family income was $11,033, .043 percent of the families made $25,000 or more. In Menlo Park, the median family income was $8,191, nearly $3,000 less, but still .047 percent of the families made $25,000 or more.

[21] One of these cities, Gilroy, has a median education of 10.3; the other, Pinole, has a median education of 12.2.

volunteers. Both of these attributes describe the political and para-political organizations which supply recruits for municipal councils. As will appear clearer later on, councilmen are ushered into and through the channels leading to office by personal associates, friends, work colleagues, neighbors, and civic associates. It is a highly personalized and informal network which identifies candidates and recruits them for the openings constantly appearing in municipal government. Unlike professions, businesses, and even administrative bureaucracies such as the federal executive, organizations involved in elective politics cannot rely on the relatively impersonal selection processes of advertisements, applications, examinations, certifications, credentials, or automatic advancement. The politically active stratum, especially in local nonpartisan politics, is formed by the day-to-day contacts one citizen has with another.

People associate with others of similar status; this observation is so obvious that we accept it as a truism. Phrased in the language of folklore, "Birds of a feather flock together." There are social structural and personal psychological reasons for this. The clustering of income levels by residential segregation leads to socioeconomic homogeneity in churches, neighborhood groups, civic organizations, and so forth. This is further buttressed by occupational patterns. Professionals spend the day with other professionals and blue collar workers with other blue collar workers. In addition, the sociometry of a community is formed as persons seek out others of similar status. It is more comfortable to spend time with persons who share background experiences and common tastes.

Combining these two observations leads to the following conclusion: The interpersonal networks which establish the political stratum in a community tend to perpetuate socioeconomic homogeneity. Keeping this conclusion in mind we can now take a second look at the evidence (in Figure 2–3) showing how the class composition of the city affects the socioeconomic traits of councilmen.

1. The wealthiest and best-educated citizens in a working-class community do not hold public office because they are social isolates. They have few contacts with the network of friends and associates who establish the politically active stratum from which, in turn, are recruited candidates for elective office. The wealthy businessman or the corporation lawyer who resides in a working-class city goes outside the city to find friends or to become involved

in civic activities. And the poorer the community the greater will be the distance between the highest status persons and the citizen-at-large, even those citizens-at-large who are among the top 40 percent in income or education.

2. Not only is the highest status person isolated from the web of friends, associates, and activists controlling political organizations, but he consciously chooses to stay isolated. For instance, since running for office requires investment of personal energy and of resources, an individual is reluctant to pay the costs unless he is given social support. It is questionable whether sufficient social support in the way of urgings and requests is forthcoming for the corporation lawyer in the working-class city. Further, to the degree Lasswell is correct in noting that men seek public office because of deference needs, men do not compete for office unless deference is a clear prize of victory. For the upper-status person in a lower-class city, the distance between him and the general public may be so great that any deference earned by holding office is of little consequence. He will not seek to gratify deference needs in the public arena. This self-elimination is particularly relevant in the low-visibility politics characteristic of municipal government.

3. Negative stereotypes about politics and politicians are more common when a stratum other than one's own dominates political life. This phenomenon operates to exclude lower-class members from political life in upper-class communities and upper-class persons from politics in working communities. The local grocer doesn't consider challenging the political elite if it is composed of corporation executives. Neither does the corporation executive get involved in city hall if its clientele are union officials and ethnic club leaders.[22]

To summarize, the natural selection processes in community life isolate from recruitment networks those citizens furthest removed from the modal socioeconomic characteristics of the active stratum. Thus the gap between leaders and led is held within bounds; it is never as great as is theoretically possible. Municipal leaders may not perfectly represent the social composition of their city

---

22 Dahl explains the self-disfranchisement of the social notables in New Haven as follows, "Rather than deal with politicians of alien stock and dubious manners, engaged in a new kind of politics that lacked the dignity and style of the old . . . [the social notables] abandoned the local political arena to the newcomers." *Who Governs?*, p. 237.

but neither will they be exclusively selected from the top echelon.[23]

Before listing all our conclusions pertinent to social bias patterns and leadership selection, one final issue should be discussed: the impact of social mobility on political recruitment.

Social Mobility and Bias in Leadership Selection

Many commentators writing about the selective effect of class characteristics in political recruitment fail to consider social mobility. To report, as many scholars have, that political leaders enjoy a higher social status than their constituents is in part to state a tautology.[24] Political success itself elevates the officeholder above the population. By the very act of selection, the person chosen to represent the group has a higher social standing than the average member. The union leader, for instance, has a higher income and a more prestigious occupation than the workers he bargains for simply because he was chosen from the rank and file, given a raise, a title, and organizational responsibilities.

In addition to this obvious link between political success and social standing, it is true that political channels are used to advance economically. The situation of immigrant groups on the Eastern seaboard is a clear case in point. As Dahl's analysis of the shift in New Haven from patricians to entrepreneurs to explebes to the new men chronicles, the ladder of politics was the route out of the ghetto.[25] Contemporary black politics tends to reflect the same trends. Political advancement is viewed in the context of social mobility. In fact, as early as 1946, twice as many black parents as

---

23 This is a conclusion similar to one advanced by Dahl. "There is probably an optimum range above the average standing of a given group within which the favorable effects of social standing are at a maximum. If a leader or subleader falls much below the optimum, he loses the esteem of the upper sections of the group; if he stands socially too far above the optimum he may seem to be alien and unsympathetic." *Ibid.*, p. 232.

24 This is one of the weaknesses in Domhoff's analysis. His charts showing that important decision-makers are also members of the social elite fail to indicate what proportion used politics as a channel to economic and social status and what proportion used their social and economic positions to move into critical political posts. See, for example, pp. 73–74, 106, and allusions to social elite membership of those 'who rule America' throughout *Who Rules America?* (Englewood Cliffs, N.J.: Prentice-Hall, 1968).

25 Dahl, *Who Governs?, passim.*

white parents were favorably disposed to politics as a career for their sons.[26]

Clearly, social and economic rewards are associated with political success. The wage earner with a successful political career does not long remain a wage earner. Strong evidence to this effect is presented by Eldersveld in his study of Detroit. Party leaders not only had higher occupational standing than their fathers but, more to the point, from one-fifth to one-fourth improved their status *during* their political career.[27] The successful politician benefits from improved salary and prestige as well as improved business contacts and the insider's knowledge of economic opportunities.

Social mobility adds a complication to analysis of the socioeconomic bias in leadership selection. How many officeholders are of higher standing than their constituents because they were to the manor born and how many have higher standing because of personal mobility, a mobility possibly accelerated by political success itself? Two important hypotheses in studies about the social composition of leadership are affected by an answer to this question.

1. Disproportionate membership in the political elite by particular economic strata, so one hypothesis goes, leads to disproportionate benefits for those strata. Since the rich dominate in leadership circles they will see to it that the rich continue to get more than their share of society's goods.[28] In its most primitive form, the hypothesis can be stated as follows: If a stratum comprises but 10 percent of the population but contributes 50 percent

---

[26] In a 1946 NORC study, "only 22 percent of the whites interviewed were favorably disposed to politics as a career for their sons, 50 percent of the Negroes viewed such a career positively." Cited in Bell, Hill, and Wright, *Public Leadership*, p. 131.

[27] Eldersveld, *Political Parties*, pp. 54–55. From his Table 3.2 (p. 54) I computed the following:

	Father's Occupation	Party Leader's First Occupation	Party Leader's Present Occupation
Proportion White Collar (professional, managerial, clerical, sales) (N = 281)	31%	35%	50%

[28] Domhoff's is the most recent and clearest example of this position. For instance, on p. 9 he writes that the power elite has its roots in the American business aristocracy "*and* serves its interests." (Italics added). Further, on p. 144, "We have emphasized . . . that the power elite is rooted in the upper class and serves the interests of members of the upper class." More specifically, "the outcome of tax legislation points to the existence of a power structure dominated by the very rich." *Who Rules America?*, p. 42.

of the governing elite, it will receive not 10 percent but closer to half the resources allocated by political authorities.

The simplistic and fallacious logic of this reasoning has been well documented elsewhere.[29] We are interested only in the consequences of social mobility for the hypothesis. If the status differences between leaders and led are at least in part due to the more rapid mobility of the leaders, then it is a doubtful assumption that officeholders will reward only the stratum to which they have climbed and never the stratum from which they departed (and, in all likelihood, continue to have many ties with). The New Haven case is relevant here; as the Irish and then the Italians gained control of city hall, the rewards dispensed by aldermen were spread much more equitably than when local government was the exclusive domain of the Yankee families. The same pattern may hold as blacks gain political office. Although the black officeholder joins the middle class, the black bourgeoisie, this does not necessarily prevent him from favoring policies which will redistribute resources.

The first reason, then, for considering how social mobility affects leadership selection is to warn us against mechanically deducing policy preferences from the social composition of the officeholders. A socially homogeneous city council may well represent very divergent social origins.

2. Differences in the social composition of leadership groups and populations are assumed to imply different political socialization experiences. If the political socialization of those destined to be leaders differs demonstrably from the socialization of those who remain in follower roles, political society will have an elite and a mass culture. Nowhere is the ramification of two cultures better expressed than by Mosca. He explored the dangers attendant on society when the ruling class is separated by its attitudes and perspectives from the masses it governs. "A ruling class is more prone to fall into errors . . . the more closed it is, actually if not legally, to elements rising from the lower classes. In the lower classes the hard necessities of life, the unending and carking scramble for bread, the lack of literary culture, keep the primordial instincts of struggle and the unfailing ruggedness of human nature alive." A ruling class morally and intellectually isolated from the mass will

---

29 The most telling critiques are Robert A. Dahl, "A Critique of the Ruling Elite Model," *American Political Science Review* 52 (1958); and Nelson Polsby, *Community Power and Political Theory* (New Haven: Yale University Press, 1963).

lose "its ability to provide against its own danger and against those of the society that has the misfortune to be guided by it."[30]

Thus, there is a second reason for considering social mobility. If officeholders are exposed during their formative years only to the culture of the upper class, they will carry into office outlooks distinctly different from those of the general population. On the other hand, if those holding office include many who are socially mobile, then there is less cause to expect two political cultures and all the attendant strains introduced into a representational system of government.

Mobility and the Selection of Councilmen

Unfortunately, the data we have available permit only some very rough estimates about social mobility. We have the occupational status of their fathers for 242 councilmen; among this group slightly better than 30 percent have been mobile. In addition, there is a smattering of indirect evidence about social mobility. This evidence points uniformly in one direction: Among the councilmen there are many who were reared in a social stratum lower than their present one.

We can also refer back to Figure 2–1. One-fifth of the councils have median incomes which represent the top 5 percent of their communities. No council has a median education which reflects this stratum. We can speculate that the status gap between councilmen and constituents grows *after* election to office. While the councillor's education is fixed before he pursues a political career, his income is a flexible commodity. Income level can be improved during the course of officeholding itself. That is, councilmen stand to benefit economically from their officeholding; they cannot, except in rare instances, improve their formal education as a result of political success. The status gap between councilmen and the population may, therefore, be in part caused by social mobility as well as by the application of class criteria in the selection process.

In Table 2–2 is evidence which shows further that councilmen have been occupationally mobile. Although councillors are in middle- and upper-middle-class occupations, their family backgrounds suggest familiarity with lower economic class conditions.

---

[30] Mosca, *The Ruling Class,* p. 119.

Table 2–2

Occupations of Councilmen and
Occupations of Their Fathers

	Fathers (N = 264)	Sons (N = 341)
Professional	17%	26%
Managerial	27	43
Clerical/Sales	9	11
Skilled Labor	24	9
Independent Farmer	16	1
Unskilled Labor	4	—
Other	3	6
Retired, No Occupation	—	5
	100%	101%

If not councilmen themselves, at least their fathers were factory workers, carpenters, truck drivers, and other wage earners.

The final, and most suggestive, data are presented in Table 2–3. The lower-class communities are somewhat more likely to have the upwardly mobile councilmen. Although not strong, the pattern is sufficiently clear to support the general argument. The socioeconomic gap between councilmen and the Bay Area population is in part attributable to mobility among the public leaders. The tendency for councilmen to be socially mobile is accentuated in the less educated and poorer communities. In these communities, then, the councilmen are even more likely to have class origins which resemble those of the governed.

Table 2–3

Proportion of Occupationally Upwardly Mobile Councilmen from Communities of Differing Class Composition (N = 246)

	COMMUNITY CHARACTERISTICS	
	Median Years of Education Twelve or More	Median Years of Education Less than Twelve
Upwardly Mobile	26% (170)	37% (76)

	Median Income Above $7,750	Median Income Between $6,750 and $7,750	Median Income Less than $6,750
Upwardly Mobile	24% (84)	31% (81)	35% (81)

Conclusions

Elected leadership in the United States is not a mirror reflection of the social and economic composition of the population it is charged to govern. Some social strata, those located toward the upper end of the stratification system, contribute more than their share of offices. Other strata, those in the lower echelons, are substantially underrepresented in political leadership circles. Class criteria, then, selectively affect the processes by which the few are chosen to manage the public affairs of the many.

Lasswell writes that rule will not be egalitarian unless all persons have equal access to the values on which political recruitment is based.[31] By this criterion, municipal government in the Bay Area is not egalitarian. The uneven distribution of the antecedent roles, the traits and skills, the self-images and aspirations, the contacts, the knowledge and experiences, and the class attributes which further political careers result in the uneven contribution of different social strata to political leadership. It is evident that, in regard to the attainment of political office, "The rich have a considerably shorter road to travel than the poor, to say nothing of the fact that the stretch of road that the rich are spared is often the roughest and most difficult."[32]

The social bias in political recruitment is, however, just the starting point for analysis. There are issues other than the presence of bias that we would like to understand. This chapter has included a discussion of three issues which take us beyond the initial finding.

First, if there is a ruling class, a social class from which rulers are overwhelmingly selected, it is the middling, white collar class. Municipal councillors (in our sample), far from being a homogeneous elite drawn exclusively from the most prestigious stratum in society, reflect the religious, ethnic, occupational, and, to a lesser degree, educational diversity of a metropolitan middle class.

---

[31] Harold D. Lasswell and Abraham Kaplan, *Power and Society* (New Haven: Yale University Press, 1950), p. 225. The authors are careful to distinguish between power itself being equally distributed and the values on which elite recruitment is based being equally distributed. They go far toward defining democracy in terms of recruitment. "What is important and what varies from one body politic to another, is the set of principles according to which the elite is recruited." P. 226.

[32] Mosca, *The Ruling Class*, p. 58.

There appears to be a range from which councillors are recruited. The lower limit of this range is approximately that point where 60 percent of the population remains below; operationally, this tends often, though not always, to be the line dividing blue collar from white collar occupations. The upper limit of the range is less precise and certainly honored less faithfully. The upper limit does, however, exclude citizens of the highest social-economic status from local office, especially in working-class cities.[33]

Second, the class composition of the community exercises a restraint on the size of the socioeconomic gap between leaders and led. The selective effect of class considerations in political recruitment clearly is a product of continuing interaction between leadership and the general population, a relationship mediated by an informal, interpersonal network which screens candidates for public office, eliminating some and recruiting others.

The range from which councilmen are selected shifts according to the social composition of the community. In the working-class city, the lower limit of the "ruling class" dips low enough to include union officials, public school teachers, craftsmen, and, from time to time, the personable skilled laborer. In the middle-class community, the lower limit is set a bit higher: The druggist, the successful car salesman, and the realtor fall within the upper two-fifths, but the union leader, school teacher, and so forth fall below the social threshold. And of course in the upper-class suburb, even the middle-class entrepreneur discovers his occupational status to be more of a liability than an asset if he should seek office.

And, third, social mobility confounds analysis of socioeconomic bias in leadership selection. In the first place, political success is itself a source of social status; thus, it is tautological to point out that officeholders are of a higher social standing than the average citizen. There is no way they could not be. In the second place, there is probably a disproportionate amount of intergenerational mobility among political careerists. Parents ambitious for their children, as well as the youths themselves, find in politics a legitimate and accessible ladder out of the working class into the middle class or out of the middle class into even higher echelons. To the extent that achievement and mobility are routes to public office, the hereditary transmission of elite status is weakened.

Consideration of the effect of social mobility on political recruitment suggests two observations. We caution against a hasty

---

[33] The idea of an "optimum range" is taken from Dahl, *Who Governs?*, Chapter 20.

assumption that the class from which rulers are selected is the class on whose behalf decisions are made. The routes into the governing group are more diversified than the composition of the group itself.[34] Second, elite-mass differences in political outlook are traced to differing social backgrounds and the consequent differences in political socialization. This is permissible practice, but we should guard against assuming differences in outlook just because in its socioeconomic traits political leadership is atypical of the general population.[35]

Those who rise from the general citizenry to occupy the seats of government are not a representative sample. The social processes shaping the governing cadre cannot be separated from factors of social and economic selectivity. In short, the narrowing of the many to the few begins with the unequal distribution of political resources and aspirations, a distribution affected by social status.

The theoretical ideas reviewed in this chapter can be generalized. Men move into political positions not haphazardly but according to structured processes. In part, the structure is given by the norms concerning qualifications for officeholding. In fact, these norms are part of the definition of an office and thus tell us a great deal about officeholders. It is equally correct to say that movement into a council position is structured by socioeconomic considerations as to say that councilmen generally come from the middle class of their community.

Criteria concerning qualifications for officeholding may be written into law (residency requirements, votes necessary to win an election, etc.) or they may be cultural norms widely accepted. In the first instance, the sanctions for violating the norms are clear and the man who violates them will not hold office. In the second instance, the sanctions for violation may be less clear and the violator may still gain office. In the latter case, however, the officeholder will probably pay certain penalties such as being ostracized by fellow councilmen or being labeled a maverick in the press or being isolated from certain influential elements in the community.

It appears to be a qualification for a council position that a citizen have middle- and upper-middle-class characteristics (that

---

34 Eldersveld reports about Detroit that both the Republican and Democratic parties "have a top leadership group which is 'middle class' in its present status, but whose background suggests considerable familiarity with lower economic class conditions." *Political Parties*, p. 51.

35 The issue of differing political socialization for leaders and led is discussed in much greater detail in the chapter following.

he comes from strata represented by those characteristics). Earlier in the chapter, we outlined three ways by which such a norm could become part of selection processes: search committees or nominating agencies could apply such criteria; self-elimination and self-selection can result in establishing office qualifications; voters can cast ballots according to some notion, however implicit, that some are more fit to govern than others. All three of these may operate concurrently; in fact, they probably do, and thereby reinforce each other.

Socioeconomic considerations, therefore, help structure the processes of movement into political office. To state this in the context of our paradigm, socioeconomic qualifications for office reduce by 60 percent the number of people who can reasonably expect to sit on the council.

From the "Ruling Class" to the Politically Active Stratum

This chapter owes much to Mosca's justly famous analysis of "the ruling class." Of course, the middle class in our cities and the aristocratic families of Southern Italy constitute a "ruling class" in very different ways, but the hypothesis that actual rulers are chosen overwhelmingly from a given social stratum remains very useful. To determine that there is to be found a range in the status hierarchy from which governors disproportionately are chosen still leaves many questions unanswered. Not every member of the middle class in our communities becomes a councilman (neither did every aristocratic family in Italy send a son to the Chamber of Deputies). To build on Mosca's question concerned with which social strata contribute the rulers, we must ask who from within those strata become political leaders.

The task is more difficult for the student of contemporary democratic politics than it would have been for Mosca. If we use the term "eligibles" to refer to citizens having the necessary social and economic traits (falling within the range), it is clear that the number of political eligibles is far greater than the number of citizens actively interested in local government. It certainly is greater than the number who consider competing for a council position.

This can be illustrated in three communities—one very large, one relatively small, and one of intermediate size.

City	Population	Population over 25	Male Population over 25	Estimated Number of Males over 25 in "Socioeconomic Range"	Number of Councilmen
Gilroy	7,500	3,800	1,800	570	7
Menlo Park	27,000	16,500	8,300	2,200	5
Oakland	370,000	230,000	108,000	9,000*	9

* The high percentage of nonwhites in Oakland accounts for the fact that the range is such a smaller proportion of the over 25 male population as compared with the other illustrative cities.

Menlo Park, for example, a city of 27,000 has a five-man city council. Slightly more than 10,000 children, adolescents, and young adults can be eliminated, thus leaving 16,500 adult citizens. By applying the ascriptive trait of sex, this number can be halved. From the remaining 8,000 or so, we estimate how many fall within the socioeconomic range, but are still left with more than two thousand citizens from whom five council positions are to be filled. Which five will it be, and why?

Obviously, we must search for social processes affecting leadership selection other than class differentiations. Since not all members of the eligible social groups become political actives, something is happening in communities to make some eligible citizens more available (or interested) than others. We need to understand who is likely to enter, and who not, the politically active stratum.

Chapter 3

Entry into the Active Stratum: Political Socialization and Leadership Selection

In any American city there are four types of citizens. First, there is the one-fourth to one-third of the population who are politically indifferent. These citizens fail to vote, ignore the comings and goings of political personalities, remain apathetic about political events, and have few opinions about public issues. Second, there are the more politically involved citizens. They do vote and often; they follow political happenings in the newspaper and on TV, discuss politics with friends and neighbors, contact their representatives from time to time, write letters to the local paper or otherwise try to influence fellow citizens to take a stand on the issues of the day. These are the citizens to be found campaigning and contributing money to their respective parties around election time. Depending on the behavior involved, from three-fifths to one-fourth of the citizens might be called politically involved. Third, there are citizens we will call the political actives. These are citizens who have a continuing interest in political matters. They work for and probably know well many public officeholders; they serve their political party on a more regular basis than quadrennial campaigning. They find in their political activities a source of gratifications, personal or psychological gratifications nearly always and more tangible, material gratifications sometimes. Depending on the social composition of the community, there are 10 percent or fewer citizens who can be called politically active. Finally, there are officeholders. These citizens may be elected

or appointed to office, hold a partisan or a nonpartisan position,
serve in the local community or travel to the state capitol or to
Washington. Some of the officeholders will be professionals with a
career at stake. Others will be citizens for whom political officeholding is more an avocation, a hobby which, however important
as a source of psychological gratification, is not a source of livelihood. Taking all the community's officeholders, from the congressional representative to the one-term appointee to the library
board, we can estimate that less than 2 percent of the citizens will
have ever been in this category.[1]

It is difficult to distinguish rigorously and satisfactorily between
these four ways in which citizens relate to political life. What one
scholar prefers to call minimal political participation another will
call active political involvement. The scholar's difficulty is compounded by the fickleness of his subjects—individual citizens shift
from one role to another, a citizen may one year be an active leader
in his community and the next year be content to leave the direction of public affairs to others. We will ignore the niceties of
rigorous distinctions, for to reduce the ambiguity of the classification would take us too far afield and produce too little of consequence. It is sufficient for present purposes to suggest rough criteria
for distinguishing between the first two categories and the second
two categories, that is, between citizens who are actively engaged
in politics on a more or less continuous basis and citizens who are
not.

The time and the energies and the resources of the political
actives are allocated to the process of selecting officeholders and
the process of maintaining control over the policies of government.[2] The active is found doing party chores, serving on committees, organizing protests, lining up candidates, accepting leadership of community organizations, and attending meetings night
after night after night.

His fellow citizens differ not so much in their level of interest
and concern as in their level of investment. Those we call politically involved but nonactive are persons who vote but seldom

---

1 See, for example, Lester Milbrath, *Political Participation* (Chicago: Rand Mc-
Nally & Co., 1965), p. 18. Additional material relevant to estimating the propor-
tion of the population engaging in various political activities can be found in
Angus Campbell, Philip Converse, Warren E. Miller, and Donald E. Stokes, *The
American Voter* (New York: John Wiley & Sons, 1964), especially Chapter 4.
2 The distinction made here is based on that suggested by Robert A. Dahl in
Who Governs? (New Haven: Yale University Press, 1961), pp. 223ff.

search out candidates, who periodically campaign but seldom
organize campaigns, who attend some meetings but seldom chair
them. In other words, they are citizens knowledgeable and concerned about public issues but who leave to others the day-by-day
control over policies.

The distinction between political actives and citizens who are
more observers of than participants in the governing process is
not entirely satisfactory but it does serve our purposes. There are
two points to be made about the distinction. First, the role of
political active is more than a simple extension of citizenship.
Whatever path leads a citizen to the politically active stratum,
once there he must rearrange his private life around the demands
of his public role. This may be an extensive rearrangement such
as leaving the law firm or the business career to engage full-time
in political activities. Or it may be a less extensive rearrangement
such as replacing Thursday night bowling with Thursday night
planning commission meeting or sacrificing a family outing for a
day-long conference on air pollution. In whatever degree the rearrangement is necessary, it is clear that the politically active role
cannot just be added to other commitments and duties. The second
point follows directly from the first. The traits and behaviors
which identify the political actives are sufficiently demanding that
membership in the active stratum is severely limited. Not many
citizens are willing to rearrange their personal lives or established
careers for the punishments of daily political involvement.

Thus, in any community, there is a distinct minority of citizens
who belong to the politically active stratum. Included in their
ranks are officeholders, candidates for office, potential candidates
for office, and actives who themselves do not intend to compete for
office but who attempt directly to influence who is to hold office
and the policies officeholders pursue.

The Research Question and Its Relevance

What social and political processes determine who is likely to
become part of the politically active stratum? This question, of
course, follows directly from our Chinese Box model of leadership
selection. Chapter 2 provided information that could only tell
us who were the most eligible citizens for the active stratum; it
could not tell us who from among the eligibles were likely to become political actives. The relevance of discovering how the active

stratum is established in a community can be outlined with respect to three topics.

—Public officeholders usually come directly from the ranks of the actives.
Barring this route to office, public officeholders will be ushered into their
positions by persons already part of the active stratum. To understand,
then, what community processes are continuously determining who from
among the many citizens will sit in the chairs of formal authority, we must
discover how people come to join the politically active minority.

—If true that public leaders are either drawn from the active stratum or are
largely recruited by persons in that stratum, then we want to know something about who populates the active stratum. More specifically, we want
to know the skills, talents, morals, resources, ideologies, and personality
characteristics of political actives. It is these skills, talents, and so forth,
which in large measure affect the policies of government.

—A study of leadership selection cannot evade the topic of oligarchy and the
question of whether passage into the leadership group is controlled by persons already established in that group. The issue of oligarchic control is
most easily presented by comparing pluralistic with oligarchic explanations
of leadership selection.
    Pluralists and oligarchists agree that to study leadership selection by
studying elections misses an important point. That is, they reject a model
of democratic politics which assumes that elections "select" leaders. Electoral outcomes decide between candidates; leadership selection has to do
with processes which produce the candidates in the first place. The point on
which pluralists and oligarchists agree is well stated by Mosca:

> *When we say that the voters "choose" their representative, we are using*
> *a language that is very inexact. The truth is that the representative has*
> *himself elected by the voters, and, if that phrase should seem too inflex-*
> *ible and too harsh to fit some cases, we might qualify it by saying that*
> *his friends have him elected.*[3]

Having agreed that processes prior to elections determine who is to hold
public authority, the pluralists and oligarchists part company. In the tradition of Michels and accepting the "iron law of oligarchy," some scholars
argue that movement into the leadership group is controlled essentially by
persons already there. Leaders develop techniques of self-perpetuation.[4]
They monopolize information and skills, and, relying on these resources,
effectively control the paths to authority. The leadership group tends to
become socially homogeneous and converges toward a common political
ideology.

---

3 Gaetano Mosca, *The Ruling Class*, translated by Hannah D. Kahn (New York:
McGraw-Hill Book Co., 1939), p. 154.
4 See Robert Michels, *Political Parties* (Glencoe, Ill.: The Free Press, 1949). For
an empirical examination of self-perpetuation among party leadership, see Samuel J. Eldersveld, *Political Parties: A Behavioral Analysis* (Chicago: Rand Mc-
Nally & Co., 1964), especially pp. 160ff. Eldersveld writes: "We have very little
support for a theory of party structure controlled by an elite which guarantees
mobility priority to socially acceptable precinct leaders." P. 163.

The pluralistic approach disagrees with oligarchic theories with respect to whether those in power can, or do, control selection of the next generation of leaders. Pluralists further disagree with the assumption that leaders share a common political ideology. The pluralist case rests in part on the assertion that channels into the leadership group are many and relatively open. Political careers are started in a variety of ways and nurtured in groups of quite divergent political viewpoints. That there are many routes into public office rules out, in the pluralist's explanation, the possibility that a few dominate either political policies or leadership selection.[5]

Data presented in this and the following chapter permit discussion of the three topics briefly outlined above. We will be able to understand the formation of the active stratum by looking at the experiences and events which lead persons to become political actives. In looking at this issue we also will be specifying the complement of skills, talents, viewpoints, and so forth likely to be represented among officeholders. Finally, as we look at the access points into the active stratum we will find clues about the relative openness of the political recruitment processes.

Pathways into the Politically Active Stratum

In describing the collective political career of four hundred or so elected officials, the first thing we learn is perhaps the most striking. Men are being "selected" for office years before their first campaign or initial political victory.[6] The experiences which direct citizens toward a career in public life are often removed by decades and by great distances from the office they actually hold. Men serving on the city councils in the San Francisco Bay Area in the 1960's were youths in the early decades of this century. Fewer than one in five (18 percent) were even reared in the city which they now help govern.

Consider the councilman of a middle-size, recently incorporated residential community in the East Bay. He was raised during the 1920's in a small, rural town in the Midwest. It was there, he tells us, that he first became interested in politics: "When I was eight, my father ran for sheriff, and I went campaigning with him. I had a couple of other relatives who were in politics, one in the state legislature. They were talked about among the family. There were

---

5 See, for instance, Dahl, *Who Governs?*
6 This same point is well put by Donald Matthews, *U.S. Senators and Their World* (New York: Random House Vintage Books, 1960), p. 12.

a few also who were not talked about. I found the family lore very fascinating." One of his colleagues on the council dates his initial interest in public life from similar childhood experiences: "As a lad I used to go to the town meetings in New England with my father. Small towns did everything at the town meetings."

A political family in the Midwest and a town meeting in New England were influencing who would serve on the council of a California city some thirty-five to forty years *before* that city even came into existence. The sifting and sorting of the general population until a relative handful from each generation is left to hold office begins long before candidacies are announced and elections held. To more clearly understand this sifting and sorting we are attempting to discover what pathways lead a few citizens into the politically active stratum.

A citizen may become a political active in one of three ways. (1) His decision to become an active may culminate many years of preoccupation with public affairs and political happenings. Put differently, as a child or youth he was an apprentice active and his adult behavior is a logical extension of interests nurtured over the better part of his lifespan. (2) Entry into the active stratum may not be continuous with long-standing interest in public affairs. It may be a more sudden decision, a decision which means that a preoccupation with public affairs occurs simultaneously with active involvement. Unlike political actives who have had a protracted active interest, persons in this category have a shorter "political" history. We can say that the experiences which ushered them into the active stratum are telescoped in time. (3) A citizen may enter the active stratum at the same time he takes office. Persons who move directly from citizen roles to public office resemble the second category with respect to suddenness of entry. Their political careers differ, however, in that they spend little or no time in general public activities prior to their appointment to or, in some cases, campaign for political office.

In specifying three pathways into the active stratum we make one general distinction and another more specific subdistinction. We first distinguish between citizens whose active roles are the result of pre-adult experiences and concerns from citizens whose political activity is not predated by years of association with politicians and political matters. Then, within the group of "sudden entrants," we distinguish further between citizens who become political activists and subsequently officeholders and citizens who begin their public careers as officeholders.

We shall call persons whose adult activity is the continuation of prior involvements and interests the *politically socialized*. Citizens whose entry into the active stratum is more sudden but whose activities occur prior to actually holding office are called the *politically mobilized*. Finally, those who are directly recruited into a public office are called *lateral entrants.*[7]

The first question in a series asking councilmen to describe their initial involvement and subsequent career in politics was posed as follows:

> I would like to shift our talk a bit and ask you a few questions about your background. We would like to find out how people first become generally aware of and interested in government and public affairs.

> Now, if you think back as far as you can, how did you first become aware of public matters? For instance, what is your very first recollection of being interested?

Interviewers were instructed to emphasize the *interest* and *awareness* dimension of this question so that respondents would not begin by discussing their specific council career. It was from answers to this question, and only this one, that we determined whether a councilman belonged in the socialized, mobilized, or lateral entry career category.

The Politically Socialized

Life experiences present to some citizens a rich array of political stimuli. Their interest in political matters—usually partisan politics—is deeply and firmly embedded in a long history. Being actively involved in public affairs is considered before conditions make such involvement an actual possibility. The protracted nature of the career is illustrated in the case where movement is from a politically active family to school politics to early adulthood involvement and finally into elected politics. The quotations below

---

[7] These terms are not completely satisfactory; certainly they are not free of ambiguity. A variety of very different phenomena have been cataloged under the headings "socialization" and "mobilization" in the general political science literature. I use the terms more as a matter of convenience than as a matter of theoretical purity. However, I have attempted to conform to the scientific norm which holds that it is not the arbitrariness of definitions so much as their looseness which hinders cumulative knowledge. Thus, while I do not presume that my usage is similar in all respects to that of other scholars, I will take care to specify exactly how the terms are used in the present context.

clearly illustrate some of the many facets of the political socialization pathway into the active stratum.

> I remember an eighth-grade civics course. I got interested in government then. All through school I was involved in politics, was in student body elections in high school and editor of the paper in college. I've always been interested in how government works. [And, we might add, in working it.]

> I read the political pages when I was six and attended caucuses when I was eight years old. I loved history in school. I was a leader in grammar school. I went to a classy high school and was on the honor society and elected to student council. In college I was president of the main student body.

> It has been in our family to be interested. No one was as interested as I to have been elected; Dad was interested in Democratic politics. We discussed it at home. I took an interest in writing to FDR. I wasn't interested in school politics but mock political conventions. I always had a desire to get into politics.

The Politically Mobilized

In contrast to the rich political backgrounds indicated above, the politically mobilized insist that no unusual interest predated their active involvement in public affairs. For these citizens experiences in their adult years triggered a commitment to political action. Conditions range all the way from "some friends asked me" to "I was mad about the way things were going and decided to do something about it." Whether a willing response to the urgings of others or a self-generated decision, the mobilized have a relatively nonpolitical background. The following quotations illustrate typical patterns.

> As soon as our children started going to school I became interested in community projects—Little League, Scouts, etc. I just developed an interest in the community and wanting to participate as a result of family growth. We were never very politically minded in our family when I was growing up.

> The city wanted to put a butane storage tank next to my house. I went out and got a petition. I got it re-zoned. It was all started when I bought a home. I became conscious of things that might lower the value of my home. This all started twenty-six years ago. I got active in the Chamber of Commerce.

> When I came to this area, it was unincorporated. I started a small law office. The way of life of an attorney brings it about that in getting a clientele you have to join organizations. I became a member of a Merchant Organization which favored incorporation. There I became active. Before, in college, I had no interest in politics.

The Lateral Entrants

We have said that persons who were neither very interested nor active in political affairs prior to their selection for a public office are lateral entrants into the active stratum. The clarity of the classification criterion, however, masks a particularly troublesome question. We often do not know just what kind of preselection activities to call political. Eisenhower, for instance, could be labeled a lateral entrant into the political arena. On the other hand, the activities of a five-star general and a college president are very much public. We cannot resolve such ambiguities here and choose to accept the face validity of the responses to the question asking about earliest interest. The following are examples of lateral entry.

> I was asked to become a member of the Council. The company I worked for, the cemetery company, was interested in having a representative on the City Council. They talked about it.

> I became interested in council affairs when I was appointed to the council by the Mayor. Prior to this appointment I had never taken an active interest in government or public affairs.

> I was bothered by some issues that I did not agree with. My wife urged me to try to do something about these things if I didn't like them, so I ran for the Council in 1964.

Frequency of the Three Pathways into the Active Stratum

Exactly half the councilmen are classified as politically socialized. A rich and varied history of political experiences serves to usher them into the active stratum. The next largest group are the politically mobilized (38 percent); their political activities are not the result of growing up with politics so much as experiences encountered in later years. Finally, 12 percent of the councilmen claim not to have been particularly aware of or active in political matters prior to holding public office. Table 3–1 presents these data.

A cautionary word about this table should be added. The distribution tells us what proportion of councilmen entered the politically active stratum along each of the three pathways. It does not tell us what proportion of political actives follow the different pathways. To answer the latter question requires a sample of

Table 3–1

Proportion of Councilmen Who Followed the
Three Pathways into the Active Stratum
(N = 431)

The Pathway of Political Socialization	50%
The Pathway of Political Mobilization	38
The Pathway of Lateral Entry	12
	100%

actives, not of officeholders. This limitation does not, however, interrupt the analysis we have proposed. Our question is how communities select the few who govern from a much larger population. A part of the answer lies in understanding how elected leaders were initially ushered into the active stratum.

In the remainder of this chapter we describe the progression of the politically socialized into the active stratum. The other two pathways, mobilization and lateral entry, will not receive separate treatment but will be described with data specifically related to the way in which all councilmen first became active in political matters.

Political Socialization and Leadership Selection

Young Americans, or at least youths in the white, middle-class America from which the councilmen come, have very similar political socialization experiences. From parents and youth leaders, from teachers and school lessons, from their friends, and from the mass media the young American learns what it means to be a citizen. A loyal and patriotic attachment to the nation is formed as the youth first learns about the nation's political heroes and is taught to revere the nation's political symbols. An understanding of the democratic creed and of the values presumably guiding government policies are acquired in Scouts and student councils and other citizenship training groups. A familiarity with and respect for the two-party system is developed as the youth learns from parental example and other adult models. In general, citizenship values and political attachments develop early in a person's life and persist, although always being modified, throughout his life.[8]

---

[8] Much of the relevant literature is reviewed in Richard E. Dawson and Kenneth Prewitt, *Political Socialization* (Boston: Little, Brown & Co., 1969), especially in Chapter 5.

For some youths, early political socialization is more than the inculcation of citizenship values. The experiences of childhood or adolescence include an exposure to politics such that a deep and lasting attachment to political activity itself occurs. Half the councilmen speak of such an exposure.[9] To explain why in their political involvement they differ so much from 90 percent of the community, they trace their active political careers back to preadult experiences which first set them on the path leading to public office.

It is appropriate to speak of an unusual or special kind of political socialization for these councilmen. In doing so, however, it is not necessary to assume that these councilmen differ from their colleagues or from the rest of middle-class Americans with respect to general citizenship socialization. Unusual political socialization experiences may make some citizens political actives. How these citizens acquired political values other than their activist dispositions need not be different from the way in which any adult citizen of this socioeconomic stratum first acquired basic political values. The issue of whether differences in early socialization relevant to political *activity* imply differences relevant to general citizenship values is an important one, and it is an issue to which we return at the end of the chapter. At this point, we assume that youths socialized into politically active roles need not differ from their peers in the way in which they acquire feelings of patriotism, a sense of political obligation, an incipient party identification, and so forth.

Councilmen Who Were Socialized into an Active Political Role

About half the councilmen (47 percent) whose pathway into the active stratum has been called political socialization date their initial preoccupation with politics in childhood or early adolescence. Illustrative is the councilman who:

> first became interested when I learned to read. I read in the Chicago Tribune about Orphan Annie. That was full of political matters. Hoover's election got me interested. That was when I was eight.

Another municipal leader recalls "campaigning for Governor Johnson when I was six," and one councilman insists that "learn-

---

[9] A more elaborate explication of "exposure" as a route into political activity can be found in Kenneth Prewitt, "Political Socialization and Leadership Selection," *Annals of the American Academy of Political and Social Science* 361 (September 1965):96–111.

ing the forty-eight state capitals in kindergarten" initially introduced him to the excitement of political matters.

The remaining councilmen in the political socialization group
(53 percent) cite high school or college years as the beginning point
of an interest which led to political activity and finally to public
office. Typical is the man who, as a high school sophomore, "had a
teacher who opened up to me the whole new world of political
science"; or the businessman who wryly recalls "leading a revolt
of the whole student body against the school administration during my college days."

Some of those who were early attracted to politics recognized the
career potential. A few of these are councilmen who spent their
childhood years in ethnic neighborhoods of Northeastern cities.
The possibilities of political mobility and its rewards did not escape them. The Boston-raised councilman who "knew I was going
to be a leader when I was still a kid" anticipates his adult role and
selectively exposes himself to experiences supporting his self-image
and furthering his ambitions. Other councilmen whose political
careers can be traced to childhood will have been less sensitive to
career possibilities but nevertheless can recount "holding office
from the third or fourth grade on."

In reminiscing about childhood, these councilmen clearly indicate that political socialization meant something more than acquir-
ing citizenship attitudes. Embedded in their preadult years are
experiences which laid the foundation for active involvement in
public life. Their political socialization experiences preselected
them for the active stratum. Salisbury states it well when he writes,
political activity "is an aspect of a life style which has uncritically
been accepted since childhood by a relatively small number of
people in the society. . . . Such people, though a very small part
of the total population, make up a very large portion of the political participants."[10]

What Was Special About Their Political Socialization?

The data suggest that their political socialization differs in three
ways: (a) the political family; (b) the political relevance of a school
experience; (c) exposure to dramatic political events or personal-

---

10 Robert Salisbury, "The Urban Party Organization Member," *Public Opinion
Quarterly* 39 (Winter 1965):564.

ities. Either singly or in some combination, these three socialization experiences are relevant to the political careers of all but seventeen of the councilmen whose adult activity is predated by long-standing preoccupation with political matters. Table 3–2 provides us with an overview.

Table 3–2

Frequency of Various Types of Political Socialization Experiences Mentioned by Those Councilmen Who Explain Their Political Activity with Reference to Preadult Political Socialization
(N = 214)

Political Family	14%
School Experience	31
Political Event/Personality	10
Family and School	7
Family and Event/Personality	10
School and Event/Personality	8
Family, School, and Event/Personality	11
Other	8
(Ideological Concern—4%)	
(Miscellaneous—4%)	
	99%

The Political Family: Inheriting an Interest

Before nobility of blood was displaced by nobility of wealth, a ruler could bestow public office on his progeny. Sons of royalty became royalty. Quite literally, the political elite reproduced themselves. Following the Industrial Revolution, as achievement criteria replaced ascriptive criteria, hereditary leadership all but disappeared. The son might still choose to follow his father's occupation, but there is no guarantee that the father's position will someday be his, especially if the parental position is elected office. "A man may bestow his land, wealth, and social connections upon his son, but he cannot bestow his corporation position, artistic pre-eminence, or elected office."[11]

Yet, even in the achievement society, political views and dispositions of offspring frequently bear close resemblance to those of parents. Community loyalties, partisan identifications, political stereotypes, and other political inclinations are transmitted from

[11] Suzanne Keller, *Beyond the Ruling Class* (New York: Random House, 1963), p. 70.

parent to child.[12] If such general political views are inherited, we should assume that a proclivity for political activity is also inherited. And, of course, the evidence, though sparse, consistently supports the reasonableness of this assumption.

A review of all available studies of the family background of political actives in American politics suggests that the proportion of the active stratum tracing their involvement to parental influence ranges between 30 and 40 percent, depending on the type of political active studied and the way the question is worded. There are studies of municipal leaders in St. Louis and New Haven in addition to those in our sample from the San Francisco area;[13] there are studies of political party workers in St. Louis, Detroit, and Los Angeles;[14] there are studies of state legislators in California, Ohio, Tennessee, New Jersey, and Connecticut.[15] Figures in the magnitude of 30 to 40 percent are significantly higher than chance. If we assume that 5 to 10 percent of American families include some member actively involved in politics, it is apparent that these comparatively few families contribute disproportionately to the political actives of the next generation. Stated differently, upwards of two-fifths of the politically active stratum come from approximately five percent of the nation's families.

Speaking about political party organizations, Marvick and Nixon note:

> Analysis suggests that the politicized family and politically active parents are peculiarly important in accounting for the nucleus that sustains a

12 See the general review in Herbert Hyman, *Political Socialization* (Glencoe, Ill.: The Free Press, 1959) and Dawson and Prewitt, *Political Socialization,* Chapter 7.

13 Results from a study of St. Louis city councilmen can be found in Bryan T. Downes, "Suburban Differentiation and Municipal Policy Choices: A Comparative Analysis of Suburban Political Systems" (St. Louis: unpublished doctoral dissertation, Washington University, 1966). For New Haven, see Dahl, *Who Governs?* For additional evidence from New Haven, see Rufus P. Browning, "Business in Politics: Motivation and Circumstances in the Rise to Power" (New Haven: unpublished doctoral dissertation, Yale University, 1960).

14 Data relevant to St. Louis are presented in Salisbury, "Urban Party Organization Member," to Detroit in Eldersveld, *Political Parties,* and to Los Angeles in Dwaine Marvick and Charles R. Nixon, "Recruitment Contrasts in Rival Campaign Groups," in Marvick (ed.), *Political Decision-Makers* (New York: The Free Press of Glencoe, 1961).

15 Data relevant to the first four states are presented in John Wahlke, Heinz Eulau, William Buchanan, and LeRoy C. Ferguson, *The Legislative System* (New York: John Wiley & Sons, 1962), p. 83. Connecticut legislators are studied in David Barber, *The Lawmakers: Recruitment and Adaptation to Legislative Life* (New Haven: Yale University Press, paperback edition, 1965), pp. 264–70.

voluntary party apparatus in campaign after campaign; thus, they are important in maintaining the continuity of talent and skill, experience and conviction, essential at this level of a democratic political order.[16]

The processes by which the political family links successive generations of political leadership operate in two general ways. There is the clear case of the child adopting the father's occupation. Hereditary politicians, common in French and British political life, are also known in American leadership. Families such as the Adamses, the Roosevelts, the La Follettes, the Tafts, the Lodges, and, more recently, the Rockefellers produce political leaders from one generation to the next. The occupational continuity characteristic of these families operates as well at less publicized levels of American political life.

A second pattern is less evident but more frequent. Many public officials inherit from their family not an occupation but an interest, even passion, for things political. The parental model need not be an officeholder, indeed, often is not. Parents need only be actively engaged in the network of associations and friendships which constitute the politically active stratum. Children of party workers, community influentials, lobbyists, union officials, or ethnic leaders are introduced to politics as a matter of course.

In Table 3–2, we see that two-fifths of the councilmen whose pathway to the active stratum was a political socialization experience mention the influence of their family. A local politician whose father had been a councilman for eighteen years tells us, "Politics was part of my life because of my father's participation." Another says his maternal grandfather "was very active in politics" and he himself first became politically aware "when I was in kindergarten." We previously quoted the councilman who very simply says: "It has been in our family to be interested." Equally direct is the son of a high school civics teacher who says, "I got my concepts of government and citizen responsibility directly from my father. Citizen responsibility, again and again and again."

In American politics, and we suspect elsewhere, there clearly is something appropriately called the political family. These families, though small in number, contribute heavily to the political leadership circles. Our data and other evidence we have reviewed runs counter to the hypothesis currently being advanced by certain students of political recruitment. The notion is best outlined in Keller's study of elite recruitment where she notes that the

---

[16] Marvick and Nixon, "Recruitment Contrasts," p. 210.

family's role in recruitment to elite positions, political and other-wise, has and will continue to diminish. "In the past, the fam-ily was the chief school for both kings and carpenters, and thereby contributed to the continuity of the social order." Today, however, the changes wrought by social and technological advancements "have deprived the family of the capacity to prepare the future generations for the lives they are to lead."[17] Keller summarizes her position by noting that the family, in being widely dispersed and fragmented into small individual units, "has lost much of its so-cial power. . . . Where it was once the springboard into society, it is now more of a refuge from it."[18]

This hypothesis does not stand the scrutiny of application to specific social spheres. Certainly, with respect to political involve-ment and leadership, families continue to serve as training ground for adult roles. Families still serve as the springboard into the politically active stratum and, thereby, into public office.

One important consequence of family transmission as a process structuring leadership selection has to do with the intensity of political attachment. The person long associated with political matters forms strong attachments to a political role, especially if that association begins under the tutelage of persons as important to his socialization as his parents are. The images of the political world conveyed by parental model are both intimate and dramatic; family exposure to political action produces more than casual commitment by offspring.

A second consequence has to do with political skills. In being closely associated with adult models actively involved in politics, the impressionable youth in the political family can acquire lead-ership talent as well as familiarity with political processes. The importance of the political family in this regard is clearly spelled out by Marvick and Nixon. They write of the political family as one in which:

> political matters receive both substantial and sustained attention, and in which skills in the analysis of public issues are supplemented by examples of adult political participation as well. In this way, the possibility is opened of developing a sense of civic responsibility that will cause each generation to "act out" its family heritage on the political stage, and, in turn, inculcate the same activist example and sense of duty in the succeeding generation.[19]

17 Keller, *Beyond the Ruling Class*, p. 217.
18 *Ibid.*, p. 262.
19 Marvick and Nixon, "Recruitment Contrasts," pp. 209–10.

The political family introduces into leadership selection processes a certain continuity of political experience and political conviction. Those who grow up with politics become sensitized to the rewards and possibilities of public leadership. They acquire a sense for the potential inherent in the levers of political power. Whether they also are trained to recognize the dangers of exceeding established limits will, of course, vary from one political family to the next. But, clearly, political families play more than a minor part in determining the composition of the active stratum.

The School Years: "Learning" to Be an Active

Public schools are undoubtedly second in importance only to the family as an agency of citizenship training.[20] Certainly in the United States, the public school undertakes a heavy share of the political socialization task. Teachers, aided by carefully designed curriculum materials, are expected to instill in the young an appreciation of citizenship responsibilities and, secondarily, citizenship rights. Civic and history classes take their place alongside reading and arithmetic instruction; proper public conduct is taught both directly and indirectly. Many states have laws insisting that the student's day include patriotic rituals: Pledging allegiance to the flag each morning, singing the national anthem, ceremonial programs honoring national heroes and events, and displaying political symbols are among the rituals in the school's repertory of socialization techniques. Research on the effectiveness of the public schools in making "good citizens" supports the common-sense observation that citizenship values are transmitted daily by teacher, curriculum, rituals, and parapolitical extracurricular activities.

Much less is known about the issue of interest to us. Does the school serve as a training ground for the role of political active? If so, how? The only systematic evidence available is about university students. For these older youths it is clear that participation in student political organizations can be a step into the active political stratum. Through his involvement in political actions, campus organizations, and student youth groups, the student moves directly into an active political role as an adult. As one

---

[20] For a study which emphasizes the public school as a political socialization agent, see Robert Hess and Judith Torney, *The Development of Basic Political Attitudes in Children* (Chicago: Aldine Publishing Co., 1967).

commentator writes, student political organizations "are usually the main source of political education for the students involved in them, and often have a vital and lasting effect on those involved."[21]

Unfortunately, it is not known whether the student political organization is joined by persons with a political career in mind or whether the organizational activity is responsible for choice of such a career. The problem is further compounded because adult political groups, especially the political parties, sponsor student political organizations, such as the Young Democrats or Young Republicans, as a means of finding and training future leaders for their own organizations. Nevertheless, whether the relationship between student activity and adult activity is to be explained by self-recruitment, by the socializing effect of the student organization, or by sponsorship, the fact remains that the pathway for some members of the active stratum is through parapolitical organizations during their student days.

With the exception of this hypothesis, however, little attention has been given to how school experiences may start some persons toward active political careers. We have even less information about why, from among a group of students receiving the same lessons or taking the same field trips, only a few are responsive. Our data are suggestive but not conclusive with respect to school-initiated political careers. To begin with, more than half (57 percent) of the councilmen whose political activity we have traced to preadulthood mention the importance of school experiences, Further, nearly a third of these councilmen mention *only* school experiences as important, more than twice as many who mention only the political family as important. (See Table 3–2.) The school's impact on who joins the politically active stratum is not just as a complementary agency supporting dispositions already learned in the family. Clearly, the school has an independent relationship to leadership selection processes.

We can provide two general answers to the question of what kinds of school experiences stimulate political activity. First, teachers and curriculum materials can instill a disposition for political action as well as the more diffuse citizenship values. Councilmen date their initial interest in politics from such moments as "when I took my first history course," or "taking all the government courses I could in high school." Other councilmen

---

[21] Philip G. Altbach, "Students and Politics," *Comparative Education Review* 10 (1966):185.

stress the importance of the teacher more than the course: "When I was a sophomore in high school, I had a teacher who opened up to me the whole new world of political science." A banker from a small town first became politically aware during his college years when he "enrolled in a political science course because it was taught by a former high school teacher of mine. I was interested in him, so I took his course." A field trip to city hall or to the state capitol can have an impact similar to that of the exciting teacher or the stimulating course. One councillor recalls visiting city hall as part of a class assignment, a visit which led to "the habit of attending city council meetings every Monday night." All together, more than fifty councilmen in our sample recount with obvious warmth the significance of an inspiring teacher or fascinating reading.

Approximately the same number of councilmen trace their careers to student politics. From first grade through college, student governments are set up, by and large, to teach the values of self-government and to familiarize students with the forms and procedures they will face in the adult political world. There is much speculation in writings of educators about the citizenship training value of extracurricular activities, especially the importance of student councils, homeroom elections, and the like. However, little systematic evidence has been marshalled establishing just how much effect these activities have.[22] Our evidence suggests that, for a few students, student governments provide direct experience in holding office and organizing collective actions. Student councils and the like are generally designed in form and title as prototypical of society's political institutions. Some students evidently find their grammar school, high school, or college offices useful training ground for leadership in the post-school years. An ex-president of his grammar school class reports his "presidency" as the experience first attracting him to political involvement. Another councilman says he had held office from third or fourth grade on. "I have always been president of classes in school and church groups," testifies a third. Some wait for high school or college honors, such as the councilman who says his "interest started about as far back as when in college I ran for class office."

These quotations support our contention that the homeroom election, the student safety patrol, the class office often serve as

---

22 A review of some of the relevant studies can be found in Roy A. Price, "Citizenship Studies in Syracuse," *Phi Delta Kappan* 33 (December 1951):180. Other studies are reviewed in Dawson and Prewitt, *Political Socialization*, Chapter 8.

training grounds for adult political roles. While what we find in the councilmen's remarks is not as dramatic as a finding that student radicals in a Brazilian university graduate to the ranks of adult revolutionaries, the findings do share common theoretical assumptions. As an educational institution, the public school has responsibilities more broadly defined than teaching basic literacy or numeric skills. The school is a training ground for a variety of adult roles. School bands produce adult musicians; school drama clubs produce adult thespians; school ham radio operators' clubs produce adult engineers; school sports produce adult athletes. With respect to political roles it has long been held that student councils and student elections will produce informed adult citizens. But it appears from our data that there is an even closer connection between school experiences and adult political roles. The availability of formal student leadership positions, patterned in name and responsibilities after adult models, can produce from among the large school population a few who will move into political leadership roles as adults.

Furthermore, some indirect data suggest that the likelihood of adult actives having started their political career in school activities may be increasing. The younger the councilman, the more likely he is to mention a school experience as relevant to his entry into the politically active stratum. For instance, 65 percent of the councilmen under forty years of age mention the socialization impact of the school; only 35 percent of councilmen over fifty-five years of age cite a school experience. (That this is not just a matter of differential recall by the younger councilmen is suggested by the fact that mention of a political family in the background does not at all vary by age of the councilman.) This pattern is consistent with the observation that schools are more and more becoming politically conscious. More courses with political material are being taught; teachers are less afraid to discuss political matters (and to take political stands as is evidenced by their strike activities); and students themselves are more likely to be politically informed and to organize themselves into political clubs. We should expect the proportion of political actives who have been influenced by school experience to increase with each successive generation of high school and college graduates.

Political Events: The Spectator Becomes Active

Political events in American life have a way of becoming spectacles, often in very spectacular ways. Politics, having to do with power and conflict and tension and larger-than-life personalities, is inherently dramatic. The issues and personalities of politics are part of a drama very much acted out on the public stage of American life, as it should be in a nation priding itself as an open democracy. Combined with the natural excitement of politics is the American knack for making any national event an occasion for entertainment. One need only watch a Presidential nominating convention to recognize the Hollywood syndrome; the convention becomes a production and the participants actors. For some citizens the drama and excitement of political life has special attraction. And when these citizens are youngsters, political drama can so whet their appetites that they aspire to be some day part of "the great game of politics." Nearly two-fifths (39 percent) of the politically socialized report that their early attraction to politics was nourished in the context of dramatic political happenings.

Campaigns, especially Presidential campaigns, lead the list of such socialization experiences. What has been said about state legislators is also applicable to city councilmen: "the excitement, the turbulence, the color, the intrusion of the campaign into the routine existence of a relatively little politicized society like America's seem to make a profound impression, so that many years later a particular election or administration may be recalled with a great deal of relish as a source of political interest. . . ."[23] One councilman recalls "getting belted for wearing a Hoover button in '32"; he was eight at the time. Another councilman, when only six, "carried campaign posters in the Alfred E. Smith campaign."

In addition to the drama of a campaign, contact with imposing political figures can attract the impressionable youth to politics. The councilman whose maternal grandfather "was very involved in politics" recalls the awe he felt when the Governor came to visit. Often, of course, such associations are facilitated because the family is politically active. The precinct meeting in the front room, the father's friend in city hall, or the neighbor leading the political parade conjure up vivid images in the child's mind. When contact with these "powerful" and just a little "mysterious" personages takes place in the personalized setting of the active family, a fascination with politics is formed.

For some councilmen, "politics was in the air" where they grew up. They needed no special event or person to portray to them the political drama. For one Californian currently holding mu-

---

[23] Wahlke, Eulau et al., *The Legislative System*, p. 89.

nicipal office, the streets of Chicago served as his political schooling ground. His vivid description is illustrative of the effective
socialization of a milieu.

> When I was a child in Chicago I saw somebody killed in a street fight.
> Police would raid bookie stores with machine guns that didn't pay protec-
> tion. Politics was moving into the schools.

Another Chicago youth whose family was never active in politics
became interested because:

> I could see what I considered a complete loss of contact with the govern-
> ment by the people and vice versa. There was corruption throughout; it
> wasn't even hidden. One party dominated the scene. Pressures were often
> ridiculous. For example, the garbage collector only got the garbage from
> party members. The citizens not serviced then got citations from the health
> department.

Both of these councilmen see a direct link between these childhood
experiences and their subsequent involvement in public life. As
one states it, "The previous council's attorney in our city was like
the attorney of Chicago. He didn't give a damn what people
thought. He refused to listen. I wanted to see what could be done
about it."

Of course, "growing up with politics" does not necessarily mean
experiencing the shock of observing street killings. A councilman
who spent his youth in the nation's capital—but whose father was
not involved politically—"just breathed politics as a kid." It is
apparent that an urban childhood is much more likely to facilitate
this "socialized by the milieu" pattern. The proximity of the child
to precinct politics formed images which are vividly recalled decades later and two thousand miles away. "I was born in Kansas
City, Missouri, close to the Pendergast and Truman machines, as
close as the average citizen could be and I was very aware."

The impact of a political event, personality, or a "political
atmosphere" is, interestingly enough, more frequently cited by
Democrats (43 percent) than Republicans (28 percent). It is also
more frequently cited by persons comparatively new to their
California cities. This indirect evidence suggests how political life
in an urban—but non-Californian—setting can initiate a political
career irrespective of family influence or school experience. Ethnic
neighborhoods in particular appear to have this consequence. This
is relevant for the mobility argument introduced in the last chapter, and is illustrated by the councilman who wanted to use
politics "to improve my station in life. I knew I was as good as

anybody, in every sense." The achievement motive is traced to a Boston neighborhood of Eastern European extraction.

Issue Concern: The Ideological Attraction of Politics

Family ties, school experiences, and exposure to the drama of politics are childhood experiences which ushered 90 percent of the politically socialized councilmen into the active stratum. The remaining councilmen, plus some of those included in the previous discussion, remark that their earliest interest in politics was actually a preoccupation with the social problems of the day.

Obviously, a concern with social problems can lead to political action, since it is within the political arena that social ills are identified and, it is hoped, social cures proffered. We should expect that among those interested in political action since youth will be a few who view their action in the context of ideological commitments. And, by stretching the term "ideological commitment" to include a sense of political indignation as well as a sense of diffuse obligation to society, we can identify fifty-six councilmen whose interest was initiated in this manner. This group (26 percent of the politically socialized) connect their political interest to a developing social consciousness. In the colorful words of one councilman: "During the war I thought. I sat around in the desert and thought about what the country was up to, thinking of political philosophy. I guess unconsciously I thought I'd actively do something about it."

Broad social issues such as war, depression, or a struggle for civil rights can, thus, help determine who will enter the politically active stratum. Parts of the population will be politically mobilized or at least become more politically aware during periods of domestic or international crisis. On the whole, however, our political philosopher is the exception. The great issues of economic deprivation, peace, or minority rights were salient for but a few of the councilmen. It has been remarked in another context that Americans tend to be pragmatist rather than idealist in their political orientation. The infrequency with which political interest is traced to ideological commitments can be interpreted in this context.[24]

Of course, note should be taken that the potential impact on

---

[24] The nonideological character of American politics is commented on in Campbell et al., *American Voter*, Chapter 8.

political socialization processes of ideological issues is subject to considerable shift from one generation to the next. The "quiet fifties" were replaced by the "active sixties" under the mounting pressure of the civil rights movement and the political polarization over the Vietnam issue. Youths today being prepared for an active role in politics tomorrow may be less indifferent than their immediate predecessors to the ideological context of politics. It remains to be seen whether American political life will be affected when the peace corps volunteer, the registrar of black voters, the antiwar marcher, and the participant democrat of the college campus move into community leadership positions. The hypothesis suggested by our data is that a higher proportion of the next generation's actives will have first been involved in politics over an ideological concern.

In addition to broad social issues, other semi-ideological motives were relevant to the political histories of some of the councilmen. In particular, a diffuse sense of obligation or responsibility can attract a person to the political arena. The councilman who was taught civic duty "again and again and again" is a case in point. We might say that the lesson of citizenship was "overlearned" by such councilmen. They have followed to the letter the injunction that the good citizen should be actively involved in the life of his community. Their zealous application of one component of the citizenship norm placed them among the minority of citizens who belong to the active stratum.

Concluding Observations: Remarks About a Democratic Theory of Leadership Selection

The way in which persons enter the politically active stratum is relevant to three general topics: the processes through which a few are chosen to govern the many; the skills and viewpoints represented among persons from whom (or by whom) officeholders are chosen; the degree of oligarchic control in political recruitment. None of these topics can be analyzed exhaustively with the evidence in the present chapter; all three of them, however, will be somewhat clarified on the basis of conclusions we can draw from the evidence.

Of the councilmen governing the nearly ninety municipalities in the Bay Area, half began their political careers long before the voters could influence their choice to be an active. Indeed, they were on the path to a council position well before any screening or selecting agencies could have had an interest in them. These councilmen entered the active minority because of experiences in their childhood and adolescent years. They became politically active—and thus available for the next stage in the leadership selection process—because their family was political, or because a teacher or reading or field trip stimulated their interest, or because the drama of political events commanded their attention, or because a social issue forced political consciousness on them.

In other words, *the accidents of personal life-experiences determine who will join the active stratum*. Now, it is true that these "accidents" are not evenly distributed throughout all of society; the kinds of life-experiences which usher the young into active political roles are biased in favor of the middle class. Nevertheless, within the group of citizens eligible for the active stratum, only a few actually belong. This minority of political actives within the larger minority of political eligibles appears to reach the active stratum as a consequence of fortuitous happenings.

Two conclusions follow from an observation about the haphazard processes determining who will join the active stratum: (a) the events and experiences determining active political involvement generally are beyond the selective manipulation of any single group intent on controlling who should be available for public office; (b) a range and variety of personal experiences determines the composition of the politically active minority; and consequently, the political motives, hopes, images, talents, and goals represented in the active stratum will be varied.

To consider these conclusions and their relevance to leadership selection in a democracy we must raise what in the discussion thus far is a new issue but what in political recruitment theory is an issue dating from Plato's *Republic*.

The Political Leader: One of the People or Specially Trained?

Although it is to oversimplify greatly, we can note two general ways in which the governing minority might be prepared for leadership responsibilities. At an early age, the future leader can be identified and then separated from the general population. The purpose of this identification and separation is to provide the leader training designed specifically for the public responsibilities he is one day to assume. He is socialized into an elite culture. The second possibility is to leave the future leader unidentified and not to separate him from the experiences normal to the general population. His political socialization would be similar to that of any other youth of his general social group. We will call the first possibility "sponsored selection" and the second possibility "contest selection."[25]

Sponsored Selection

In the *Republic*, Plato elaborates a basic principle he has learned from Socrates: Government is not something to be put in the hands of wayward amateurs or the untutored. Men who rule should be trained and disciplined and prepared for managing public affairs. Once he has been tapped by his teachers for possible membership in the ruling elite, the Athenian youth begins a long and grueling preparation. The future Guardian receives one type of education; his friends who someday will become craftsmen, soldiers, merchants, farmers, and common citizens receive another.

Separating rulers from the population at large and providing for their special instruction is a practice known to many societies. Certainly, wherever biological reproduction is the leadership selection technique, the political elite will receive a political education which can only make them "different" from the people they rule. In hereditary monarchies, this practice is elevated to the state of prescription. Exposure to the royal court is considered an indispensable part of the young prince's socialization. A similar practice was observed in the African Kingdom of Buganda. Sons of chiefs took up residence at the Court of the Kabaka (the priest-king of Buganda) in order to learn and benefit from daily contact with the royalty. No man could hope for political importance unless his youth was spent at the Court.

---

25 These terms are taken from Ralph H. Turner, "Sponsored and Contest Mobility," *American Sociological Review* 25, No. 6 (December 1960):855–67. We use them to a slightly different purpose from Turner who has compared American and British schooling in terms of the different mobility norms. Sponsored mobility, characteristic of the British public school system, is mobility which favors a controlled selection process. "In this process the elite or their agents, deemed to be best qualified to judge merit, choose individuals for elite status who have the appropriate qualities. Individuals do not win or seize elite status; mobility is rather a process of sponsored induction into the elite." Contest mobility, on the other hand, is "like a sporting event in which many compete for a few recognized prizes." P. 287.

Contest Selection

Democratic or competitive theories of leadership selection come to conclusions very different from what is outlined in the *Republic*. It is better for the political order if those who are to occupy places of political power are first socialized into the general political culture. Political socialization, broadly defined, and leadership training, narrowly defined, are sequential. First comes general socialization and only after this initial baptism is the leader identified and given special training. The intent is to guarantee that political leaders will have internalized the norms and values of the common citizens. Leaders should be products of the same socialization experienced by those they rule.

These two models differ in specifying the best training for future leaders but, even more importantly, they differ in outlining the preferable relationship between the leaders and the people. The different relationships follow from the different values maximized in the two models.

Plato, and most of the historical variants on the Platonic model, stressed the *quality* of the leadership. The best leader is the disinterested leader. The Guardians, it will be remembered, were to remain untouched by the squabbles, the corruptions, and the petty differences of the common citizens. They were to govern by philosophizing, by concerning themselves with what the people should have, not with what the people wanted. There is, then, in Plato, an intent to create and maintain distance between the experiences of the rulers and the experiences of the ruled.

A consequence, not necessarily intended by Plato, but, as history shows, scarcely avoidable under his rules, is that leadership circles will be relatively closed and self-perpetuating. Who but the already chosen would know how to recognize and train future leaders?

Under assumptions of contest selection, *variety* in leadership is stressed. Leaders should not be disinterested and removed, but representative of the moods, viewpoints, and habits of the people. Leaders govern by representing what the people want, not by philosophizing about what they need. The intent is to close as much as possible the gap between rulers and ruled. It is preferable if leaders have had the same formative experiences which shape the values of the average citizens. Since populations are almost always heterogeneous in their political preferences and experiences, it follows that leaders must be a varied lot. Since no one is sure who will make a good ruler and since no single group should have its views unequally represented, the processes through which leaders are selected should remain as open and flexible as possible. Further, if the leaders are to be responsive to the people, they should come from the people.

In outlining the differences between the two positions on leadership selection, it has been necessary to be brief. Nevertheless, even if oversimplified and overstated, these two models as ideal-types are useful guides against which to interpret the materials reported in this chapter.

Interpreting the Data

Of course, our data do not help us decide which of the alternative modes of socializing the leaders is ethically preferable or even which is more efficient if measured against some external standards. We can describe what actually seems to happen in eighty-seven American communities, communities in which the elitist assumptions of sponsored selection are formally rejected and the democratic assumptions of contest selection formally accepted. As is ever the case in the real world, what we find is a mixture.

In many important respects, the evidence conforms to the prescriptions of the contest selection. Early socialization of leaders and citizens is very similar. To begin with, half the councilmen (those not discussed in this chapter) fail to even discuss their political socialization in explaining how they came to be politically active. We assume that no agencies selected them and initiated training to prepare them for public office.[26]

A reasonable conclusion can be drawn: As youths, these councilmen acquired their basic citizenship values in ways similar to that of friends and peers. Democratic norms were learned in permissive families, student councils, Boy Scouts, Little Leagues, Future Farmers of America, and equivalent settings. Patriotism and a sense of national identification were formed at the urging of parents and teachers. In other words, we are confident that at least

---

26 The alternative explanation—that these councilmen deliberately falsified their past and attempted to hide important aspects of their political socialization—cannot be disproven with our data but is not credible. Nothing in our general understanding of American politics could sustain such an interpretation.

half the councilmen did not experience political-social training in ways markedly different from other middle-class youths.

What about the councilmen who did cite "unusual" political socialization experiences? The initial fact to keep in mind is that these councilmen acquired their taste for politics from the same socialization agencies responsible for teaching citizenship norms. Youths acquire citizenship values from families and teachers, in the classroom, and through observing political life. Councilmen who trace their initial involvement to a socialization experience cite, therefore, the identical agencies which also provided them and their age peers with the basic values of American political life. No special group prepared them for leadership.

Nevertheless, we still have avoided the most difficult question. Half the councilmen did have unusual political socialization experiences; they did begin to take, or to consider, an active role in politics well before their adult years. We want to know more about the unusual nature of their political socialization. The distinctive factor appears to be exposure to political life and a responsiveness to its attractions. Some portion of American youth, concentrated in the middle class but not identical with it, spend significantly more time exposed to politics than do their age-cohorts. As children, they are raised in a politically charged atmo-sphere, often in an active family. Or, as adolescents, they are busy in school politics or enrolled in politically relevant courses. They learn to accept politics as a normal part of their life activities.

To accept political activity as normal or to be fascinated with politics is, to be sure, a distinguishing trait in our society. Few youths grow up with thoughts about active political involvement. But to be *distinguished* in terms of such a trait is not to be *separated* from those lacking it. Youths whose early experiences put them on a pathway leading into the politically active stratum are not pulled out of the general population and subjected to spe-cialized training.

Similar conclusions are drawn in even the most exaggerated pic-ture of American society as an elite-controlled oligarchy. Mills writes that "What is lacking [in the political order] is a truly common elite program of recruitment and training." He quotes a British critic of American politics, Field Marshall Viscount Mont-gomery, who urged Americans to adopt a system "under which a minority of high-caliber young students could be separated from the mediocre and given the best education possible to supply the country with leadership."[27] Whether Americans should reject or accept this advice is not our question; that they have rejected it in practice is clear from our data.

27 Quoted in C. Wright Mills, *The Power Elite* (New York: Oxford University Press, 1957), p. 295.

Chapter 4

Entry into the Active Stratum: Three Pathways

A clue to community political life is the way in which the people are sifted and sorted until only a handful are left to hold political office. Governing bodies are constituted not in some random manner but according to patterns which crystallize as political precedents become established, political norms agreed upon, political groups organized, and political actives chosen. To uncover leadership selection patterns led us first to ask how the politically active stratum is formed. This inquiry in turn led to the question: What life experiences and social conditions affect citizens in such a way that some—but not many—volunteer themselves for the active stratum? Chapter 3 dealt in part with this issue. Among citizens who become involved politically, some are taking adult roles anticipated in childhood. Adult activity is an extension of interests and attachments formed in younger years. Political socialization, then, is to be counted among the processes which sift and sort until only the few remain.

Investigating political socialization established that half the councilmen reached the threshold of adult activity as a result of childhood exposure to politics. To establish this does not, however, explain their actual involvement. We have only described why they are available for those public roles more demanding of time and energy than their citizenship roles. Nor have we accounted for the initial activity of councilmen whose entry into the active stratum was not preceded by a lengthy interest in politics. In this chapter, we shift attention from earliest interest to earliest activity. The underlying question remains the same however: What factors determine the composition of the politically active stratum?

Studying the Earliest Political Activity of Elected Leaders

In Chapter 3, we reported the questionnaire item which elicited the "earliest interest" responses. The following query in the interview schedule directed the respondent's attention away from political interest and directed it explicitly to initial political activity:

> Now, thinking back over your own career in public life, can you recall when you first considered being actively involved in public matters?

In the follow-up questions and probes, councilmen were asked about the situations, conditions, and persons associated with their initial activity.

We have shown that councilmen can be classified according to three paths leading into the active stratum. Half the councilmen came to public life as a result of political socialization experiences; another 38 percent were mobilized by activating conditions; the remainder, the lateral entrants, moved directly into an official or quasi-official position in the community. It is obvious that political experiences associated with earliest activity will be differentially related to the three entry patterns. Therefore, in addition to a general description of earliest activity, we will pay some attention to how different experiences are associated with the three pathways. Of course we do not hypothesize that different experiences will be related to different entry patterns; such would be tautological. The intent is not to test hypotheses but to explicate the shaping of the active stratum.

Personal Experiences and Community Conditions Associated with Initial Activity

Table 4–1 presents the frequency with which councilmen were ushered into the politically active stratum by different personal experiences and community conditions.

Civic Activities

To step from a civic role into the politically active stratum is the most frequent route for the nonpartisan councilmen. For nearly half (44 percent), their journey to public office begins when they take on a civic responsibility—PTA committee, service club

Table 4–1

Experiences and Conditions Associated with Initial Activity
(N = 431)*

Civic Activities	44%
Partisan Involvements	13
Occupational Ties	26
Sense of Personal Investment in the Community	22
Communitywide Political Event	23

* Percentages total more than 100 because councilmen report more than one condition.

officer, church leadership, United Crusade Chairman, Chamber of Commerce position, library board, Little League organizer, or any one of many similar tasks. This is neither surprising nor, as we shall see, unimportant for community political life. Two facts about American social life will help us interpret the influence of the structure of civic life on the politically active stratum.

1. Americans are joiners. Given the opportunity, they flock to the literally thousands of organizations, groups, clubs, voluntary associations, and fraternities which form the social fabric of American life. Initially and perceptively noted by de Tocqueville, this observation recently has been investigated in dozens of empirical studies; these studies consistently show high rates of organizational membership in the United States.[1]

2. Associational membership is related to political participation. The citizen who belongs to organizations, especially if he is active in them, is more likely than the nonjoining citizen to be politically informed, to vote and otherwise participate in political life, to take an interest in and to care about politics, and to view himself as competent with respect to his citizen role.[2]

These two facts suggest that political activity is a subset of more general social activity. There are many more citizens in society who belong to organizations and associations than there are citizens who belong to the politically active stratum. There are probably very few citizens, however, who are politically active without

[1] See, for instance, Gabriel Almond and Sidney Verba, *The Civic Culture* (Princeton: Princeton University Press, 1963), Chapter 11.
[2] For extensive analysis of the relationship between organizational membership and political activity, see Norman Nie, G. Bingham Powell, and Kenneth Prewitt, "Social Structure and Political Participation: Development Relationships—Part I," *American Political Science Review* 63, No. 2 (June 1969):361–78; and Part II of the analysis in *American Political Science Review* 63, No. 3 (September 1969):808–32.

also being involved in the general organizational life of their community.

In the communities of the kind we are studying, there is an overlap between the politically active stratum and organized civic life. It is to be expected, therefore, that a community's many organizations and associations are a breeding ground for political officialdom. Persons initially drawn into civic roles become aware of and involved in municipal politics. In the words of one councilman, "It is a natural step from the kind of community activities I was in to the council." It is also likely that persons with council ambitions recognize that civic groups are a useful springboard into elected office; the civic role is chosen to attain other goals.

Not unexpectedly, the frequency with which a civic role ushers persons into the active stratum is important in two respects:

It means that civic organizations and activities dominate the shaping of the politically active stratum.

This, in turn, clarifies why councilmen so often think and behave as "volunteers." The elected position is an extension of a community role formed by and spelled out in the numerous volunteer organizations.

The causes councilmen serve and the gratifications they seek must be understood in the context of this norm of volunteerism. At least, some councilmen view their position as no different from that of being president of the Chamber of Commerce, chairman of the United Crusade, library board member, or church leader. The public-minded citizen volunteers his services to the city as a councilman just as he has volunteered his services as a PTA officer. But many of the volunteer roles which serve as entry points into the active stratum are very unlike "political" roles in one important respect. There is no constituency which periodically reviews policies of persons in these volunteer roles; there certainly are no routinized procedures by which voters can replace the inept church leader, the misguided Little League organizer, or the irresponsible library board member.[3]

The tradition of volunteerism may, therefore, run counter to our theory about democratic elections. To state the same argument from a different perspective, some political theorists suggest that democracy is viable to the extent—and only to the extent

---

[3] This is not to say that persons in such roles have no constituencies, nor that they operate without restraints. But the constituencies to which they are "responsible" and the constraints on their behavior are different from those we normally associate with electoral politics.

—that elected leaders want to stay in office. The politician is responsive to the mass public because he anticipates in today's action the coming election. It is an axiom of some democratic theory that officials stand in fear of the ballot box. Dahl, in particular, is a strong advocate of this theoretical argument. He notes, for instance, that though elections are poor clues to the preferences of the people, nevertheless they "are a crucial device for controlling leaders." It is elections, along with competition, which "make governmental leaders so responsive to non-leaders that the distinction between democracy and dictatorship still makes sense."[4] Dahl submits his notion to an empirical test in New Haven and concludes, according to my reading, that in part pluralistic democracy works because the mayor wants to stay in office.

Other theorists of democracy have taken the argument a step further. If the elected leader is indifferent to future contests, he is a dangerous leader. The "volunteer" is a man free to ignore constituent wishes. Representative democracy depends on a supply of men who desire election and then reelection. And it is the elected leader's desire to be reelected which "becomes the electorate's restraint upon its public officials. No more irresponsible government is imaginable than one of highminded men unconcerned for their political futures."[5]

We find that civic activities are a major factor in determining who belongs to the politically active stratum, and, second, that councilmen frequently graduate from volunteer civic roles to elected office. A possible consequence is to introduce into the circles of elected leadership a tradition of volunteerism; this, in turn, can severely cripple representative democracy as commonly understood. The volunteer in elected office may be a devoted public servant as he understands that role; he may or may not be solicitous regarding voter preferences. If he serves causes of his own choosing, it is because he can afford to. His political calculus offers no formula taking into account shifts in voter sentiment.

Partisan Activities

In striking contrast to civic roles, partisan roles usher many fewer councilmen (13 percent) into the active stratum. It is evi-

---

[4] Robert A. Dahl, *Preface to Democratic Theory* (Chicago: University of Chicago Press, 1956), pp. 131–32.

[5] Joseph Schlesinger, *Ambition and Politics* (Chicago: Rand McNally & Co., 1966), p. 2. These notions will be explored in much more depth in Chapter 8.

dent that the active stratum we are describing is shaped by institutions other than the political parties. This is consistent with a point to be developed at greater length in the next chapter. Persons who want to make a career in nonpartisan politics in these Northern California communities are well advised to expend energies in service clubs, youth organizations, and other civic groups rather than in party precinct work. Conversely, those whose life-goals include a career in partisan politics find their time is best spent in party roles. The network of friends, organizations, activities, and ad hoc groups supplying persons for council office undoubtedly somewhat overlap the network characterizing party activity. But in general, the norm of nonpartisanship of city councils is deeply embedded in the processes selecting those who are to become councilmen.

This does not mean that the political parties are totally inactive in council politics.[6] Party activists may campaign for council candidates, they may appear before the council to petition their causes, and they may even recruit for partisan elections from among the more attractive and successful councilmen. Later material will indicate that in some communities all three of these things happen. Nevertheless, party activity itself is not a frequent route into the particular stratum from which councilmen come.

Further evidence is clear from data in Table 4-2. The relatively few councilmen who cited partisan activities as instrumental in their initial political involvement are overwhelmingly those whose political roots reach back into childhood years. We have already seen that partisan events were important for councilmen whose interest in politics predates adult activities. It follows that partisan childhood associations and predispositions might be carried into the adult years.

Table 4-2 also reveals that councilmen not drawn into the active stratum by partisan roles are likely to be mobilized by their civic roles; this again shows the importance of civic groups in shaping the active stratum. Civic organizations step into the vacuum created by the comparative absence of party organizations. With respect to leadership selection in the nonpartisan milieu, civic organizations are the functional equivalents of party orga-

---

6 For a report analyzing the conditions under which the political parties do become active, see Heinz Eulau, Betty H. Zisk, and Kenneth Prewitt, "Latent Partisanship in Non-Partisan Elections: Effects of Political Milieu and Mobilization," in Kent Jennings and Harmon Ziegler (eds.), *The Electoral Process* (Englewood Cliffs, N.J.: Prentice-Hall, 1966).

Table 4–2

Relationship Between the Three Entry Patterns and Whether Civic
and Partisan Roles Were Associated with Initial Activity

	Politically Socialized (N = 214)	Politically Mobilized (N = 163)	Lateral Entrants (N = 54)
Initial Activity Associated with a Civic Role	36%	51%	13%
Initial Activity Associated with a Partisan Role*	21%	4%	4%

* Put differently, 85 percent of those who mention a partisan role in connection with their initial activity come from the politically socialized
group, 11 percent from the mobilized group, and only four percent (two
councilmen) from the lateral entrants.

nizations. They play a major part in the screening, selecting, and
nominating processes.

One implication following from this is that the political process
in our municipalities resembles a multiparty system more than a
two-party system. Civic organizations do not coalesce into two distinct groupings. Second, the candidate is seldom identified by any
clearly recognizable ideological or policy position. Thus, the voter
is denied even the minimal information about candidates that he
has in partisan elections. Third, councilmen may reflect the values
of the civic group which ushered them into office, but seldom will
they vote with anything approaching what we call "party loyalty"
in partisan legislatures. Councilmen may be more autonomous in
this sense than Democratic or Republican legislators.

The Occupational Nexus

It is well known that certain occupations are overrepresented
among political leaders.[7] Lawyers and businessmen, for instance,
always hold a larger number of legislative and executive posts than
their relative numbers in the population merit. The evidence
showing the unequal representation of certain occupations has
come from documentary data, usually from biographical records
and *Who's Who* compilations. This type of evidence has some-

[7] See, for instance, Donald Matthews, *The Social Background of Political
Decision-Makers* (Garden City, N.Y.: Doubleday & Co., 1954), especially Chapter
3. For an extended analysis of lawyers in politics, see Heinz Eulau and John
Sprague, *Lawyers in Politics* (Indianapolis: Bobbs-Merrill Co., 1964).

what limited the explanations advanced to account for such unequal representation. For the most part, scholars have simply
noted that the prestige and resources of professionals and entrepreneurs give them an edge in the competition for political positions, that is, the explanation depends on a social bias argument.
Interview data permits us to advance a somewhat different, though
not incompatible, explanation, one not easily teased out of biographical sources.

Professional and occupational roles can be so located in the
social network that they facilitate movement into the active
stratum. Once these roles dominate the active stratum, it is to be
expected that they will dominate among elected leaders as well.
Lawyers, union leaders, lobbyists, and some businessmen and educators, by virtue of their occupational duties, are closely linked
to the public sector. Thus it is that the occupational makeup of
the community shapes the active stratum; some community members are pushed into more intimate contact with political happenings than are other members.

Our data illustrate this. Twenty-six percent of the councilmen
trace their initial public involvement to contacts or concerns attributable to their occupational roles. Lawyers effectively illustrate
this pathway into the active stratum. In response to the query
"How did you first get active?" one lawyer-councilman says, "My
profession, it's inevitable. I don't know which came first, it's like
the question of the chicken and the egg." Another, recognizing as
do most young lawyers that his livelihood depends on social contacts, "joined organizations as a way of getting clientele."

Occupations other than law also place their members in contact
with the active stratum. A grocery-store owner says, "When you
are in business, you are always having an interest in city hall." A
clergyman with a social conscience first got actively involved in
community affairs "because of duties associated with my pastorate."
Even an architect traces his interest to professional duties; appointed a member of the city's architectural advisory commission,
he reports that his activities in connection with that post drew him
further and further into local affairs.

The convergence of professional-occupational roles and political
activity has a major consequence for political life. The skills and
perspectives available in the leadership group are those available
in the active stratum. The proximity of certain occupations to
the public sector means that the talents and outlooks dominant in

the active stratum are those provided by the training characteristic of the favorably located occupations. Political life, therefore, is influenced by the occupational outlooks and the professional training officeholders bring to their public duties. If American politics is "legalistic," this is in part related to the historical preponderance of lawyer-politicians. If American politics lacks a self-consciousness about "purpose" and "ideology," this may be attributed to the traditional isolation of clergy, educators, and the general intellectual community from political roles.

Of course, the occupational makeup of political leadership is subject to change. Educators appear currently to be taking active political roles. This is the case for a variety of reasons: the growth of public education, the need for consultants in the educational sector, the close relationship between educational institutions and their communities, as well as the awareness on the part of educators that they have a stake in decisions made in Washington, in state capitals, and in local councils. The reawakening of a social action norm in churches may augment the ranks of clergy in the active stratum. If new occupational groups come to dominate in political roles, political life may reflect different perspectives and be governed by different norms.

Duties associated with occupational roles will, then, be more or less proximate to the public sector. In addition, the absolute size of the occupational group in the community will affect the manner of formation of the active stratum. A community with comparatively few realtors and contractors will be lacking in its active stratum the attitudes and skills associated with those occupations.[8]

We have reviewed three community roles—civic, partisan, and occupational—which, in varying amounts, influence formation of the active stratum in the nonpartisan municipalities being studied. We have initiated, but by no means concluded, several discussions about the influence of the composition of the active stratum on democratic political life. To continue these general discussions, we turn now to two influential community conditions.

---

[8] In his study of Connecticut legislators, David Barber shows "how dependent the skills and attitudes available to the political order are on occupational changes among the general population." See, in particular, p. 235, where he shows how fluctuations in the proportion of lawyer-legislators is related to fluctuations in the proportions of lawyers in the general population. *The Lawmakers: Recruitment and Adaptation to Legislative Life* (New Haven: Yale University Press, paperback edition, 1965).

Sense of Personal Investment in the Community

Among the country's founding fathers were numbered those who felt that some citizens were more deserving of political influence than were others. Persons with a "stake-in-society," to use John Adams' famous phrase, should have more say in running society than persons with no investment to protect. In Adams' day, therefore, the propertied should be enfranchised, the propertyless denied the vote. The latter have nothing to lose and turn too often to attacks on property.

A variant on this theme, more descriptive than normative, is well known to contemporary scholars. Persons who feel they have a stake in their community do attempt to control political resources. At the local level, persons become politically involved because of home ownership, children in school, or business investments. They enfranchise themselves to shape the community in a manner consistent with their values. The homeowner who "put every dime I had into a house in 1956" soon thereafter became active to "keep apartments out of the neighborhood." The parent with school-age children "thought the schools were going downhill and became active in the PTA to do something about it." A businessman joined an organization to "get more businessmen in politics" because "we contribute a great deal to government in the way of taxes"; he wants to control the ways in which "his money is spent." For some councilmen, the investment they intended to protect was more uncommon than a home, children's education, or business. A boatowner, for example, "got mad when the city sold the yacht harbor to a group of men who made it into a shopping center"; this irate citizen became politically active to protect the remaining shore line.

About one-fifth of the councilmen (22 percent) report getting involved in the community leadership network because of a life-experience which reminded them that political levers could be pulled to advantage. Buying property, sending children off to school, going into business, or just moving into a new community are viewed as investments which may be protected by taking an active political role. People who feel "this is my community, my home" acknowledge the obligations attendant on citizenship; they also recognize the inherent possibilities of political power.

Of course, purchasing a home, having school-age children, and so forth are normal experiences for most Americans at some time or another in their life-cycle. We cannot say why one mother, when her child starts school, immediately becomes active in the PTA, whereas another mother, only too happy to have the public school babysit her offspring, fills her leisure hours with bridge or golf.

This need not be a matter of concern, however. Our task is not to explain the motivations of political actives. The goal is a quite different one: to understand the social processes which form the politically active stratum. Important clues to these social processes are revealed, we assume, through the histories of those who have become elected leaders. Once we have understood the formation of the active stratum we will be better equipped to describe the values and dispositions represented among actives and, consequently, among elected leaders. That a sizable group of municipal leaders first became politically active to protect some community investment suggests a reason why the prevailing ideology in so many of these communities is protective of the status quo.

Communitywide Political Events

Political history is written around events that mark turning points for a nation. The depression marked the end of laissez-faire economics and the beginning of government intervention in the economy, the Second World War marked the end of isolationism and the beginning of internationalism, the civil rights movement marked the end of legal segregation and the groping for a new social structure. Under the pressure of economic, social, or international crises, a nation alters its political course, never again to be quite the same. What is true of nations is true of smaller political communities. Local municipalities measure time from those watershed experiences that radically alter the political makeup of the community.

In the previous chapter, we saw how national crises can be "socialization agents." Turning points in personal political histories coincide with turning points in national political histories. The pressures and consequences of a national crisis work to rearrange individual lives just as they work to rearrange the political order. In a similar way, community upheavals act as socializing-mobilizing agencies. Prominent among such community events are recall elections, incorporation movements, and annexation drives.

Large segments of the population, previously indifferent to local politics, become agitated and activated in response to the sense of community urgency implicit in times of recall, incorporation, or annexation. Some portion of these newly aroused citizens will continue their involvement after the crisis has subsided. Nearly one in four (23 percent) of the councilmen date the beginning of their public careers from a period of major community change. One councilman, previously uninterested in local matters, got involved in a recall election because it was apparent to him "that this city needed upgrading." It took the recall election, however, to bring community conditions to his attention. Once mobilized by the election, he maintained active interest until "after eight years of supporting people, I felt I would become a candidate."

A movement to incorporate a city—or forestall annexation by a neighboring city—is a frequent happening in Northern California. Municipal boundaries are still in flux. Large expanses of area near urban centers remain unincorporated. Within the geographical region covered by our study, three cities were added between the pretest stage and final data collection. Other municipalities added new lands to their communities.

Seldom will incorporation or annexation proceed without controversy. Inevitably this controversy brings new faces to local politics—a young lawyer representing the neighborhood eager to move from county to municipal rule, a developer working to obtain favorable zoning of a tract soon to be annexed, a conservationist hoping to protect open land. Always, a few of these new faces remain active after the issue initiating their involvement is settled.

In one sense, the communitywide event and the sense of investment in the community are similar. Each attracts persons into the active stratum and involves them in the ongoing political life of the community. In another sense, they are very dissimilar. The former condition, what we called "investment in the community," is individualistic in its impact. "Community crises," on the other hand, are more universal in their impact. Large segments of the population are simultaneously activated by community upheavals. Just as at the national level we say that "today's leaders were formed during the war years," we can say at the local level that "the current city councilmen were activated during the incorporation years." Further, a community investment, being individualistic, can easily be experienced as nonpolitical. A community crisis, flushing to the surface as it does public tensions and conflicts, is both more collective and more political.

Considered jointly, the two community conditions helped usher nearly half the councilmen (45 percent) into the active stratum.

But the impact of these experiences should not be randomly distributed across all career types. If the dissimilarities between the two conditions are relevant, they should be differentially associated with the three career patterns previously identified: the socialized, the mobilized, and the lateral entrants. Table 4–3 demonstrates this to be the case. Those with deeply rooted commitments to politics were more likely than their colleagues to be activated in the context of politically charged community events. Correspondingly, the concern to protect one's investment in the community was salient to the lateral entrants. With respect to both community conditions, the politically mobilized fell between the socialized and the lateral entrants.

Table 4–3

Comparison of the Impact of Community Experiences on the
Three Entry Patterns

	Politically Socialized (N = 214)	Politically Mobilized (N = 163)	Lateral Entrants (N = 54)
Mention Community Investment	7%	11%	19%
Mention Community Political Event	28%	20%	9%

Attitudes and Values Associated with Initial Activity

Persons who seek out or accept the relatively demanding and time-consuming role of political active will have a variety of motivations. Some seek to further personal wealth; some hope to gain in social status; some wish to release psychological tension rooted in deeply embedded drives to exercise power; some expect to satisfy sociability wants in community activity; some simply need to achieve. Students of the "political personality" have speculated about all these needs or drives—economic, deference, power, affiliation, and achievement.[9] The data are inadequate, however, and

[9] See, for example, Harold Lasswell, *Power and Personality* (New York: W.W. Norton & Co., 1948) where the power accentuation hypothesis is formulated. Lasswell writes, "If there is a political type . . . the basic characteristic will be the accentuation of power in relation to other values with the personality when compared with other persons." P. 22. For a modified statement, see Lasswell, "The Selective Effect of Personality on Political Participation," in Richard Christie and Marie Jahoda (eds.), *Studies in the Scope and Method of "The Authoritarian Personality"* (Glencoe, Ill.: The Free Press, 1954), pp. 197–225.

conclusions remain ambiguous. One difficulty in studies of political personality stems from the way in which the question is posed. All too often, students have asked how the individual politician maximizes his need satisfaction. The question is stated in social-psychological terminology: "Of what use to a man is his political involvement?"

We raise the "motivational question" somewhat differently. We do not attempt to account for *why* particular persons seek out a political role. The guiding model of this study turns attention to those conditions under which a minority of the population comes to hold public office. The motivational question, if indeed it should even be labeled as such, has to do with conditions of political life affecting self-selection to an active role. In other words, it is not the *personal needs* of the politician we include in our model of leadership selection: of interest is the way in which the *conditions of political life* affect recruitment. Our approach is guided more by studies which employ a model of "situation and recruitment" than those more purely interested in "personality and recruitment."

Phrasing the question as we have directs attention to two considerations: First, what political attitudes are associated with initial activity? and, second, what political stereotypes affect self-selection patterns?

Four Attitudes Associated with Initial Activity

Councilmen were not asked "why" they got involved in politics, but were asked to recount the circumstances associated with their initial activity. From their responses to several open-ended questions, it was apparent that four "attitude sets" affected their decision to join the active stratum.

Councilmen explain initial activity in public life with respect to four dispositions: (1) a sense of political indignation or protest; (2) a feeling of civic obligation; (3) an attitude of pragmatism and problem-solving; and (4) a sense of general interest, even curiosity. These four features of the attitudinal makeup of the active stratum are familiar to any student of American politics. They touch on

---

For a useful empirical study of other "personality drives," see Rufus P. Browning and Herbert Jacob, "Power Motivation and Political Personality," *Public Opinion Quarterly* 28 (Spring 1964):75–90. Other studies are reviewed in Prewitt, "Political Socialization and Leadership Selection," *Annals of the American Academy of Political and Social Science* 361 (September 1965):96–111.

the major issues of American political life. Reformers, pragmatists, the socially conscious, and the generally interested are always energizing forces in national and local politics.

It is equally clear that the conditions of political life call forth these four types of actives in different mixtures. Reformers will dominate when the times call for large-scale social change. The pragmatists often attempt to consolidate and routinize new political advances. When community values are to be preserved, persons who place a premium on obligation and duty will be attracted to office. The generally interested constitute a diffuse, almost residual category. They will be represented in the active stratum under nearly any political conditions.

Table 4–4 shows that the kind of career entry pattern followed by councilmen is differentially associated with the attitudes they express. The longer one has been associated with political matters, the more likely is simple "interest" salient at the time of his initial activity. Both the socialized and the mobilized councilmen see their early involvement in the context of pragmatic goals and problem-solving activities. Those who come to political matters by seeking or being sought for an office, the lateral entrants, are less likely to mention any basic attitude. When they do, they express a sense of righteous indignation toward some feature of the community or simply report that they felt obligated to respond to a request for their services.

Table 4–4

Attitudes Associated with Initial Activity Related to the
Three Entry Patterns

	Politically Socialized (N = 214)	Politically Mobilized (N = 163)	Lateral Entrants (N = 54)	Totals (N = 431)
Sense of Indignation	16%	18%	15%	17%
Feeling of Obligation	7	10	17	10
Pragmatism Orientation	20	21	2	18
General Interest	25	16	6	19
Miscellaneous	3	1	0	2
No Attitude Mentioned	29	33	59	34
	100%	99%	100%	100%

Public Stereotypes and Political Activism

Generalized images about politics and politicians abound in any community. These cultural stereotypes serve as selective devices affecting who joins the active stratum. If it is widely thought that "politics is dirty and attractive only to the dishonest," we expect the self-seeking to become active politically. If it is believed that "politics is public service and attractive to the statesman-like person," we expect the civic-minded to seek active roles. We can paraphrase Easton to good purpose here: The effect of cultural norms in political life is to impose outer limits on the number and kinds of persons seeking entry into the active stratum.[10] Community beliefs, then, affect self-selective tendencies of potential actives.

This assumption is not a new one. That the public's view of political life affects who chooses a political career has been a topic of much speculation, though, unfortunately, infrequent systematic investigation. The most common argument is that a generalized negative view of politics in the United States inhibits entrance into the active stratum of the more able citizens. Klain illustrates this position clearly. The American public, he allowed, responds to public leaders with hostility, suspicion, or indifference, views, he felt, almost always fortified by ignorance.[11] A few years after Klain wrote, Mitchell addressed himself to the same problem:

> The fact that Americans have tended to regard political offices as not requiring any special training and the fact that political office has been so accessible to the poor and formally uneducated has in turn attracted persons whose performances in office have not always been very exemplary. Thus, a vicious circle developed in which offices with low status attracted less desirable officeholders and their inadequate or corrupt actions further confirmed the low status of public office.[12]

In *Who Governs?* Dahl continues the theme in noting that the supply of political recruits in New Haven is limited "by the rela-

---

10 Easton's interest is with how demands rather than persons are affected by cultural norms. He writes, "The effect of cultural norms in political life is to impose some kind of outer limits on the number and kinds of wants seeking entry as demands." David Easton, *A Systems Analysis of Political Life* (New York: John Wiley & Sons, 1965), p. 102.

11 Maurice Klain, "Politics—Still a Dirty Word," *The Antioch Review* 15 (December 1955):459–60. For a general review of this issue, see Wendell Bell, Richard J. Hill, and Charles R. Wright, *Public Leadership* (San Francisco: Chandler Publishing Co., 1961), Chapter 7.

12 William C. Mitchell, "The Ambivalent Social Status of the American Politician," *Western Political Quarterly* 12 (September 1959):696. I will take issue a bit later with the implicit assumption in Mitchell's statement that the "poor and formally uneducated" behave in nonexemplary fashion and the "rich and educated," one can only assume, are honest and virtuous as officeholders.

tively low attraction of politics."[13] He reports that 28 percent of New Haven citizens gave an unqualified "yes" and 57 percent gave an unqualified "no" to the question, "If you had a son just getting out of school, would you like to see him go into politics as a life-work?" Leaving aside the methodological difficulties with this item, the notion guiding the assertion is an important one. *If* community political life is viewed as dominated by ward bosses, party hacks, dishonest businessmen and the personally ambitious, the politically active stratum will be attractive to persons whose char-acter permits them to feel comfortable in such a crowd.

The hypothesis admits of more general applicability as well. For example, if public office is viewed as rightfully belonging to the young, vigorous, and well-educated, as for example it is in many African states, then the middle-aged, the tiring, and the illiterate do not consider politics a career option. If, as seemed to have been the case in early America, only native-stock Protestant fam-ilies were expected to govern, then only native-stock Protestants joined the politically active stratum. The list could be extended at some length. Those characteristics considered "appropriate" for public office exercise a selective and self-fulfilling effect on leadership selection processes.

Before presenting relevant data, a complication should be dis-cussed. The notion that cultural stereotypes affect selection processes has a theoretical affinity with a point made earlier. We have noted that a community's political life tends to become domi-nated by a particular social-economic stratum, and that this domi-nation, in turn, affects leadership selection patterns in very defi-nite ways. Here we argue that political life can also be dominated by images and stereotypes, and that these, in turn, affect who will choose, and be chosen for, leadership positions. We do not assume, as does Mitchell in the passage cited, that there is necessarily a tendency for "low performance" or "corruption" in office to be associated with places or times when political office is "accessible to the poor and formally uneducated." The wealthy have no mo-nopoly on exemplary behavior either in reality or in cultural norms; witness, for instance, the suspicion among American citi-zens that the rich bribe and buy their way into political favor. Neither, of course, do the poor and uneducated who make their

---

13 Robert A. Dahl, *Who Governs?* (New Haven: Yale University Press, 1961), p. 179.

way into public life have a monopoly on vice. The "log cabin to White House" myth is part of the American political culture; it is a myth which sanctifies the honesty and diligence of the poor who find their rewards in public service. We prefer to treat as a hypothesis rather than as an axiom the notion that civic virtue is generally assumed to be differentially associated with class position.[14]

Another caveat, and one which links up the argument here with the evidence presented earlier, is that with respect to cultural norms "the public" is a misnomer. It assumes more homogeneity than is the case. The familiar observation that political orientations are differentially associated with class, ethnic, religious, and geographical groups in society works to the advantage of our argument in the following way. The poorer and less educated the community, the more suspicious will be its view of the wealthy few. The absentee owner, the large developer, the rich doctor who belongs to the country club of another community, will be viewed with suspicion if they suddenly show an interest in local politics. Similarly, the ambitious labor leader or local ethnic club president will be suspected as a radical in the community dominated by middle-class stereotypes. Thus it is that when "your own kind" hold public office, you tend to form favorable images about political life. When those alien to your way of life dominate the political sector, your views will be informed by the negative stereotypes commonly associated with outgroups.

Although guided by the thinking which connects public images to leadership selection, the specific research question we pose is somewhat different from the politics-is-dirty vs. politics-is-clean dichotomy. The nonpartisan milieu, as well as theoretical considerations, dictated phrasing the question as a choice between the political or nonpolitical label. Councilmen were asked whether they considered their job to be a political one; and they were asked whether they thought people in the community viewed the council as a political body.

Tables 4–5 and 4–6 present these data. Clearly, councilmen avoid labeling themselves as politicians and feel that the public eschews such labels as well.

The disinterested public servant is considered appropriate for nonpartisan, council-manager cities. The public-regarding ethos

---

14 See, on this issue, Donald Stokes, "Popular Evaluations of Government: An Empirical Assessment," in Harland Cleveland and Harold Lasswell (eds.), *Ethics and Bigness* (New York: Harper & Brothers, 1962), pp. 61–72.

Table 4–5

Councilman's Conception of the Job of Councilman
(N = 360)

Requires that you be a real politician	9%
Requires political skills but not a political job	39
Job is not in any way a matter of politics	52
	100%

Table 4–6

Councilman's Conception of How the Public Views the Job of
Councilman (N = 322)

Public sees the councilman as real politician	16%
Public sees the councilman more as a public servant	62
Public sees the councilman as just another citizen	23
	101%

presumed to be dominant in reformed cities is reflected in Tables
4–5 and 4–6.[15]

There are alternate interpretations to these tables, interpretations not necessarily in disagreement, but one of which probes more deeply than the other. We initially observe that the term "politics" is in bad repute among these councilmen. Under the best of circumstances, to be politic is to be manipulative and clever; more often, it means to be conniving and tricky, or even something more devilish. Although true that politics is a term with negative connotations, to explain away Tables 4–5 and 4–6 in such a manner misses a second and more important point.

The second interpretation for these tables raises a larger question about democracy in these municipalities. As well as being "antipolitical," these municipal leaders are "nonpolitical." Governing the city is no different from running a business. The managerial, administrative ethos replaces a political one. This argument is consistent with earlier findings that civic roles dominate the shaping of the active stratum. The "business as usual" approach to municipal government may indeed be caused by leadership selection mechanisms. Community expectations combine with

---

15 See James Q. Wilson and Edward C. Banfield, "Public-Regardingness as a Value Premise in Voting Behavior," *American Political Science Review* 58 (December 1964):876–87; see also their *City Politics* (Cambridge, Mass.: Harvard University Press and the M. I. T. Press, 1963). Raymond E. Wolfinger and John Osgood Field, "Political Ethos and the Structure of City Government," *American Political Science Review* 60 (June 1966):306–26.

self-selective tendencies to produce not just antipolitical but also nonpolitical leadership.

If true, what does this mean for political life? First, common vocabulary includes phrases in which the term "political" is not nearly as narrow and negative as we just suggested. We are not surprised to see the word "political" in conjunction with lofty terms. The daily press as well as scholarly writing frequently makes use of phrases such as political vision, political wisdom, or political purpose. Indeed, we often assume that the man who claims to be political is the man claiming to be committed. In other words, if the term "politics" has narrow and negative connotations, it also has more visionary and positive referents.

Further, it is recognized that politics as vision and commitment has deep roots in conditions of conflict and fundamental differences. The political man is not so naive as to believe that communities are without disagreements. But the apolitical man prefers to gloss over serious differences; for him, the community should be governed according to enlightened principles. There is risk to the community in this, however. To evolve a philosophy which precludes conflict and value differences may be to escape from commitment and political vision. In being nonpolitical, city councilmen chance being parochial as well.

The parochial nature of city politics is a theme reflected in much of the material presented throughout our study. For now, the case may rest on two additional pieces of evidence: Table 4–7 demonstrates that councilmen define their role as they think the public defines it; Table 4–8 shows that the few councilmen who are willing to be called "political" come from those longest and most intimately connected with political matters.

Table 4–7

Relationship Between Job Self-Conception and How the Public
Is Thought to Define the Councilman's Job

| | SELF-CONCEPTION | | |
	Political (N = 24)	Quasi-Political (N = 124)	Nonpolitical (N = 174)
PUBLIC VIEWS			
Political	46%	23%	6%
Public servant	54	66	60
Just a citizen	0	11	34
	100%	100%	100%

This agreement with respect to role definitions is indirect, although persuasive, evidence that beliefs assumed to be current among the public affect self-conceptions of public leaders. At the least, the councilmen project their images onto the public. It is reasonable to think that such beliefs affect self-selection patterns as well. According to this interpretation, public stereotypes place a premium on candidates willing to be "nonpolitical" as well as "antipolitical."

Table 4–8

Job Self-Conceptions Related to Entry Patterns

| | ENTRY PATTERNS | | |
	Socialization (N = 180)	Mobilization (N = 138)	Lateral Entry (N = 42)
SELF-CONCEPTION			
Political or quasi-political	54%	42%	36%
Nonpolitical	46	58	64
	100%	100%	100%

In Table 4–8 we see that councilmen attached to the political sector since youth are less reluctant than their colleagues to identify with the political component of the councilman's job. This finding is not easily explained by assuming that councilmen socialized as youth are less bothered by negative connotations of the term "political." Quotations in Chapter 3 clearly illustrate that an early introduction to political matters often includes knowledge of political corruption. When a youth acquires his image of politics on the streets of Chicago or in the ghettoes of Boston, he hardly equates politician with public servant. The interpretation of Table 4–8 must probe deeper than this; we prefer an explanation consistent with the argument that most councilmen are apolitical as well as antipolitical. A minority of the councilmen, however, do have a more fundamental grasp of what it means to be political. They recognize that governing a city is not like running a business. The issues at stake are more complex, the causes to be served more urgent, and, of even more importance, their constituents differ widely in their vision of the good life. In value disagreement is rooted community conflict; in community conflict is rooted politics. Table 4–8 indicates that a long acquaintance with political matters is compatible with a deeper understanding of political life.

Summary Observations

Chapters 2, 3, and 4 depict as fully as our data allow the community conditions, the historical processes, the social-economic considerations, and the personal backgrounds which ushered councilmen into the politically active stratum. It is evident that a complex mixture of life-histories, personal characteristics, local and national events, mobilization agencies, political conditions, and public beliefs combine in different blends to attract—or push—a minority of citizens into active roles.

In one form or another, we have indicated conclusions to be drawn from the material. It will be useful to collect these conclusions here and to provide a more general summary.

1. As youths, elected officials did not receive any special political schooling or training. Although half the councilmen experienced greater exposure to things political than is usual during their preadult years, the evidence disallows the possibility that there occurred systematic schooling for future leadership. Councilmen learned to be good American citizens from the same social agencies—parents, teachers, classroom ritual life, peers, and personal experiences—instructing all youths in citizenship.

Everything we know about American political life argues that this observation is appropriately generalized well beyond the confines of our sample. Within the United States, basic political socialization precedes political recruitment and any in-role socialization associated with leadership status. During the years in which society is forming any given generation of citizens, there is no gap intended nor is there one observed between the political instruction available to the citizen-at-large and that available to the few who will someday occupy political authority positions.

2. The personal experiences which facilitated a political career were exceedingly varied. For some councilmen, their preactive careers were deeply embedded in a network of political contacts; active families, school politics, and partisan involvement predispose some youths toward political activity. Other councilmen first developed their unusual political interest as adults. Within this second group, the personal experiences generating commitment were varied; civic roles, community conditions, and occupational contacts were the most frequent channels into the active stratum. A few leaders moved directly into public office.

Friendship ties or occupational prestige were resources available to these councilmen.

The variety of personal experiences causing councilmen to first become actives were classified into three general categories: the politically socialized (councilmen with a long-standing political interest, one predating actual involvement); the politically mobilized (councilmen whose political interest coincides with active involvement); and the lateral entrants (councilmen who emphasize that holding an official, or quasi-official, position in government marked their initiation into the active sphere).

3. A corollary to the observation that a variety of life experiences ushers persons into the active stratum is the observation that a wide range of values and ideologies will be represented in that stratum. Scattered throughout the political stratum are partisans, reformers, pragmatists, as well as the civic-minded, the interested, and the curious.

There is an important exception to the variety of viewpoints represented in the active stratum. There appears to be widespread, though not universal, agreement that the councilman's task is nonpolitical. With this exception—an important one, as our earlier discussion intended to convey—the active stratum is populated with a variety of political views.

4. It is consistent with our observation that a variety of experiences can initiate a career that there are many access points into the active stratum. Further, the more numerous the routes to a destination, the easier it is to get there. Entry into the active stratum is facilitated by its porous boundaries and by its numerous access points.

We conclude from this that the active stratum in these communities is relatively open. A model of democratic pluralism rather than one of oligarchic self-perpetuation characterizes this stage of leadership selection. It appears that penetrating the active stratum is more a result of youthful political exposure, chance factors, or personal desire than permission from the already established. Control over entry into the active stratum is haphazard at most. (This, of course, tells us nothing about control over selection to political office itself. An oligarchic elite still can exercise control over who among the actives will receive nominations to candidacy or appointments to office.)

This conclusion is also applicable, we suspect, beyond nonpartisan councilmen in California. A close reading of the empirical literature on careers of American politicians reveals time and again that the active stratum in American political life is shaped by the accidents of life-experiences more than the sponsorship of elites bent on perpetuating their control. Studies of local officials, party workers, state legislators, federal bureaucrats, governors, and congressmen confirm this observation.

Within limits set by considerations of socioeconomic advantage, the social processes shaping the active stratum guarantee a diversity of opinion and background among actives that strongly contradicts the oligarchic assumptions.

Pointing Toward Chapter Five

Studies of leadership selection in the United States have too often been limited to elections or, at best, to the screening and nomination of candidates. The first part of this book has been an attempt to push an analysis to a prior stage—to show how a group of elected leaders first became actively involved in public matters. Selecting political leaders actually begins whenever and wherever a few American citizens, perhaps every twentieth one, decide to "enter politics actively, work at it, accept its terms, and sometimes to wish to rise in it."[16] For some, a decision is anticipated in childhood socialization; for others, it is the consequence of adult experiences. With a few exceptions (the lateral entrants in our terminology), the processes determining who becomes a councilman in the Bay Area communities begin well before apprenticeship, sponsorship, search committees, or nominations.

No political system, least of all a democracy, carries out a universal search for political talent. Communities select their leaders from persons who by accident or by design have become part of the active stratum. The picking and choosing of actual candidates takes place within this group. Or, in the few cases where a candidate is sought from outside, it is members of the active stratum who are doing the seeking. The infrastructure of American politics is probably too well established to permit many authentic outside challengers.

The next task, then, is to understand the screening, the eliminating, and the selecting processes which do locate the candidates from within the active stratum. We will shift from extramural to

---

16 Dwaine Marvick, "Political Recruitment and Careers," *International Encyclopedia of the Social Sciences* 12 (New York: Macmillan Co., and The Free Press, 1968):281.

intramural processes, from the vocabulary of socialization and mobilization to the vocabulary of sponsorship, nomination, apprenticeship, and winnowing. We have saved the term "recruitment," in particular, to describe the processes grooming an even smaller group within the active stratum for public office.

Thus, whereas in Chapter 2 we found that socioeconomic criteria produce a pool of eligibles smaller by far than the general population, and whereas in Chapters 3 and 4 we found that within the eligibles an even smaller group enters the active stratum, in Chapter 5 we look for the minority within the active minority who actually become candidates for public office.

Chapter 5

Recruitment and Apprenticeship: The Grooming Process

The task of locating candidates for political office is faced by any community which expects its political system to outlive the particular men who currently manage public affairs. Finding candidates is an obligation lending itself to a wide variety of solutions: Very complicated or quite simple procedures can be used; the search and selection may be haphazard or carefully routinized; the task can be shared by many or left in the hands of a few. However resolved, the job of recruiting candidates for public office is never ignored.

Throughout much of Western history there was employed a very simple procedure for finding political candidates. Public office was inherited. This fact greatly eased the burden of locating candidates—biological reproduction fixed the supply. With the decline of hereditary elites, the political recruitment process has become much more complex. It is especially clear that the growth of democratic practices has complicated the formal and informal processes which locate the small minority who hold public office. In fact, it is likely that the more widely accepted are democratic norms, the more complicated are the procedures for choosing officeholders. Somehow, the contradiction between a belief in popular sovereignty, on the one hand, and the inescapable fact that minorities rule, on the other, must be reconciled, at least in the thinking of a public expected simultaneously to hold democratic beliefs and to comply with rules made by minorities.

The important issue of legitimacy is affected by the way in which the contradiction between popular sovereignty and rule by the

few is managed. In a democracy, leaders will be legitimate only if
the populace feels its preferences form part of the processes which
choose leaders. The complicated procedures which pick and help
legitimate political leaders in the United States have been studied
at the national level. The vast machinery of party politics—nominating committees, party conventions, caucuses, primaries, and
competitive elections—convey to most American citizens the belief that the minorities finally chosen to govern have been selected
by procedures which permit an acceptable measure of popular control. Those who govern, therefore, should be generally supported
and the rules they make generally complied with. In nonpartisan
municipalities, it is not so clear what the formal and informal
processes are which recruit and presumably legitimate officeholders. We attempt in this and the next chapter to understand
these processes.

A Description of the Recruitment Process

The Interpersonal Context of Political Recruitment

The political careers of councilmen, as most politicians, are nurtured in small, informal, and often intimate recruitment groups.
This, of course, is consistent with a general fact of social life: Personal choices, including choices of vocations and avocations, are
affected in substantial ways by primary group experiences. The
college student decides on a pre-med rather than pre-law course
because his fraternity brothers are pursuing that course. The junior
law firm members take up skiing because it is a favorite sport of
firm members. The housewife tunes in *Dr. Kildare* because her
weekly bridge partners constantly refer to the program. Examples
could be multiplied. Primary group influence in personal choices
is one of the defining characteristics of social life.

The influence of the small group is accentuated by self-selection
tendencies. A person gravitates toward groups having habits and
values compatible with his own. In electing a fraternity, the under-
graduate intent on a professional career rejects bids from the
athletes' house or the party group. Although the student may be
undecided about his major, he does intend his college years to
be preparatory for a professional career. The junior law firm member chooses, as well as is chosen by, a firm of relaxed and young
fellows, persons likely to have attractive leisure-time activities. The
housewife plays bridge with neighbors who watch daytime TV

rather than neighbors active in the local garden club. Primary group influence, then, is a combination of the influencing ability of small face-to-face groups *and* the tendency for persons to seek out groups which accord with their values.

Political choices are no less influenced by primary groups than other types of choices. We expect to find, and we do, that a man's decision to become politically active and eventually to seek a council position will have been influenced by the advice, the suggestions, and the social pressures from other individuals. In tracing the experiences which led from their general interest in politics to their political activities to their candidacy for office, two-thirds of the councilmen cite the importance of small, informal groups of friends or acquaintances. Table 5–1 presents these data.

Table 5–1

Proportion of Councilmen Who Link Their
Political Recruitment to Influence of Other
Persons (N = 431)

NO PERSONS MENTIONED	32%
AT LEAST ONE MENTIONED	68
	100%
PERSONS MENTIONED:	
Friends, family	30%
Community activities	27
Councilmen, local officials	23
Work associates	8

It is likely that the proportion who report that no persons influenced their political choices and activities is an inflated figure. Persons like to think of themselves as "self-starters," a self-image, especially attractive to politicians, which precludes dependence on others. To admit that your political career choices were influenced by others is to risk the charge that you are not a free agent. But, whatever we make of those disclaiming outside influence, ties with small groups and particular persons are instrumental in the careers of at least two out of three councilmen.

The most striking aspect of Table 5–1 is the frequency with which persons already established in community politics assisted the current leaders along the path to office. Nearly a quarter of the councilmen report that councilmen or other local officials helped shape and nourish their ambitions for political office. As one incumbent stated it, "The former mayor appointed me to the planning commission; I had campaigned for him in the last election."

Another reports that "Some city councilmen and the mayor requested several times that I run for the city council and I finally gave in to them." For a third councilman, "The superintendent of schools urged me to run for the school board; from there I came to the council."

A second sizable group, 27 percent, were aided and urged by community actives and local influentials. A councilman in one of the largest cities in the area "was asked by influential people to be a candidate and was urged and supported by the two local papers with the greatest circulation." One retired businessman claims to be "a political accident"; important businessmen came to him and urged him to run. He does recognize, however, that "it was a natural progression from my interest in local and community affairs."

It is clear from Table 5–1 that working your way through the channels leading to public office is simply not something you "just decide to do." For most councilmen, it is the result of social experiences and personal contacts which draw them into and up through the network of relationships which control—whether by design or not—access to political office. For a sizable contingent of councilmen, their personal contacts include incumbent officeholders and other community actives. It is the rare councilman who insists, as one man did, that "No one helped me; it was just my own disgust at the way things were done when I knew they could be done better."

Additional evidence, though of an indirect sort, testifying to the frequency with which councilmen were recruited by persons in leadership positions is shown in Table 5–2. Respondents were asked whether, prior to running for the council, they knew councilmen who were then serving. Half knew the incumbents very well; they were friends with all or nearly all of them. Less than a third initially sought office without benefit of close relationships with incumbents; only 15 percent without benefit of any contacts.

Apprenticeship and Political Recruitment

The second observation clearly suggested by the descriptive data on recruitment is that councilmen frequently served an apprenticeship prior to their candidacy. More than half had actually held an official or quasi-official position in local government. One of every five had served on the city planning commission; an equal number had served on some other city commission or board. Table 5–3 presents these data as well as material on other precandidacy roles.

Table 5–2

How Well the Respondent Knew Incumbent Councilman Prior to Running for Office (N = 431)

KNEW INCUMBENTS	
Very well	50%
Moderately well	11
Slightly	17
Not at all	15
Not ascertained*	7
	100%

* The nonascertained are almost always persons who ran to be on the charter council in a newly incorporated city. They will have known the other persons running for they will have all shared in the incorporation movement. Thus, if anything, the "very well" category underestimates how many candidates knew incumbents.

Table 5–3

Apprenticeship and Other Community Positions Held Prior to Seeking a Council Seat (N = 431)*

HELD COMMUNITY OFFICE		54%
Planning Commission	19%	
Other city commission	19	
Other appointive post	9	
Elective position	7	
CIVIC LEADERSHIP		50
INCORPORATION MOVEMENT, ANNEXATION DRIVE, LOCAL CAMPAIGNING, ETC.		20
PARTISAN POSITION		8

* Percentages total to more than 100 because councilmen could give more than one answer.

The part played by an apprenticeship system in choosing the few who govern has several important consequences. Viewed from the perspective of the aspirant to office, an apprentice role on the planning commission or library board is where he demonstrates his worth. As one councilman explains his candidacy, "I had served on the planning commission. Prior to that I campaigned for councilmen and mayors. There was an opening on the council; *I had done my prework.*" In this incumbent's view, his claim to the council opening was legitimated by his apprenticeship on the planning commission, itself an appointment to reward his campaign activities.

Viewed from the perspective of selection agencies, an institutionalized apprenticeship program helps locate potential candidates. It also provides selectors (whether they be incumbent councilmen, community actives, or voters) with criteria as to the candidate's skills and values. This latter benefit is particularly helpful in nonpartisan municipalities. In such communities, leaders must be screened and selected in the absence of commonly understood and widely shared labels which identify in some general way a candidate's orientations toward government, his political associates, and his policy views. An apprentice system can partially fill the vacuum created by the absence of party labels.

Finally, and to anticipate a point to be made later, an apprentice system reduces the training burden on government. The task of instructing a freshman member in the council rules, formal and informal, is measurably eased when the inductee has already been a peripheral participant, as when he has served on an ancillary board to the council.

For present purposes, however, we are interested in the precandidacy recruitment experiences of councilmen for what they tell us about the connections between leadership selection and political processes. The descriptive data make it clear that the modal pattern for councilmen is recruitment in the context of informal, interpersonal contacts and service to the city in some official or civic capacity prior to their candidacy.

Three Themes to Be Explored

The selection of leaders is related to the skills and talents available to government. The recruitment process, then, determines in part which qualities of judgment and which skills of management are present among elected leaders. Stated differently, to meet the demands of the day, governments rely on many kinds of resources. The skill with which these resources are marshaled and deployed is itself a resource, one that we usually call the "quality of leadership."[1]

---

[1] A useful discussion can be found in David Easton, *A Systems Analysis of Political Life* (New York: John Wiley & Sons, 1965), pp. 451–54.

> *How then, do leadership selection processes place differential premiums on skills, talents, and other qualities?*

The choosing of candidates for office raises the issue of tension between leaders already established and challengers hoping to win political positions.[2] Those in office are cross-pressured by two considerations. Manpower needs prompt authorities to recruit persons for commissions, boards, and similar ancillary posts in government. For the recruits, these posts often are the springboards into leadership circles. Persons who have authority, however, share it grudgingly. To sponsor the career of a talented and ambitious recruit may be to issue one's own discharge papers.

> *How, then, are tensions between established authorities and new recruits affected by political recruitment processes?*

An issue in political scholarship as ancient as Aristotle and as contemporary as Easton is "recruitment as representation."[3] Selecting the governors is a major way in which demands from citizens are represented or are repressed. In a democracy, it is assumed that all viewpoints receive a hearing in the halls of decision. A guarantee that this is so is for all viewpoints to influence who will be making the decisions.

> *How, then, does leadership selection affect the flow of political demands from citizens to authorities?*

The Successful Recruit

Nearly four decades ago Harold Lasswell startled the social science community by daring to apply psychoanalytic concepts to political analysis.[4] What, asked Lasswell, is the relationship be-

---

2 See the discussion, for instance, in Dwaine Marvick, "Political Recruitment and Careers," *International Encyclopedia of the Social Sciences* 12 (New York: Macmillan Co., and The Free Press, 1968):273–82.

3 Easton, *Systems Analysis*, pp. 254ff. He writes, for example, "The modifications in recruitment criteria to permit the admission of others can be viewed as an adjustment in the representative system and not just as a purely administrative measure." P. 255. Using historical data, Robert A. Dahl makes a similar point in the first seven chapters of *Who Governs?* (New Haven: Yale University Press, 1961). In her chapter on "descriptive representation," Hanna Pitkin pursues a similar theme; Pitkin writes, here, of how the selection of leadership affects the representational process. See *The Concept of Representation* (Berkeley: University of California Press, 1967), pp. 60–91.

4 Harold D. Lasswell, *Psychopathology and Politics* (Chicago: University of Chicago Press, 1930). See also his *Politics: Who Gets What, When, How* (New York: McGraw-Hill Book Co., 1936).

tween private motives and public acts? His efforts to answer this question raised, in turn, new and stimulating problems for political scholarship. One issue, of immediate relevance to us, treats the personal traits and characteristics which make for success in a political career.

Lasswell in his early writings thought that political man emphasized the value of power over all other values. To understand political man, one need only trace out the life-histories of politicians and discover what personal traumas created in some men a power-centered personality. Those who crave deference and power will be overrepresented among political careerists.

The theory of leadership implicit in this hypothesis is one which stresses the mutual interaction of situation and personality. In his earliest work, Lasswell assumed (incorrectly, as he subsequently noted) that politics overwhelmingly had to do with the search for and exercise of power. It followed, therefore, that the political personality is the power-centered personality. Lasswell subsequently altered his power and personality hypothesis, though he retained the general theory of leadership which explains the traits of a politician through the analysis of politics. In the mid-fifties, Lasswell took another look at the political "situation" and drew quite different conclusions about the traits politicians are likely to have.[5]

Democratic politics, Lasswell noted, puts a premium on cooperative, compromising activity. Success in such a political environment is withheld from rigid personality types, from those who are unable to adapt, adjust, and realistically appraise the situation. The selection process weeds out the intensely power-oriented person; his personality equipment precludes flexible give-and-take politicking. "Young people with rigid personalities may discover that the ladder of advance in politics is less congenial than the more regular steps provided by standard professions and vocations." If in politics at all, the power-centered individual will "be relegated to comparatively minor roles." Those who will be successful in democratic politics are relatively free of internal conflicts; they "get along" because they can "go along." In a typical Lasswell sentence, "a basically healthy personality is

5 Harold D. Lasswell, "The Selective Effect of Personality on Political Participation," in Richard Christie and Marie Jahoda (eds.), *Studies in the Scope and Method of "The Authoritarian Personality"* (Glencoe, Ill.: The Free Press, 1954), pp. 197–225.

essential to survive the perpetual uncertainties of political life."[6]

The key to Lasswell's argument, and the linkage between his thesis and our findings about city councilmen, is in the following sentence: "As we move up the ladders of modern industrial society [or the ladders of modern democratic society] the number of links with other human beings that must be maintained is a factor in success that reduces the usefulness of arbitrariness."[7] It is clear from our material that the successful political career is nurtured in small, informal groups. The interpersonal context of activation into the political stratum and movement upwards through it exercises a selective effect on those who are likely to be successful in political life. The face-to-face character of political interaction is as true of selection stages as it is of officeholding itself. The individual who attaches importance to coercive action in face-to-face relations will be eliminated during the recruitment stage; by and large, he will not make it into the ranks of elected officials.[8]

Our first observation, then, about the data patterns in Tables 5–1, 5–2, and 5–3 can be summarily stated as follows: Leadership selection processes place a premium on interpersonal skills. The "democratic man" who can compromise, negotiate, and comfortably interact in face-to-face politics will have an edge over persons lacking these skills. A coercive style is likely to be noted and eliminated at an early stage in leadership selection. The screening and sorting processes going on within the political stratum will eliminate persons deficient in interpersonal skills.

One way in which to make clear the importance of this observation for democratic politics is to compare political careers with careers in other social spheres. Success in the economic sphere, the academic sphere, the entertainment sphere, or the athletic sphere is measured by tangible products. In the business world success is measured by profits; in the academic world, by research; in the entertainment world, by box-office receipts; in the athletic world, by victory.

---

[6] *Ibid.*, pp. 222–23.

[7] *Ibid.*, p. 222.

[8] In a very different context, Charles E. Lindblom pursues a similar theoretical argument. He explores the adjustment mechanisms which affect political decision-making. The mechanisms, in some instances, are similar to those affecting political recruitment and self-selection for political office. See *The Intelligence of Democracy* (New York: The Free Press of Glencoe, 1965).

In electoral politics the only analogous product is victory at the polls. This is a measuring rod not applied until one has already worked his way up through recruitment channels. How then is the neophyte recruit to prove his abilities? It is possible that social acceptance is a critical test. Political ascent (as well as ascent in other spheres) is available to the favored few who make a good impression, who get along with people, who can sway others in the interpersonal context of politics.

Governors are both selected and self-selected; selection mechanisms reward those with interpersonal skills. If our point is only partially correct, then leadership selection helps define the kind of politics we expect to witness in "pluralistic" and "democratic" America. The politics of compromise, coalition-formation, and bargaining should be more prevalent than the politics of polarization, splinter groups, and doctrinaire defensiveness. In the words of Easton, "the process of competing for positions of authority in itself trains the leadership in many of the competences required by the system."[9]

Who Influences the Recruit?

As we have said, political involvement is heavily influenced by interpersonal situations. The anticipations and expectations acquired along the path from initial activation to political candidacy are nurtured in small, informal groups. These groups are socializing as well as recruiting; they instruct in the norms of political interaction. If this be the case, it is important to ask who populates these small socializing and recruiting groups.

Councilmen in large numbers were partly assisted up the career ladder by persons with considerable experience in running the political community. Nearly 50 percent of all councilmen allow that those already in established positions helped channel their political interests. Further, a sizable majority knew incumbents fairly well before they ran. Finally, more than half the councilmen were actually involved in city government prior to their candidacy.

---

[9] Easton, *Systems Analysis*, p. 451. Easton's observation is anticipated, of course, in the famous Weber sentence: "According to all experience there is no stronger means of breeding traits than through the necessity of holding one's own in the circle of one's associates." Our data indicate that "holding one's own" may well be dependent on having excelled in interpersonal skills." See Max Weber, "The Protestant Sects and the Spirit of Capitalism," in H. H. Gerth and C. Wright Mills (eds.), *From Max Weber: Essays in Sociology* (New York: Oxford University Press, 1946), p. 320.

We can conclude that the recruitment of councilmen is affected by the sponsoring and co-optive strategies of established leadership. This conclusion raises additional questions.

We have noted that the recruitment process tends to place power-holders under pressure from two conflicting considerations. On the one hand, persons in leadership positions are under constant pressure to attract talented lieutenants. Committees have to be staffed, leg work must be done, apprenticeship slots filled, and, over the long haul, new blood must be brought into the inner circles. As Marvick has put it:

> There are both recurrent and emergent manpower needs in the institutional processes ancillary to control of government; these manpower needs prompt those in politics to recruit others, offer them appropriate rewards and gratifications, and help some to rise politically.[10]

On the other hand, persons in authority generally do not like to have that authority challenged. Recruiting younger and more vigorous talent is to risk a challenge, if not immediately, at least in the future.

The solution to this dilemma is for the senior politician (or businessman, professor, or administrator) to sponsor careers in a selective fashion. The ideal recruit is one who combines ability with a proper measure of deference. The tension between the manpower needs of the institution and the status needs of the recruiter is managed by selective sponsorship.

Barber has written of political recruitment that the recruiter's self-image depends to some extent on how he compares himself with new recruits. The recruiter is tempted "to choose nominees who are not glaringly superior to him. . . ." Those responsible for seeking new talent may, consciously or not, prefer pushing persons "who will not do quite so good a job."[11] Barber's thesis is a useful one, but, we suspect, flawed in one regard. It is less the absolute quality of the new recruit which is scrutinized than his attitude toward his "superiors." The assumption that recruiters seek persons with less talent than themselves is recursive. It is to assume a process which can end only when the least able men in society govern. The check which prevents this from happening is that elected officials in part are evaluated by the behavior and abilities of those they place in apprentice positions. A poorly functioning

---

10 Marvick, "Political Recruitment," p. 281.
11 David Barber, *The Lawmakers: Recruitment and Adaptation to Legislative Life* (New Haven: Yale University Press, paperback edition, 1965), p. 240.

planning commission discredits the council. It also increases the council's burdens.

We share Barber's general idea, but prefer to state the specific hypothesis differently. The potential tension between recruiter and recruited is managed not through the selection of low quality but through the selection of like-minded individuals. Through selection processes as well as through direct teaching and imitation learning, the values of those already in established positions will be transmitted to new recruits. Persons who inherit the positions of their sponsors tend to inherit their views as well. "Probably as individuals move into the ranks of leadership . . . they receive an indoctrination into the mores of the subculture of political activists."[12] There may well be, then, a perpetuation of preferred "community values" from one generation of leadership to the next.[13]

If the reasoning is correct thus far (and we deliberately advance very broad generalizations in this chapter), we should next ask, "What are the values being perpetuated in these communities?" A tentative and somewhat complicated answer can be suggested.

In the United States, commitment to democratic procedures— by which we mean faith in majority votes, belief in political competition, tolerance of dissident views, support of due process, protection of minority rights, etc.—is stronger among persons most politically involved. Further, commitment to these procedures increases with socioeconomic status.[14] Since the political actives come disproportionately from higher status groups, these tendencies

---

[12] V.O. Key, *Public Opinion and American Democracy* (New York: Alfred A. Knopf, 1963), p. 52.

[13] Evidence providing additional support for this thesis is presented in Chapter 7. There we will suggest that there is little need for in-role socialization among councilmen because their anticipatory socialization was so effective. Inductees have comparatively few things to learn as freshmen council members because their proximity to the council prior to their selection familiarized them with the rituals, the values, and the orientations appropriate to holding a council position.

[14] Data relevant to this point are found in Samuel A. Stouffer, *Communism, Conformity, and Civil Liberties* (New York: Doubleday & Co., 1955); in James W. Prothro and Charles M. Grigg, "Fundamental Principles of Democracy: Bases of Agreement and Disagreement," *Journal of Politics* 22 (1960):276–94; in Herbert McClosky, "Consensus and Ideology in American Politics," *American Political Science Review* 58 (June 1964):361–82. There is also a useful discussion in V.O. Key, "Public Opinion and the Decay of Democracy," *Virginia Quarterly Review* 37, No. 4 (Autumn 1961):481–94; and in the final chapter of Dahl, *Who Governs?*

are mutually reinforcing. Adherence to democratic procedures, therefore, should be typical of the politically active stratum in the municipalities we are studying.

Political recruitment in these cities is clearly influenced by individuals already holding office and by community actives in general. Thus candidates who are successful in this recruitment system are likely to share a strong commitment to democratic procedures. The implications of this notion should be made clear. According to Madison, de Tocqueville, and other theorists, a tendency toward self-perpetuation of leaders protects democratic society from the excesses of the untutored. That the politically advantaged in society are committed to democratic norms and that these persons use their resources to influence successive generations of officeholders is, in the long run, likely to protect democratic procedures more than would be the case if political recruitment were completely open.

We present this notion not as a hypothesis, for, as such, it would rest on a fragile data base indeed. But it is plausible, as a general interpretation of the kinds of adjustments going on in democratic communities all the time. It may help to make the logic of such a general interpretation more explicit.

A normative goal can sometimes be most closely approximated by practices which themselves appear to contradict that goal.[15] This often is the case when the conditions necessary for attaining the goal are absent and cannot, realistically, ever be expected to hold. Assume the goal to be something we can call "democratic political recruitment"; meaning, in this instance, equal chance for all citizens (who meet minimal, nonarbitrary legal criteria) to hold public office. Further, no one already in office or having similar political resources exercises any influence on the processes which select the few from the many. Ideally, all adult citizens would be candidates and all adult citizens would vote.

Among the conditions which would have to be met for the ideal to be realized are: universal willingness to serve, universal ability to hold office, and consensus that unequal social and political resources were not to be used in determining who is to hold office (or, a more difficult condition, that there were no unequal resources). Of course, such conditions cannot be met. Probably it is also true that any attempt to design political recruitment as if

---

[15] In some respects, this is the thesis of Robert A. Dahl, *A Preface to Democratic Theory* (Chicago: University of Chicago Press, 1956).

the conditions could be met would only further becloud matters.

Communities, and here we speak of communities which pride themselves on being democratic, appear to be satisfied with a very different alternative for selecting officeholders, an alternative which nevertheless may be consistent with democratic ideology. Persons most committed to democratic procedures are also the persons who are most active in the recruiting and selecting of candidates for public office.

Leadership Selection and Political Demands

Easton has written at length and persuasively regarding the consequences for political life of the way in which interested parties communicate political demands to their leadership. Any political system will have some more or less institutionalized channels through which demands flow from the governed to the governing. The effectiveness of these channels in permitting expression from divergent segments of society *and* in controlling the type and amount of demands is, in Easton's theory, a critical factor in the operation of a political system. He explores a great many facets of demand expression and demand regulation; we concentrate on one aspect of his analysis.[16]

Easton points out that recruitment affects which segments in society have the ear of the political authorities. Does leadership selection improve the chances of some demands being heard more than others? Does leadership selection systematically exclude any segments of society? If we answer either of these questions positively, do we have cause for suspecting serious tensions between citizens who are heard and those who are not? Since we have already explored several aspects of this general issue, it will profit us to briefly review what the data presented thus far indicate.

We first raised the question of whether disproportionate council membership by some socioeconomic groups resulted in unequal representation of their opinions and in unfair allocation of goods. We concluded, somewhat tentatively, that there is undoubtedly some favoring, but that there is little evidence for assuming systematic exploitation of the ruled by the ruling. Too many safeguards are built into leadership selection processes. One safeguard, upward mobility for the politically ambitious, guarantees at least minimal representation for most socioeconomic groupings. Fur-

---

16 Easton, *Systems Analysis, passim.*

ther, elected leaders tend to come not from the most socially advantaged sectors of the community, but from within a range apparently set by middle-class values.[17]

We then posed the question as one of the "socialization gap" between the leaders and the followers. Is there any reason to suppose that leaders get inducted into an elite culture which provides them with political views strikingly dissimilar from views of the public at large? Our data suggest this view is unwarranted. Those who govern were not specially trained and prepared for leadership roles. We concur with Key, who wrote, "it may be supposed that a compatibility exists between the modal expectations, values, opinions, and attitudes of the population generally and the ways of behavior of the political activists."[18]

We have explored the question of recruitment and representation in yet another way. The evidence presented demonstrates that the routes to an active political career are many and that among actives are represented a variety of political backgrounds, expectations, and viewpoints. There are many access points into the active stratum; it is unlikely that the shaping of the active stratum is much controlled by an oligarchic elite. We cannot determine, but we do suppose that the backgrounds, the expectations, and the viewpoints represented in the active stratum more or less reflect what we would find in a random sample of middle-class voting citizens.

We did find the councilmen to be fairly homogeneous with respect to one perspective. They shared a bias against the label "politics." But this makes them more similar to than dissimilar from the people they represent. The antipolitics attitude characteristic of the American public is reflected in the orientations of these municipal leaders.

By combining the several ways in which data prior to this chapter touch on the issue of leadership selection and representation, we concluded that selection mechanisms tend *not* to create severe gaps between the governed and the governing. The flow of demands from population to authorities should proceed relatively

---

[17] This analysis, like, unfortunately, much political analysis in the United States, must proceed with the disclaimer "except with respect to the black citizens." The safeguard of "upward mobility" operates for the working class in middle-class cities. It does not operate for the black minorities (nor, as is the case in several of our cities, the Mexican-American minority) in those few cities where they are concentrated.

[18] Key, *Public Opinion and American Democracy*, p. 52.

unhindered by major disjunctions between what the people want and what the leaders hear.

Materials presented in this chapter permit us to pose the question in yet another manner. From many studies we know that, although large numbers of people in a community might have wishes or wants, a much smaller group actually takes responsibility for articulating these as political demands. Variously labeled opinion leaders or members of the attentive public, these are the citizens who press their views on government. In the communities we are studying, they are the civic activists. They attend council meetings, write letters to the local newspaper, pass resolutions in their groups, petition officials, campaign for or against bond issues, serve on advisory boards, and dominate the civic roles in the community. Do the data give us reason for thinking that there exist any major gaps between this articulate minority and the elected leaders? That is, although we have concluded that leadership selection processes minimize the inevitable distance between leaders and led, might these processes not increase the gap between those who actually voice demands and those who must act on them?

Our data discount this possibility. Political demands are voiced by the same stratum which produces the leadership. In our municipalities, we do not have social groups pressing their views on government which do not also play a role in deciding who is to occupy council positions. It is Mosca who reminds us that the closer the ties between the first and the second strata of the ruling class, the more will the top group be imbued with the "ideas, sentiments, passions, and therefore, policies" of the intermediate level.[19] The affinity between councilmen and the attentive public is suggested by the frequency with which civic roles usher persons into the active stratum and the frequency with which councilmen served out their apprentice years in civic roles. There is other supportive evidence as well. The preponderance of businessmen on the council and the general attitude that running the council is like running a business suggests shared perspectives among dominant elements in the community and the elected leaders. So also is the finding (reported in Chapter 8) that councilmen willingly relinquish their seats to newcomers. This is due to the tendency for recruits to come from the same stratum producing the incumbents.

[19] Gaetano Mosca, *The Ruling Class*, translated by Hannah D. Kahn (New York: McGraw-Hill Book Co., 1939), p. 430.

The data presented in this chapter suggest, then, that the transition for the councilmen from private life to semipublic roles to public office is such that the major demands made on the council are handled by persons very familiar with them. Movement into and out of the council proceeds in a way guaranteeing that mutual expectations are shared between the private and the public sector. This does not mean that all groups in the community will be satisfied with city policies. It does suggest that tension between those who most frequently voice demands and those who must process them will be kept at a minimum.

Implicit in our discussion is a particular theory of representation; our point may be clarified by making this theory more explicit. We assume that men do not represent other men. Men represent interests. When interests are shared by a legislator and those who chose him, we say that representation occurs. In the more concrete language of Cole, "We say . . . that you never ought try to represent Smith and Jones and Brown by means of Robinson, but that, if Smith, Jones, and Brown have a common interest in some particular thing . . . it is quite legitimate for them to choose Robinson to execute for them and on their behalf their common purpose."[20]

If the link is to be made between recruitment theory and representation theory, the idea advanced by Cole must be taken into account. Our position is that a great deal of representation of the attentive public by means of councilmen does take place because councilmen are recruited from that public, quite possibly because they share common interests with members of it. In this respect, the recruitment process substantially affects the scope of demands likely to receive the attention of councilmen.

Conclusions and Speculations

By now the reader has noted an inconsistency with respect to one of the major issues in this monograph. In previous chapters we more or less discounted the possibility that a "ruling group" exercised much control over successive generations of leaders. Themes introduced in this chapter run counter to this position.

---

[20] G.D.H. Cole, "Guild Socialism," in *Introduction to Contemporary Civilization in the West*, published and prepared by Columbia University, Vol. II, p. 889. Quoted in Mancur Olson, Jr., *The Logic of Collective Action* (Cambridge, Mass.: Harvard University Press, 1965), p. 115.

We can best resolve the inconsistency by spelling out a very general thesis, a thesis which puts into perspective much of the material thus far presented.

A group in society intent on affecting the qualities and values of future leaders can do so at any of five stages in the processes which successively select smaller and smaller minorities:

1. When a political generation is receiving its earliest political socialization;
2. When the population is being divided into citizens and actives;
3. When potential candidates are being recruited from within the active stratum;
4. When the final selection between candidates occurs;
5. When freshmen members reach the political bodies in which they are to serve.

1. Through a rigorous program of selective socialization and political training of the young, interested groups can guarantee that appropriate traits are bred into those few destined by birthright (or some other criterion which can be applied early in life) to be future rulers. We have seen that this is not an option directly exercised in the United States. If this pattern operates at all, it does so very informally and irregularly through the tendency for middle-status persons to have an edge in the competition for political resources. Since socioeconomic status is correlated, though far from perfectly, with differences in early political socialization, an argument could be made that future leaders receive different political training from the citizen-at-large. This is a tenuous argument, at best: Social mobility reduces the effect of the social basis of leadership; only a very few of the eligibles choose political careers; the gap between socialization experiences of the different socioeconomic groups is not that great. On the basis of our material, we concluded that leadership socialization operates independently of efforts by any groups with an interest in manipulating this stage for purposes of sponsoring "suitable" leaders.

2. At some point in the political maturing process of a generation, some very few join the active stratum. The remainder perform their citizenship duties but avoid direct involvement in political matters. Clearly the separation of the actives and the citizens is a point at which interested groups could control the qualities they prefer to be dominant in leaders. Any combination of dozens of selective criteria could be used. Does the potential active have the appropriate personality traits? Desired policy views? Acceptable ideology? Suitable loyalties and commitments?

Requisite skills? Correct friends? And so forth. Persons who failed to measure up to whatever standards were considered appropriate would be precluded from the activist stratum. Persons with suitable characteristics would be sought and urged to join the active stratum. Something of this sort seems to happen in one-party states when the party cadre is in control of membership and when membership is a requisite for political office.

Our materials indicate that there is little, if any, self-conscious shaping of the active stratum. Personal motivation and accidents of life-experiences are as important to determining who from among the general population will become actives as are choices by persons already established in active circles.

3. The shift of some few persons from an active role to a candidate role is the third point at which interested groups may attempt to guarantee the kind of person who will hold elective office. This stage is called "political recruitment" to refer to the processes through which screening, sorting, sponsoring, and eliminating take place within the active stratum.

In the Bay Area cities, there is evidence that this stage is more self-consciously directed than the previous two stages. Both through interpersonal contacts and through the allocation of apprentice roles there is an opportunity to give some actives an edge in the competition for office. We suggest, then, a very general conclusion. Though socialization and mobilization occur outside the purview of established selection agencies, political recruitment does not. Up to this point, finding and choosing political leaders has been left pretty much to chance or to the operation of processes part and parcel of American political life (the class bias, the impact of public stereotypes, the tendency for active roles to be inherited,[21] and so forth) though not controlled by any selection agencies.

With material presented in this chapter, we have the first indication that communities may have routines and procedures for keeping "misfits" out of office. It is not surprising that attempts at conscious selection are instituted at the recruitment stage rather

---

[21] The proportion of councilmen who join the active stratum because of a political family appears to contradict the idea being advanced here. However, one datum discounts the possibility that politically established families dominate leadership selection in any given community from one generation to the next. More than half (55 percent) of the councilmen have lived in the city where they currently hold office for less than twenty years. This is to say that they are not officeholders in the same communities where family members were politically active.

than at prior stages (or, as we shall see, at subsequent stages). To "control" political socialization runs counter to the norm that public leaders should be chosen on the basis of contest rather than sponsorship. To enforce some selection-training program on the young would necessarily raise the issue of which youth; democratic ideology prohibits making a choice which would permanently exclude some citizens from the possibility of political office. The famous eleven-plus examinations in Great Britain (with all their implications for an early choosing of public leaders) came under attack for just such a violation of democratic procedures.

It is also reasonable that efforts are seldom directed toward influencing who is to populate the active stratum. The boundaries enclosing the active stratum are too vague to be easily manipulated. Unlike the situation in nations where clear lines can be drawn separating party cadre, party members, and nonmembers, the active stratum in the United States is generally self-defined. It would take a tremendous commitment of political resources and energies to seriously establish and apply membership credentials. Although there is some selection and shaping at the edges, as, for instance, among the lateral entrants among our councilmen, those hopeful of guaranteeing certain traits or viewpoints among elected leaders recognize that controlling entry into the active stratum is not a productive arena for their efforts.

The latter two stages—influencing elections and in-role socialization—are discussed in the next two chapters. We continue the general thesis after these materials have been presented.

Chapter 6

Elections and Leadership Selection

In the democratic community, elections are the final screening and choosing process influencing who from among the many will hold public office. The many citizens legally qualified to become councilmen are finally narrowed to the very few who actually do so. Elections determine who will occupy (and who vacate) the chairs of government; they do so by separating the candidates into two groups: winners and losers. Elections have been spoken of as "rituals of choice." It is in the act of voting that the average citizen appears to recognize, and accept, that the larger collective is choosing the smaller number to govern. In *electing* their political rulers, the choosers confer legitimacy on the chosen.

These observations are part and parcel of any writer's discussion of democracy. Elections, by which is normally assumed competitive elections, are at the core of theories of democracy, at least of those theories purporting to explain how American democracy works. It is no surprise, then, that research resources have been heavily committed to the study of voters and of elections. Particularly in the United States, voter choice and candidate election have dominated empirical research.[1]

However, in spite of the preeminent role ceded to elections and the massive amount of data analyzed, there remain significant questions which are unanswered about the relationship of elections to representative democracy. Some of these unanswered questions can be initially explored with data at hand. For instance, we will inquire into the frequency of appointment as a route into elective

---

[1] The literature is far too extensive to be fully cited. A recent summary is found in Lester Milbrath, *Political Participation* (Chicago: Rand McNally & Co., 1965).

office. Further, we examine the extent to which elected office-holders appear to concern themselves with reelection. Finally, we speculate about the relationship between the form and ideology of nonpartisan elections and the type of leadership selection processes described in the foregoing pages.

Other questions could be raised as well, but, for two reasons, it would be difficult to give to elections the attention they merit. First, the range of questions which might be explored is considerable: competition, party activity, political organization, campaign behavior, and so forth. It would divert us from our major preoccupations to raise and examine the full complement of relevant questions. These issues are being investigated in a separate volume in this series.[2] We refer the reader to that work for a more extensive treatment of how elections affect the leadership selection process.

Second, elections more, perhaps, than any other topic reviewed in this book, would be difficult to analyze by limiting ourselves to the modalities in the data. The variations in the influence of elections on leadership selection are great; it would be misleading to limit analysis to the central tendencies and it would be inconsistent with the structure of the book to do otherwise. Thus, since the companion volume presents the election data in detail and does so with attention to variations between cities, the treatment in this chapter is designedly truncated.

Appointment: An Alternative Route to Elective Office

It normally is taken for granted that persons holding elected office earned it by competing for voter support. Much of our theory about democratic politics makes this tacit assumption and looks no further. But one should not too quickly assume that an election is always the route to elective office. Nearly one-fourth of the office-holders in our sample initially reached office *without* competing for voter support. Table 6–1 presents relevant data for the councilmen we interviewed and also aggregate statistics collected about all candidates in the cities over a ten-year period (five elections from approximately 1955 to 1965).

---

2 See Gordon Black, *Patterns of Contention in Small Democracies* (Indianapolis: Bobbs-Merrill Co., forthcoming). Preliminary analysis can also be found in Prewitt, "Political Ambitions, Volunteerism, and Electoral Accountability," *American Political Science Review* 64, No. 1 (March 1970):5–18.

Table 6–1

Frequency with Which City Councilmen
Are Appointed to Office

	Interviewed Councilmen (N = 433)	Aggregate Data on Candidates for Office* (N = 764)
Proportion Appointed	24	23

* The figure 764 are all those candidates for a council position who ran as incumbents. The proportion appointed, then, is of incumbent candidates who were appointed to office for their previous term. Aggregate election data were available for only 86 cities; the remaining city had been incorporated too recently to be included.

Table 6–1 clearly indicates that the strategy of appointment is well established in the Bay Area cities.[3] That nearly one-quarter of all councilmen initially gain office through appointment is consistent with our discussion of the apprenticeship system. This system combines with an appointment strategy to guarantee that at least some sizable proportion of councilmen will have been sponsored by their predecessors. As we would expect, those appointed to office were on more familiar terms with the incumbents than were those who campaigned for office. Table 6–2 presents evidence.

Table 6–2

Elected and Appointed Councilmen Compared with Respect to Preselection
Contact with Incumbents

	Elected (N = 327)	Appointed (N = 97)
Proportion Who Knew Incumbents Well Prior to Becoming a Councilman	58	72
Proportion for Whom a Councilman Was Important in Initially Getting Them Active in Political Affairs	21	33

[3] Eugene Lee reports data from six California cities over an eight-year period (1947–55). In these cities (two of which also appear in our sample), the percentage of councilmen who were appointed was twenty-six. See his *The Politics of Non-Partisanship* (Berkeley and Los Angeles: University of California Press, 1960), p. 66.

Further, as we would expect, the appointees are more likely than their colleagues elected to office to have held prior appointed positions in city government: planning commission, library board, recreation commission, etc. One-half of the appointed councilmen previously had been members of the auxiliary government; 39 percent of those elected had served in such a capacity. This confirms the earlier reasoning that apprenticeship positions in the auxiliary government are proving grounds for the aspirant to office. Just as the partisan candidate must have done his party chores, the nonpartisan candidate, and especially the appointee, will have served his predecessors on commissions and boards.

There is one additional difference between the elected and the appointed which merits note before drawing some general conclusions. We noted that councilmen give four different types of reasons for wanting (or being willing to accept) a council position: a sense of political indignation, a feeling of civic obligation, a general interest and curiosity about political matters, and a concern to solve specific problems. In ways which we might expect, those who were appointed to office and those who sought office through an election differ in the relative emphasis they place on these four reasons. Table 6–3 presents data.

Table 6–3

Elected and Appointed Councilmen Compared with Respect to Reasons Given for Wanting a Council Position*

	Elected (N = 327)	Appointed (N = 97)
Sense of Indignation	22%	6%
Feeling of Obligation	6	21
General Interest	20	18
Problem-solving	20	11
No Reason Given	32	44

* Percentages total more than 100 because of multiple responses.

Persons initially elected to office were more likely than their appointed colleagues to express a sense of indignation; conversely, a higher proportion of the appointed councilmen reported feeling obligated to serve their community. The tendency for those feeling indignant to have been elected is understandable; though not many councilmen are "challengers" in the sense of running to

turn out incumbents, there are some candidates who are so moti-
vated. They often will be disturbed by the personal behavior or
the policies of those presently in office. We have no way of knowing what proportion of all candidates are challengers, but we do
know that most of those who gain office do not report these reasons
for seeking (or accepting) office. Still, there are a few and it is
reasonable that they first gained office in an election rather than
through appointment. It is equally understandable that the appointed councilmen have a greater proportion of those who speak
about their obligation to the community. The appointees often
are councilmen who, when friends or business associates pressure
them to serve, respond out of the same sense of civic duty which
makes them officers in the Chamber of Commerce or chairman of
the United Fund Drive.

With these initial observations in mind, it is relevant to examine
appointment as a route to office in more detail. We have alluded
to the potential importance of the apprenticeship program insofar as it permits those in office to influence the selection of their
successors. The pattern of recruitment by sponsorship is thrown
into even sharper relief by considering the strategy of appointment
to elective office. In reviewing the interview protocols of those initially appointed, three important political purposes stand out: (1)
appointment as a strategy for insuring like-minded successors, (2)
appointment as a strategy for co-opting spokesmen from dissident
groups, and (3) appointment as a strategy for building a coalition
within the council.

Appointment and Political Continuity

The strategy of appointment is ideally suited to insure a procession of like-minded people through the council.[4] This use of
the political appointment is very clearly, if in an extreme way,
illustrated in one of our cities: Any councilman wishing to leave
office does so prior to an election; his successor is appointed and
runs for office, therefore, as an incumbent; no incumbent is chal-

---

[4] Lee's earlier study discusses the same issue. He writes of one city, "this
power of appointment to vacancies had been used as a stratagem of the dominant political group in the community in the retention of power. An incumbent
who decided not to seek reelection would resign a few months before his term
expired; the remaining council members then appointed a successor who appeared on the next ballot with the designation 'incumbent,' providing him an
advantage not otherwise possible." *Ibid.*, p. 67.

lenged. The strategy of appointment simply replaces electoral politics. During the twelve-year period for which data were available on this city, there was not one single deviation from the pattern. One hundred percent of the councilmen were first appointed to office; 100 percent stood for election at the next formal election; 100 percent were unchallenged; and, of course, 100 percent were returned. The route into the council is outlined by one of the members:

> I moved here about fifteen years ago or so. I joined the Civic Improvement Group, became treasurer in 1950—it is a nice group of people. Finally, they asked me to be president. Then came an invitation to become appointed to the city council—"Would you like to join?" they asked. "We think that you think what we think," that is about how they put it. Then I decided to accept their invitation; they seemed like a nice bunch of guys.

He reports, in response to the query of whether he would eventually have run had he not been appointed, "You don't run—at least if you know what is going on." One of his colleagues provides corroborative evidence. In response to a question about "informal rules of the game" on the council, he replied:

> There is one thing that is unique here, we are all appointed. When you are not going to rerun you have to resign a few months before the election so that the present council can appoint some good man in order to get the same mood maintained in the council.

Thus is continuity of political viewpoint maintained. New councilmen are carefully chosen to guarantee a procession through office of like-minded persons. That the strategy appears to work is confirmed by another councillor who explains to us why so many council decisions are unanimous:

> Probably the main reason that we make so many unanimous decisions goes back to how people get on the council. We are very careful about who we appoint and we make sure that they want the community to develop in the same way the rest of us feel is best.

Although this city represents a very exaggerated case, the strategy of appointment is used in other cities to the same effect. Appointment coupled with a well-established apprenticeship system preserves some continuity to policy in spite of personnel turnover. As a councilman from another community explains in response to our query about how new members learn their duties:

> Easy. He wouldn't be a councilman if not quite familiar with the city and the present council. New members are carefully controlled. For twenty years we have been a government by appointment—no one ran for office unless he has been appointed first.

Of course, the strategy is more available to some city governments than others; it is the deviant case when appointment to office can occur so frequently as to render elections superfluous.

Appointment and Co-optation

A second purpose to which the appointment strategy can be put is that of silencing, or attempting to silence, dissident elements in the community. Co-optation means bringing someone into the establishment for fear that if he is left out he will become a disruptive influence. Several of the councilmen initially appointed to the council fall into this group. One councilman, for example, was active in an opposition group representing a group of merchants. "The council heard about it. They wanted a voice from the group and asked me to accept an appointment. Now things are harmonious. It was mostly a matter of communication." Another councillor, one of the few blacks serving, was appointed not because he was a disruptive element but to forestall the election of a more militant black. "There was terrific disappointment on the part of many groups because a more militant individual had not been appointed. Some still are upset at my appointment." This councilman comes from "the worst district and had worked there for years and knew the people's problems. I don't want to ask for handouts for these people—but I did want to get better opportunities for them." It appears that the council members hoped to silence the rising pressure of black demands by a strategy of partial incorporation, that is, by appointing a black, but one who would not make "unreasonable" demands.[5]

Appointment and Coalition Building

The strategy of appointment is a time-tested way to improve the relative strength of one group over another. When a council is polarized and an opening occurs, the majority faction might well seize this opportunity to expand its ranks by appointing a person

[5] The strategy was not very successful in the city in question. Those citizens within the black community who felt excluded from municipal politics finally organized their own political organization, a very militant one. The tension between city officials and the black group has been, at times, unmanageable and both sides have resorted to violence. This suggests that a co-optive strategy is likely to be useful only if the actual leadership of the dissident groups are allowed a share of the political authority.

sharing its viewpoint. As one respondent informs us, "I was appointed by the antimayor group; it was a split vote." However, we do not find the strategy of appointment put to this purpose very often. The smallness of the councils and the infrequency with which a member of the minority faction can be counted on to retire prevents much use of appointment in this regard. In the majority of cases, appointment as a method to select a new councilman who has desired policy views is used in the more consensual councils where perpetuating "like-mindedness" is the goal.

We can offer only an educated estimate of the relative frequency with which these three different purposes are served by the appointment strategy. Consistent with material presented in the chapter on apprenticeship and recruitment, it appears that of the 24 percent of councilmen initially appointed, about four out of five were selected by councils intent on selecting like-minded successors. Appointment as co-optation and appointment as coalition-building are strategies far less frequently used.

It does remain, however, that nearly one-fourth of the councilmen in these municipalities first gained office without having to compete in an election. There are two general inferences we can suggest at this point. First, this finding further corroborates the thesis already introduced that political recruitment is not completely left to chance by those in a position to influence which citizens will hold political office. Although the shaping of the attentive stratum is relatively unregulated, movement from a role as active citizen to council position is apparently influenced by the manipulation of an apprenticeship system and by the effective use of appointment powers.

Second, we have seen clues elsewhere that there is a tendency toward apolitical patterns in the leadership selection process we are describing. Businessmen and civic leaders move into, and out of, elected political positions seemingly indifferent to their new role which, we might expect, should demand very different perspectives and life-styles. One component of councilmen's career perspectives appears to be a certain nonchalance about elections and the power of the ballot box. It is now clearer why this is the case. Since one out of four councilmen gains office initially without campaigning for votes and since 80 percent of these are returned to office as incumbent candidates, elections probably do not play a major role in their political career calculations. This does not mean that councilmen are not concerned about votes and elections; it does suggest that when a large minority of officeholders are "atypical" with respect to election processes, new perspectives and norms will be introduced into the way officeholders think about what is "normal" in leadership selection.

The "Success" of the Appointment Strategy

There are many ways to measure the success of the appointment strategy. For instance, does a high appointment council have more group cohesion and policy agreement? Does the appointment strategy effectively silence (through co-opting) dissident elements in the community? Does an effective coalition become established through appointment? To examine the success of appointments from such perspectives would take us into questions far removed from our primary interest in leadership selection. We will be content, therefore, to inquire further into the strategy of appointment by simply seeing whether the appointed councilman has an electoral advantage when he does run for office.

In Table 6–4 we present the proportion of winners among three groups of councilmen running as incumbents: those who were appointed and are competing in an election for the first time, those who were elected but have served only one term, and those who were elected and have served more than one term. There are no differences. Having been appointed to office neither improves nor hurts one's chances of winning in a subsequent election.

Table 6–4

Proportion of Winners Among Three Groups of Candidates Running
as Incumbent Councilmen*

	Appointed (N = 178)	Elected and Concluding First Term (N = 304)	Elected and Served More than One Term (N = 282)
Proportion Winning	79	80	79

* These data are from the records of all councils in eighty-six cities over a ten-year period (1955 to 1965). They include but are not limited to the interviewed councilmen.

This finding is instructive in two respects. First, and most obviously, the incumbent initially appointed is not advantaged over his elected colleague when he first seeks office in a campaign. Incumbency rather than a particular route into office is the advantaging factor. Four out of five incumbents win when they stand for reelection; they win just as frequently if they were appointed or not and if they have served only one term or have held office for a longer period.

That four out of five incumbents standing for reelection are successful raises another question, one again relevant to the relationship between elections and democratic theory. Democratic theorists place much emphasis on elections as a social control device; presumably the elected officeholder is restrained in his behavior by his estimate of voter response to his actions. The apparent ease with which incumbents are returned to office, when they so desire, raises questions about this assumption. It may well be that the "upcoming election" plays a very small role in the councilman's considerations as he chooses between policies. If so, then a reexamination of democratic theory is in order. For this suggests that anticipating voter reaction is not what makes the officeholder responsive to public preferences.

Of course, the incumbent's success at being returned to office varies from one community to the next. There are twenty-one cities in our sample which, over the ten-year period for which we have aggregate data, never failed to return an incumbent. There are five communities which turned down three of every five incumbents who stood for reelection. Table 6–5 presents the proportion of cities having different incumbent win ratios.

Table 6–5

Proportion of Cities with Different Incumbent Win Ratios

Percentage of Incumbents Returned: Averaged for Five Elections	Proportion of Cities (N = 86)
90 to 100	30%
80 to 89	17
70 to 79	22
60 to 69	13
50 to 59	7
40 to 49	5
30 to 39	4
less than 30	2
	100%

There is a second inference to be made from the finding that those initially appointed do not have an electoral advantage (nor are they disadvantaged) over those initially elected to office. In an indirect way, this finding supports a point made in the previous chapters. Among the small group of citizens active in community political life, there is a high degree of interchangeability. Persons move from a civic role to a position in the auxiliary government to a council seat and then back into a quasi-public (though non-elected) role. Who is actually holding a council seat at any given time is less significant than that he belong to that active cadre.

The data in Table 6–4 permit us to expand this idea of interchangeability. At least from the viewpoint of the voters, it appears that there are no major differences seen between those incumbents initially appointed and those who initially campaigned for office. We might have expected voters to support those initially appointed at a differential rate for one of two reasons. The appointed may have been returned to office less frequently because the voters resented the manner in which an appointment strategy circumvents the electoral process. Or, the appointed may have been returned at a higher rate because they were chosen for traits which might maximize voter support. That neither of these interpretations can be advanced at least opens the possibility that voters do not discriminate between the appointed and the nonappointed. Without survey data, this can be only a speculation. It is a speculation, however, which fits with our more general argument that establishing the small pool from which councilmen are chosen is more important to the leadership selection process than the actual choice of councilmen.

The observations about the frequency and implications of appointment as a route to elected office are a useful introduction to two other questions: First, what part does the desire for reelection play in democratic theory and what can our data say about this issue? And, second, at the most general level, what is the relationship between the election process and the more inclusive leadership selection process? The first of these questions is explored in Chapter 8; to the second we now turn our attention.

Nonpartisan Elections and Leadership Selection

In Chapters 2 through 5 we presented in some detail the social processes and the personal behaviors which combine to select the governing authorities in our California cities. In drawing a general portrait of leadership selection, we paid little attention to important contextual variables. We have not, for instance, compared cities of different sizes or of different demographic mixtures; rather, we reasoned that the analysis of the successive "boxes" in the paradigm was sufficient to uncover in a general way the political and social processes through which the few are selected to govern the many.

There is one contextual factor, however, which we should examine: the nonpartisan election system. Nonpartisanship is a characteristic shared (in law, though not necessarily in fact) equally by all the cities. It is a political trait which, it has been supposed, "alters the relative balance of power of various segments of society as well as the functions of various social and political institutions."[6] With such claims having been made about the nonpartisan ballot, we would be remiss if we failed to at least briefly discuss how the philosophy and operation of nonpartisanship affected those leadership selection processes taking place prior to the actual election, or appointment, of councilmen. The probable impact of nonpartisanship is increased because all of the cities studied have at-large elections.[7]

The ideology of nonpartisanship has been explicated in great detail elsewhere, particularly in the work of Lee and of Adrian, as well as in the official publications of the National Municipal League.[8] We need not repeat at length what the nonpartisan ballot was expected to introduce into city government. Suffice it to say that the reformist impulse which in the early decades of the twentieth century ushered nonpartisan elections into being had as its goal putting local government "on a business basis." Ideally, the creators of nonpartisanship "wanted to see the principles of 'sound business management' applied to government, not by professional politicians, but by established and successful businessmen of the community."[9] The political and social ideology of Main Street America held that local policy issues are unrelated to national party programs and personalities. The community is best served not by politicians beholden to a party boss but by civic-

---

6 Charles R. Adrian, "Nonpartisanship," in *International Encyclopedia of the Social Sciences* 11 (New York: Macmillan Co., and The Free Press, 1968):201.

7 Three cities have electoral arrangements which combine at-large elections and district elections; a candidate stands in a particular district but is elected, or defeated, by voters from the entire city.

8 Lee, *Non-Partisanship*. Adrian, "Nonpartisanship." See as well Adrian's "Some General Characteristics of Non-partisan Elections," *American Political Science Review* 46 (September 1952):766–76.

9 Adrian, "Some General Characteristics," p. 768.

minded public servants (i.e., business leaders) beholden to an informed and, as it turned out, largely middle-class electorate.

Though the success of nonpartisanship as a reform movement can be disputed, that it is firmly installed in California cities and appreciated by those who hold office under its protective shield are issues beyond debate. When asked if they felt cities would be better or worse off if elections became partisan, the councilmen responded "worse off" by a twenty-to-one ratio.[10] The degree to which the ideology of the reform movement has been internalized by these California office-holders is clear from their reasoning:

> We don't have a Democratic police department; or a Republican fire department.

> On a local level, government should be on issues and not parties. In national government, it is support of a philosophy. In local government, people simply want the local issues solved.

> Because candidates should represent all the people.

> I don't think party politics should play any part in city government. That would set up a lot of 3–2 votes. With the nonpartisan setup it gives the individual a better chance to weigh the matter under discussion from a nonparty standpoint without feeling he is letting the party down.

> Grass roots government in a community this size would be split unnecessarily by partisan issues. If you ignore party lines, you can get better unity and cohesion all the way through.

Further, approximately 85 percent of the councilmen feel that "better people" run and serve on city councils in nonpartisan cities. Of course this may be a self-serving response; however, it does suggest that the self-images probably conform to the idealized image of the public servant envisioned in the early reform literature. Councilmen give public support to the nonpartisan principle that "better candidates" are recruited for local office if unencumbered by an awkward and often corrupt party machinery.

> If it were partisan, it would be the parties' duty to elect certain people regardless of their ability. We have good people who do a good job on the level of city council and there are those who would stay away from it because of party politics and this would eliminate the good group of people.

> I think when you run as an individual, an individual can take the time and be willing to be judged on his merits as an individual, but when it gets into party politics and you have to expend so very much effort to work up

---

[10] The complete distribution for the "N" of 434 was: 84 percent said worse off, 9 percent said it would make no difference, four percent said better off, and the remaining three percent gave no response.

through the precinct level, and get cut up in the back rooms, it discourages
the finer element.

Whether in fact nonpartisan ballots completely eliminate the
active presence of political parties is, of course, a separate question. It is not an issue we deal with here, but two items do suggest
that the separation of party and council is not perfect, at least in
a few of the cities. Nearly one-third (31 percent) remark that
one or both of the parties are at least sometimes active in local
elections, though often this activity is by party members working
as individuals rather than by the organizations as such. Nearly
three-fifths of the councilmen (58 percent) feel that political parties
sometimes look to the councils for possible recruits for partisan
office at other levels of government.[11]

It is not our task at this time to decipher the implications of
this latent party activity in the nonpartisan communities.[12] We
are more interested in how nonpartisanship as an ideology and as
the general practice in the communities sustains the type of leadership selection processes described in previous pages. In two important ways nonpartisanship as a set of legal constraints and as
norms generally shared by community actives serves to sustain the
particular system through which a few come to govern the many.

Nonpartisanship, Disfranchisement, and the Sixtieth Percentile

Councilmen tend almost entirely to be selected from the upper
two-fifths of the population of their community arrayed along
traditional measures of social status. Nonpartisanship is related

---

[11] A finding reported by Lee is interesting in this connection. He asked party
chairmen in California if they ever looked to the ranks of city, county, or school
officeholders to seek candidates for state or national office. "Slightly more than
half of the 58 chairmen reported that they had looked 'often' (15 percent) or
'sometimes' (38 percent); 43 percent that they had never done so; and the remaining number did not reply." He adds that there were no differences between
Republicans and Democrats, though chairmen from larger counties were more
likely to reply affirmatively than those from smaller counties. Though Lee's data
do not provide the breaks, I suspect that county supervisors are much more
likely to be sought out as candidates for higher office than city councilmen, the
former having by far the larger "natural" constituency to offer the party leaders.
See Lee, *Non-Partisanship*, p. 106.

[12] This issue is in part explored in Heinz Eulau, Betty H. Zisk, and Kenneth
Prewitt, "Latent Partisanship in Nonpartisan Elections: Effects of Political
Milieu and Mobilization," in M. Kent Jennings and L. Harmon Zeigler (eds.),
The Electoral Process (Englewood Cliffs, N.J.: Prentice-Hall, 1966), pp. 208–37.

to this finding. Citizens of every socioeconomic stratum participate in politics less than the opportunities available to them make possible, but different strata disfranchise themselves at different rates. Middle- and upper-middle-class citizens, for instance, are more active in politics and vote with more regularity than working-class and lower-class citizens. It is also the case, though the generalization admits of many exceptions, that those groups which tend on the whole to be already less politically active also disfranchise themselves in local elections at a greater rate.

Nonpartisanship as practiced in the cities in our sample can further accelerate this trend; "nonpartisanship is a structural device that favors the values held by those on the upper end of the socioeconomic continuum."[13] The average middle-class voter is less dependent on a party organization to keep him involved in politics than is the average working-class voter. The network of largely middle-class service clubs, businessmen's groups, civic associations, and so forth form natural parapolitical organizations— organizations which help find and prepare candidates, which activate their members at election time, and which petition office-holders once elected. In contrast, the working- and lower-class citizen has no natural political organization in the community. Labor unions, which might play this role, are much more oriented toward partisan offices at the state and national levels where, after all, the decisions affecting the laboring man as a worker, not as a community resident, are most often made. There is a scattering of ethnic associations and a few emerging racial organizations, where the black population is large, but such groups are nowhere nearly as abundant as the middle-class equivalents and certainly nowhere as intertwined with local government. The blue collar voter is not likely to get politically involved in the absence of organized efforts. Without a political party to provide either expressive gratification or instrumental rewards, the voter must look to other organizations to link him to local government. These "other organizations" are simply more accessible to the voter in the upper two-fifths of the population than for the voter who in his socioeconomic traits falls below the sixtieth percentile.[14]

---

13 Oliver P. Williams and Charles R. Adrian, *Four Cities: A Study in Comparative Policy Making* (Philadelphia: University of Pennsylvania Press, 1963), p. 103.
14 For similar reasons, the nonpartisan ballot is assumed to favor Republicans over Democrats. The impact of nonpartisanship on the political parties is not an issue we review here. Some of the election data have been processed in this regard, however. If the distribution of council and mayoral positions in the

In this sense, nonpartisan elections help sustain the tendency for
candidates to be selected from the higher socioeconomic echelons.
It is persons from these strata, who usually are also Republican,
who have natural ties to a local government expected to operate
"on a businesslike basis." The lack of a political party to organize
the middle class is less of a hindrance to their political involvement.
Thus, the population groupings most underrepresented on councils, in the sense of having no members holding office, are the racial,
the religious, and the ethnic minorities. The argument has been
succinctly summarized by Lane.

> . . . the municipal reform ideal of non-partisan, efficient, apolitical politics
> is certain to seem attractive to white native, Protestant, middle-class citi-
> zens. By abolishing party labels, the lower-status groups are disoriented and
> become the unwitting clients of the upper-status press. By . . . abolishing the
> small constituencies, and making the election of councilmen citywide, eth-
> nic solidarity is weakened. . . . Municipal reforms of this nature, non-
> partisanship, smaller city councils, the replacement of mayors by city-
> managers, may serve admirable technical purposes, and in the long run be
> in the best interest of most groups in the community—but they weaken the
> political ties of the disorganized and depressed groups in the community.[15]

Although survey data are necessary to directly examine these notions, we can present some indirect evidence which corroborates
the thesis that where political parties are active in nonpartisan
elections those organizations most reflective of working-class sentiments are also active. Table 6–6 shows that in cities where councilmen say the parties are active, the presence of labor groups and
ethnic associations is more likely to be felt in council elections.

In general, it is likely that the nonpartisanship of the ballot
systematically favors the social stratum benefiting from easy access
to the network of civic associations and service clubs. It is in this
way that, as an election system, nonpartisanship along with at-large
elections enhances the odds of the upper two-fifths of the population monopolizing public office just as they monopolize the active
stratum from which candidates nearly always come.

---

eighty-eight cities for which we have relevant data were reassigned to conform
with the partisan voting behavior of the city residents (in state and national
elections), the Republicans would gain seventy-five council seats; the Democrats,
158 seats. This computation was done by Willis D. Hawley and presented in
"The Partisan Bias of Nonpartisanship: A Reexamination of the Conventional
Wisdom" (Institute of Governmental Studies, University of California, forthcoming).
[15] Robert Lane, *Political Life* (Glencoe, Ill.: The Free Press, 1959), p. 270.

Table 6–6

Proportion of Councilmen Saying Labor or Ethnic Groups
Are Active in Elections in Cities Where Political Parties
Are Active Versus Inactive

	Parties Are Active (N = 147)	Parties Are Inactive (N = 285)
Labor Unions Provided Election Support	13%	6%
Ethnic Groups Provided Election Support	11	1

Nonpartisanship and the Politics of Acquaintance

Earlier we stressed the way in which personal and informal contacts influenced which citizens from among the many join that small circle of actives who are considered, or consider themselves, appropriate candidates for office. This "politics of acquaintance" is equally relevant during the election stage of leadership selection. Lee states it well when he writes,

> Particularly important in the local election is "the politics of acquaintance," that is, the informal word-of-mouth politicking between friends and associates that occurs at such places as the service-club luncheon, the legion hall, the women's book club, the union headquarters, the lodge, the chamber of commerce, the charity organization. It is a form of politics not generally identifiable as such. Rather, it is the byproduct of a highly organized community in which these groups provide the principal avenues of the day-to-day communication and contact pertinent to city politics. Usually, such activity is no more than a conversation between friends concerning their choice on election day. The cumulative effect of these informal discussions, repeated by the hundreds, however, looms as one of the most important aspects of any local campaign, particularly in small to medium-sized cities. This is true not only in influencing the choice of a particular candidate but also in stimulating a person to go to the polls.[16]

Nonpartisanship contributes to a strongly interpersonal politics in three ways. First, as the previous section indicates, local elections run under the nonpartisan ballot tend to be freed "from the more organized structure and activity implied by the partisan ballot."[17] Smaller and more homogeneous political groupings such as the civic improvement league or the taxpayer's association

[16] Lee, *Non-Partisanship*, p. 120.
[17] *Ibid.*, p. 120.

or the politically sensitive service club or, less often, the union local fill the organizational vacuum left by the absence of political parties. Members of these groups will know each other by sight if not by name; they will know which of their officers might make good councilmen; and they will often act politically on the basis of their personal knowledge. Thus the very smallness and intimacy of the groups which, around election time, take on a political coloring contribute to the politics of acquaintance.

Second, quite often the nonpartisan election will be relatively "issue-free" or at least it will appear that way to the generally uninterested and uninformed public. Even when there are issues, they tend not to be the same ones from election to election. This lessens tendencies toward the formation of stable, organized coalitions of voter groups. For the council candidate, it heightens the importance of being known. As Adrian has put it,

> And since under nonpartisanship the voter seldom can associate a candidate with a position, he comes, as a last resort in his confusion, to choose a "name" candidate. This means that there is a premium upon personal publicity. . . .[18]

To us it means as well that there is a premium on having many acquaintances in town. Without a party label to introduce him, the "unknown" candidate must either wage a major campaign (something which violates campaign norms in many cities) or bide his time until his personal following is sufficiently large to guarantee election.

Finally, nonpartisanship as a form of the ballot is very often coupled with at-large elections (it always is in the cities under discussion). In such an election system, the two or three candidates with the most votes, even if well under a majority, win office. The politics of plurality elections tend to sustain the interpersonal politics previously described. Even in a fairly large city, it does not take many votes to gain the plurality necessary for a council seat. This means that the candidate who has the advantage of many associates and acquaintances can be elected solely on the basis of votes he captures from persons who already know him personally. Table 6–7 presents some data on the minimum number of votes it has taken to gain a council seat in cities of different sizes. That even in a city with a population of thirteen thousand, only eight hundred or so voters can repeatedly send a man to office emphasizes how important the politics of direct acquaintance can

---

18 Adrian, "Some General Characteristics," p. 773.

Table 6–7

Average Minimum Number of Votes Needed to Win
Office in Cities of Different Size

City Population (1964 Estimate)	Average Total Vote of Lowest Winner—Five Elections
71,000	5,298
28,750	1,931
13,450	810
6,675	518
500	64

be. As one councilman puts it, "I don't campaign much. I know nearly everyone in town." (By which he means, we assume, everyone who normally votes.)

There are three facts, then, which help us understand why interpersonal contacts play such an important role in prelection leadership selection processes: (1) a comparatively small electorate can choose a councilman; (2) nearly one-fourth of the councilmen gain office solely through the politics of acquaintance, these are the appointees; and (3) once in office, councilmen have an 80 percent chance of being returned. The cumulative effect of these three characteristics of nonpartisan elections is to sustain the emphasis on interpersonal politics which is so prevalent in the leadership selection processes. This, then, is an important way in which the election system molds the processes which narrow the many to the few during the preelection stages.

Conclusions

Although we have abbreviated this discussion, we have attempted to show connections between the leadership selection processes described in the previous four chapters and the election system. Nonpartisan balloting and at-large elections constitute a set of arrangements which lead to some recruitment processes and lessen the likelihood of others. Because this is so, the arrangements also favor some social groups and disfavor others. Making allowances for the dispersion around the central tendencies, we suggest that the upper echelons of the community are favored by the election system. Second, the type of recruitment, nomination, and election activities which benefit the citizens already organized work further to their advantage in the nonpartisan community.

These activities in turn are heavily influenced by interpersonal contacts. Finally, the frequent use of the strategy of appointment works to sustain the apprenticeship system.

We are left with a seeming anomaly. On the one hand, we have intimated (and propose more clearly in Chapter 8) that elections are not very salient in the thinking of many councilmen. On the other hand, we have seen in this chapter that it probably is the special characteristics of municipal elections in our cities which sustain the leadership selection processes discovered.

This anomaly presents a challenge to any political theory which would attempt to incorporate elections into an analysis of leadership selection. For the time being, we resolve the issue as follows: The election *system* sustains a type of politics which minimizes the significance of individual *elections*. The election system provides advantages to those citizens who already have social and political resources; to those located favorably in the network of friendships and associates which play such an important part in city politics; to those whose apprentice roles identify them as likely candidates for political office; to those who have natural organizational ties and support; and, finally, to those already in office if they choose to stand for reelection.

These advantages have a cumulative effect. In a variety of ways they tend to benefit some of the same people. In many cases, these advantages become so politically useful that persons become *selected* to the council even though they are indifferent to the *election* itself. Once there, they are so benefited by their incumbent status and their natural political allies in the community that they can afford to remain generally indifferent to elections. Thus, even when councilmen hope for reelection (and many times, as we see later, they plan an early and completely voluntary retirement from office), on the whole they retain this indifference.

We might restate this set of influences in terms of in-role socialization. The path to elected office taken by many councilmen is not one which sensitizes them to the ballot box. As businessmen, professionals, civic leaders, and so forth, they are accustomed to exercising authority. However, they are not accustomed to an authority which is periodically accountable to a large, and unknown, voting constituency. Their specific selection into the council failed to reverse the images of how one exercises authority provided by previous experiences. The nonpartisan election coupled with a heavy reliance on the appointment strategy tends to transfer citizens from a civic or business role to public office with but a passing nod to campaigning and elections. The question of who is to serve on the council is more an issue resolved by the comparatively small core of permanently active citizens than by the masses of voters. Even when this is not, in truth, the situation, it remains the image in the minds of many councilmen.

The election system, then, is clearly very relevant to leadership selection. But we may have to reformulate our understanding of how it is relevant. The importance of nonpartisan, at-large elections in our cities may lie less in the specific candidate choices made than in how the election system buoys up a distinct leadership selection process, one which, as it were, lessens the importance of elections.

Chapter 7

Becoming a Councilman: What Is There to Learn?

Although, in a literal sense, the process of leadership selection is completed when the ballots are counted and the victors named, it would be a mistake to end a discussion of political recruitment at this point. The elected leader must eventually become part of an already established political group. The newly elected is leader in name only until he begins to govern, until he lends his political weight and voice to council decisions. The way in which the freshman councillor becomes part of his council and the consequences of this merging of new member with established group have to do with induction.[1] In adding an analysis of induction to a general political recruitment study, we hope that we can show a connection between the method of choosing leaders and the operation of governing units.

As a political process, induction can be investigated profitably from three perspectives: (1) from that of the individual who is faced with the challenge of learning a new role; (2) from that of the group which as an ongoing political unit is faced with the task of integrating new personnel; (3) from that of political life more generally construed, especially with respect to maintaining policy continuity in spite of personnel change.

The Individual Copes and Adapts

Induction, from the perspective of the freshman councillor, is a problem of in-role socialization. How is the neophyte to deal

---

[1] With the exception of David Barber's study, little attention has been paid to this issue in political research. See his *The Lawmakers: Recruitment and Adaptation to Legislative Life* (New Haven: Yale University Press, paperback edition, 1965).

with the demands and duties of officeholding? How does he learn what is expected of him as a councilman? New members fresh from a campaign victory arrive at city hall on their first meeting night with more or less information about their new chores. The intricacies of formal duties as well as the subtleties of council norms present challenges to even the best prepared freshman.

His imperfect information is probably compounded with uninformed expectations. It is reasonable to hypothesize that what Barber found among state legislators is descriptive of city councilmen as well:

> Based on his experiences of politics so far, the new legislator begins the first session with expectations which are both inaccurate and overly optimistic. His information about the legislature and its work is almost entirely second-hand and is conveyed to him by persons who have an interest in stressing the brighter side of legislative life. . . .[2]

We have more to say about a presumed disjunction between "experiences thus far" and the council role later on. For now it is useful to take Barber's finding about legislators as a working hypothesis. The imperfect knowledge councilmen have about their role requires them to devote considerable energy to coping and adjusting during the first months of incumbency.

How successfully does the new member adapt? The rewards which a councilman receives for serving must, for the most part, be intrinsic: a sense of satisfaction and personal accomplishment, a feeling of being important and of contributing, maybe even the awareness that he has helped shape the community and made it a better place for raising his children. These are the kind of rewards which are taken in lieu of pay for the unending meetings, the nuisance phone calls, the distorted press stories, the cost of campaigning, the interference with leisure activities, and the time away from family.

Since municipalities depend on volunteer talent, it is necessary to keep the volunteers happy. Citizens can neither be bribed nor coerced into serving on the council or any other of dozens of auxilliary groups. To keep volunteers at their tasks requires that a balance be struck between the costs and the benefits of serving, between the disagreeable aspects of incumbency and the satisfaction associated with occupying a council seat. Among other things, dissatisfied volunteers lead to high personnel turnover, a condition putting considerable stress on municipal government.

Satisfaction with a new role can be greatly affected by initial

---

[2] *Ibid.*, p. 246.

introduction to it. The freshman councillor adapts or he does not to the new demands on his time, to the complexities of collegial decision-making, and to the glare of publicity. The better he adapts, the more he will find satisfaction in the council position. His morale is, of course, linked to his effectiveness as a councilman. The neophyte councilman's initial response to duties and demands will influence his council career, and it may in some cases either foreshorten or lengthen that career. It is for these reasons that we inspect induction processes from the perspective of the freshman.

The Group Integrates and Absorbs

Induction, from the perspective of the council, is an issue of group cohesion. City councils share with most legislative bodies a distinct trait—there is never complete membership turnover. Staggered terms insure that each election is followed by the continuing presence of previous legislators. Even in the absence of staggered terms, the usual concomitants of electoral politics (high ratio of incumbent victories and safe seats) guarantee that any legislative body will include some old and some new.

The new members must somehow be integrated into the group and, further, integrated in a way so as to minimize disruption of established decision-making practices. In many ways, a five-man city council is like any other task group. Its effectiveness as a purposeful, deciding group cannot be separated from the way in which it solves problems of social relations. The induction of new members provides a clue to how successfully the group can resolve the natural tensions of a face-to-face group which must make frequent and consequential decisions.

Whether a council will be cohesive is not decided during the months immediately following an election. As a group, the council is a constantly changing enterprise. Members learn more and more about each other and shift their perspectives and allegiances accordingly. Nevertheless, we can assume that it is during a councilman's earliest months in office that he first encounters the group's norms, the subtle rules of the game without which collective decision-making is made very difficult. Whether the new member learns these norms—and how group norms change with arrival of new personnel—affects the decision-style as well as decision-content of council policy making.

The second perspective for investigating induction, therefore, is

with respect to group norms and their initial perception by new
members. What is it that councilmen learn during the period immediately following an election victory? From whom do they learn?
We will be interested in answers to these questions for what they
tell us about the way in which groups respond to a leadership
selection process which continually feeds them new members.

Maintaining Policy Continuity

Induction as a political process is relevant not only to the adaptation of the individual and the integration of the group; it is
related as well to broader issues of political life. One of these
broader issues is how to guarantee some continuity to policy as
successive waves of decision-makers come to occupy the seats of
government. This issue in turn is related to an even more serious
problem in politics—controlling the arbitrary exercise of power.
In practice the nonarbitrary exercise of power often means the continuation of programs and policies established by past leaders. A
severe break with prior policy is viewed suspiciously by the political onlooker; it violates the incremental, cumulative nature of
political decision-making.

What restraints are available to the constitutional engineer
hopeful of institutionalizing nonarbitrary rule? From the beginning of recorded history, a means of avoiding tyrants and of pre-
serving policy continuity has been to control those who are to
manage society. There is a persuasive logic to this. Outlining and
enforcing rigid recruitment criteria can guarantee appropriate
views among the governing group. This is especially the case if
the governing group has undergone extensive preparation prior
to ruling. Hereditary castes are the best historical example. Birth
was the one criterion determining entry into ruling circles. Qualification for office was established by bloodline; moral behavior
in office was guaranteed (presumably) by exposure to the court
and its etiquette. A similar logic is today used in single-party states
(though without the hereditary implications). Carefully applied
recruitment criteria—party membership, party service, and party
training—insure, or attempt to insure, that acceptable views will
dominate among the political leaders.

Democratic politics have moved away from a reliance on recruitment criteria as a technique to impose policies or to weed
out political misfits. Only the most minimal and most neutral recruitment criteria are allowed (age, citizenship, and residency).

Broader recruitment criteria have been replaced with other safeguards against arbitrary rule: periodic and overlapping elections,
separation of powers, a checks and balances system, and federalism. However, students of politics have noted that these formal
checks are buttressed with a complex network of informal safeguards. And, as we have already begun to show, recruitment is
one of these informal safeguards. The selection of new leaders is
not completely left to chance. Persons who enter and move through
political channels either have or acquire certain "appropriate"
characteristics.

It is profitable to examine induction as a stage in leadership selection with respect to the issue of how appropriate characteristics
are insured. If legislative bodies must take whatever persons are
selected by the electoral process, at least attempts can be made to
shape and mold the inductees. In this sense, a legislative body is
like a military camp where the emphasis is not on selective recruitment so much as on intense (and highly successful) induction. Boot
camp is part indoctrination, part socialization, and part coercion.
The result is to take very divergent raw materials and produce
very uniform and suitable military personnel.[3]

Of course the city council is not faced with nearly as great a challenge as is a group of army sergeants. As we have begun to see,
selective criteria are at work long before the stage of political
candidacy, let alone officeholding. On the other hand, city councils do operate under the formal constraints of not being able to
impose strict recruitment criteria. From the perspective of the
political system, this means that leadership traits can never be
fully guaranteed. In looking closely at the induction stage, we will
be searching for clues as to practices which might serve the twin
needs of avoiding arbitrary rule and insuring some continuity
to policy.

The Council Role and Continuity with Prior Experiences

Much of social life can be examined as the processes by which
persons shift from one role to another—from bachelor to husband,
student to employee, child to teen-ager, criminal to inmate, or, in

[3] A useful theoretical discussion of induction within a military setting can be
found in Sanford M. Dornbusch, "The Military Academy as an Assimilating Institution," *Social Forces* 33 (May 1955):316–21. Dornbusch writes of how the
U.S. Coast Guard Academy, by isolating cadets from the outside world, provides
the new recruit with a self-conception appropriate to his role.

our case, political candidate to officeholder. It is thought, perhaps too readily, that assumption of a new role implies major shifts in expectations. As an organizational theorist states it, "In every situation in which a member or an aspirant is to be transformed into a successful incumbent, there are at least four requirements that must be met. The candidate must acquire: (a) a new self-image, (b) new involvements, (c) new values, (d) new accomplishments."[4] Although this requisite argument is practically tautological, we can still borrow from organizational theory the notion that incumbency in a new role implies a change in values and orientations.

The question remains, however, how much of a change? At one extreme is the case where assuming a new role entails a complete break with all that has gone before. Goffman's powerful analysis of the new patient's induction into a mental asylum illustrates how a totally new role can be thrust upon someone, a role for which nothing in his previous experience could have prepared him.[5] Under such conditions, the individual probably does acquire new self-images, new involvements, and so forth. At the other extreme is the new role which requires only minor readjustments. Anticipatory socialization was sufficiently detailed—possibly through an apprentice program—that little in-role socialization is required. The well-prepared senior from the elite university finds that graduate life holds few surprises and requires only moderate shifts in his outlook.

To what degree does the newly elected councilman view his new role as an extension of preincumbent roles? One perspective for investigating this question is determination of what from a councilman's past he views as relevant to his council work. We asked councilmen,

> We are wondering what in your previous experience, before you became a councilman, has been of most help to you in your work on the Council?

Table 7–1 presents the responses.

The councilmen were very explicit in explaining why and how they draw upon preincumbent experiences for lessons regarding conduct as councilmen. As the table shows, more than half cited skills relevant to occupations. A large proportion also are able to smooth the transition to the new role by drawing on prior com-

---

[4] Theodore Caplow, *Principles of Organization* (New York: Harcourt, Brace & World, 1964), p. 170.
[5] Irving Goffman, *Asylums* (Garden City, N.Y.: Doubleday Anchor, 1961).

Table 7–1

Prior Experiences Found to Be Useful in Council Work (N = 435)*

MENTION OCCUPATIONAL SKILLS		57%
Business, accounting	24%	
Law	8	
Engineer, developer, realtor	6	
Teaching	2	
Other (military, etc.)	15	
MENTION PRIOR COMMUNITY POSITION		39
City commission	16	
Civic position	20	
Partisan activity	3	
MENTION PRIOR KNOWLEDGE OR CONTACTS		12
Knowledge of council activities, previous attend-		
ance at council meetings	8	
General knowledge of the city	4	
INTERPERSONAL SKILLS, PHILOSOPHY		37
Ability to work with people	20	
Legislative skills	8	
General philosophy of life	9	
NONE		19

* Percentages total more than 100 due to multiple responses.

munity positions or on knowledge gained from prior community activities. It appears that these elected officeholders view their positions as continuous with other roles. What aspects of these prior experiences do councilmen view as preparatory for office-holding?

We begin with occupational skills. Clearly, it is business skills which are most often found appropriate to council duties. This is consistent with the proportion of businessmen on the councils. For instance, they outnumber lawyers nearly five to one (157 and 30 respectively). Explanations of why businessmen are in politics and why they transfer their occupational skills to political positions are rather sparse. This is obvious if we compare the "lawyers in politics" literature with the "businessmen in politics" studies. In the latter, the only hypotheses one can find are the economic ones which posit that businessmen seek out political roles in hopes of gaining financial rewards. Though this explanation is partially true, it is unlikely the complete story.

For one thing, gaining public office can hurt as well as help a man's business. We asked councilmen, "Would you say that being a councilman has helped you or hindered you in your private occupation? Or doesn't it make a difference?" Table 7–2 presents the responses.

Table 7–2

Whether Being a Councilman Has Helped
or Hindered the Councilman in His Private
Occupation (N = 431)

Helped	29%
Hindered	23
Both Helped and Hindered	11
Made No Difference	37
	100%

Although, clearly, the honesty of answers to such a question is suspect, the open-ended probe which followed produced responses indicating that holding a council seat indeed is a mixed blessing for the local businessman. Of those who said that being a councilman hurt them in their private occupations, nearly all could cite a specific case when time given to the council was time away from business or when customers had been alienated by an unpopular decision.

> It's been a disaster. My average income before the council was $25,000. Income while on the council has been $14,000. I don't have time to do my job well.

> I am on a salaried position in another jurisdiction. But other councilmen have told me that the people will boycott their business if [their] decisions don't please them. I think this is bad because it will tend to keep businessmen off the councils. One guy won't run next time because of this very thing.

> My photographic business has suffered 50 percent at least. I have no time for it and now I can't sell pictures to the city or in several areas.

Other councilmen have found their political activity improves their business contacts, impresses their superiors, and provides them with information about contracts, information easily converted into business advantages. One contractor was enthusiastic in his reply:

> Being a councilman has been immensely helpful. It has allowed me to meet a lot of people I would never have met before and at a different level. Business to me, a great amount of it, is a matter of personal relationships and the council has given me more stature in the community. I have just come in contact with more people who can do things *for* me.

Another businessman is even more to the point, "Sure it helps you. It's opened some doors. It should help you in your endeavor. There has to be some monetary value. The amount of time put in should be compensated for." An insurance man said, "I was raised from a claims adjuster to a salesman because of my work on the council. I have business contacts and they know me."

Another 11 percent noted that being a councilman can both help and hinder a business career. As one local businessman stated it, "You make new friends and lose old ones. It balances itself out. I have had some large accounts that were referred to me because of my community standing, because my name appeared frequently. But I lost one very large account because I voted against someone. This cost me about $2,000 to $3,000 a year."

Businessmen in municipal government can improve their financial standing. But they can also be hurt. Any council is likely to include those who are benefiting, those who are not, and possibly those for whom "it balances itself out." What the data do show is that the frequency with which businessmen appear in local government is not entirely to be explained by resorting to an economic advantage hypothesis. The activities of the council—providing services, letting contracts, allowing variances, construction, affecting taxation policies, and so forth—are undoubtedly of great interest to the business community. It does not follow, however, that businessmen always seek a council seat for private gain. Economic advantage will motivate some business aspirants, not necessarily all of them.

Beyond the "economic advantage" hypothesis there is little scholarly discussion which would help us account for the high incidence of businessmen in municipal government. However, since so many councillors are businessmen, it is important to devote attention to this issue. For ideas, we turned to the sizable literature that analyzes the frequency with which lawyers appear on legislative bodies at the state and national levels. It was hoped that the hypotheses about lawyer-legislators in state and national politics would hold clues relevent to understanding businessmen-councillors at the local level.

Eulau and Sprague conveniently summarize the more important theories accounting for lawyers in public life. Taking as their starting point the observation that "no occupational group stands in more regular and intimate relation to American politics than the legal profession," they review the familiar explana-

tions.[6] Lawyers have the appropriate status requirements.[7] Lawyers
have the appropriate skills for a legalistic political system which, it
is contended, the United States is.[8] Lawyers belong to an independent profession, one that allows of the career risks incurred whenever political office is sought.[9] Lawyers monopolize one of the major
avenues to public office, law enforcement positions.[10]

To these explanations, Eulau and Sprague add another. The
legal profession is structurally isomorphic with public careers.[11]
To treat in detail this interpretation would take us too far afield
here. Put most briefly, Eulau and Sprague suggest that, because of
their convergent development as professions, law and politics are
similar in structure. The private skills and roles of the legal profession are similar to those of public life. This isomorphism facili-
tates the lawyer's adaptation to a political career. Incidentally,
Table 7–3 provides interesting support for the Eulau-Sprague
hypothesis. Lawyers more than other occupational groups see
the link between their professional training and council duties.
Whereas 80 percent of the lawyer-councilmen recognize the connection between their professional life and their council role, only
38 percent of the businessmen and accountants see the same connection. At least from the view of the participants, the argument
that the lawyers constitute more of a profession and that the legal

---

6 Heinz Eulau and John D. Sprague, *Lawyers in Politics* (Indianapolis: Bobbs-
Merrill Co., 1964), p. 11.

7 *Ibid.*, pp. 32–39. This explanation is presented as well in Donald R. Matthews,
The Social Background of Political Decision-Makers (Garden City, N.Y.: Doubleday & Co., 1954).

8 They write, for instance, "The prominence of the legal profession in politics,
then, is traditionally attributed to the American reverence for law. . . . This
traditional explanation has some aspects that commend it—lawyers do play an
important role in politics as legal technicians." *Lawyers*, p. 15. Eulau and
Sprague trace this particular hypothesis to de Tocqueville's *Democracy in
America* (New York: Oxford University Press, 1947), a study first published in
France, in two parts, in 1835 and 1840. De Tocqueville writes, "Scarcely any
question arises in the United States which does not become, sooner or later, a
subject for judicial debate." P. 177.

9 Eulau and Sprague, *Lawyers*, pp. 39–50. This hypothesis is traced to Weber,
especially his "Politics as a Vocation," in H. H. Gerth and C. Wright Mills
(eds.), *From Max Weber: Essays in Sociology* (New York: Oxford University
Press, 1946).

10 Eulau and Sprague, *Lawyers*, pp. 50–53. The work of Joseph Schlesinger is
the primary source cited for this hypothesis. See his "Lawyers and American
Politics: A Clarified View," *Midwest Journal of Political Science* 1 (May 1957):
26–39.

11 Eulau and Sprague, *Lawyers*, p. 125.

profession is convergent with political duties is given some support.

Nevertheless, it is not lawyers but businessmen who are predominant among councilmen. And it is business and accounting skills which most frequently are transferred to council activities. A strategy for analyzing this mesh between municipal government and the business community is to investigate which of the lawyer-legislator hypotheses can be used, if transformed, to account for the businessman-councillor.

Hypothesis 1. Lawyers are members of a high-prestige occupation. This hypothesis, initially advanced by de Tocqueville, is easily converted into a statement about the frequency with which businessmen serve on municipal councils. Local businessmen are located exactly in that status group contributing such a large proportion of councillors. The material in Chapter 2 shows that it is from the middle class that municipal leadership comes. If lawyers have the requisite status for state and national office, certainly the local businessman does for municipal office. We should not be too satisfied with this explanation, however. There is an implicit functionalism in this argument which, like most functional hypotheses, is tautological. To "discover" that (a) officeholders come from prestigious occupations and to conclude that (b) occupational prestige is a prerequisite for officeholding partakes of a suspect logic. We should turn to other explanations.

Hypothesis 2. Lawyers monopolize a major avenue leading to public office. Schlesinger provides the best statement of this theory;[12] again it is one easily transformed to account for businessmen on local councils. The channels leading to council positions are dominated by local businessmen. In Chapter 5 we saw that apprenticeships are frequently served in local civic activities. These activities—service clubs, school groups, the Chamber of Commerce, charity drives—are, in turn, populated by the businessmen of the

Table 7–3

Proportion of Lawyers and of Businessmen Who Mention
Skills Learned in Their Professions as Relevant to the
Performance of Council Duties

	Lawyers (N = 30)	Businessmen, Accountants (N = 157)
Mention Skill from Occupational Training	80%	38%

[12] Schlesinger, "Lawyers," p. 31.

community, or by their wives. As one respondent stated it, "Well, I was president of the Chamber of Commerce two years, that helped a lot. In a small town when you're on the Chamber, you work very close with city officials on lots of matters."

In other words, the argument that lawyers enjoy a competitive advantage in the quest for public office because of their "control over a major avenue to public office,"[13] can be restated as follows: Businessmen enjoy a competitive advantage in the quest for council positions because they dominate the avenues leading to the council. Businessmen are conveniently located in the social structure of the community; their positions make them visible targets for recruiting agencies and give them an edge if they choose to pursue a political career.

Hypothesis 3. Lawyers belong to an independent professsion. This Weberian hypothesis has been aptly summarized by Bendix, who notes that, "for Weber, lawyers are the prototype of the modern professional politician. They are available for political activities in economic terms. Through arrangements with their associates they can free their time for politics and continue to receive an income or at least can expect to return to a secure and profitable profession when their political activity has come to an end."[14] Or, in Weber's words, more than the worker or entrepreneur, "it is easier for the lawyer to be dispensable; and therefore the lawyer has played an incomparably greater, and often even a dominant, role as a professional politician."[15] This hypothesis cannot be transposed for our purposes, but a word about council duties does suggest why it is irrelevant. To become a councilman does not require sacrifice of present employment, moving to Sacramento or Washington, keeping two homes, or even taking a temporary leave of absence. Persons in "dispensable" occupations do not, therefore, have a competitive advantage with respect to council positions. The local businessman, who can adjust his working hours, is as free to pursue politics as a hobby, "to live for politics," as is the lawyer.

Hypothesis 4. Lawyers possess the appropriate skills for a political career. Or, in the more refined version of Eulau and Sprague, a legal career and a political career are analytically convergent.[16]

---

13 *Ibid.*, p. 31.
14 Reinhard Bendix, *Max Weber: An Intellectual Portrait* (Garden City, N.Y.: Doubleday & Co., 1960), p. 436.
15 Weber, "Politics," p. 85.
16 Eulau and Sprague, *Lawyers*, pp. 122–30.

This is a more complicated theory to work with, but we do think it holds an important clue for understanding the preponderance of businessmen in local government. But it is necessary to detour at this point and make an observation about municipal government.

Matthews writes, "The skills developed by the lawyer in the practice of his profession give him an advantage in the race for office, if not actual training for the performance of public duties. His job involves skill in interpersonal mediation and conciliation and facility in the use of words. Both of these skills are indispensable to the politician."[17] This argument has been advanced, in one guise or another, from de Tocqueville to the present. It implies two things. First, lawyers have the skills most necessary for managing a "government of law," which, it is widely held, the United States preeminently is. Second, the two-party system of American political life puts a premium on skills of mediation and conciliation. The lawyer presumably has acquired these skills.

It is interesting to speculate, and speculation is all we can offer, about the consequences of the comparatively low salience of problems of constitutional interpretation and problems of partisan adjustment in council government. For example, the constant battles over constitutional interpretations so prevalent in federal and state politics are largely absent from municipal politics. The legal parameters within which city governments operate are determined by persons *other than* councilmen and their staff. It is the legislature in Sacramento which decides the basic election laws and the debt ceiling, and which assesses the property of public utilities for local tax rolls. The doctrine of *State preemption* forbids cities from making regulations in an area in which the State has already acted.

Second, the rhetoric of nonpartisanship is accepted by most councilmen. For the most part, major policies and programs are articulated and pursued without reference to persisting partisan groupings. As we have observed, an overwhelming proportion of all council decisions are made unanimously.

We should not wish to push the argument too far, however. Certainly, councils must be preoccupied at times with constitutional matters and, certainly there occur conflict situations when the skills of mediation are required. However, in comparison with state and federal politics, we are safe in suggesting that municipal politics less often concern legal matters or partisan groupings.

---

17 Matthews, *Social Background*, p. 30.

Issues left for municipal government to act upon are similar to issues encountered in business. In the words of the councilmen:

> I am in insurance and this experience in business helped me gain some administrative ability. Government is like running a business.

> My business experiences have been of help to me. The city is not unlike a business. You deal with people and finances, personalities and budgets.

> Personnel, production problems are similar both in business and public life.

> Fundamentally, I am an accountant. I understand working with figures. City government is just a business and a matter of handling money. My background gives me an understanding of working with the city budget and expenditures.

These quotations, and the many others which could be listed, are suggestive of the "convergence hypothesis" used to explain the presence of lawyers in legislative politics. We can usefully paraphrase Eulau and Sprague. In many instances, the distinction between a community's public life and its business life is difficult to discern. Rightly or wrongly, it is thought that business leaders and government leaders have the same purposes and use, to accomplish these purposes, similar skills. As a result, the occupation of businessman and the role of councilman converge. This convergence means that businessmen, more than other occupational groups, find in public life opportunities that facilitate "the actual interchange of institutional positions, careers, and professional roles."[18]

This lengthy discussion of why businessmen so often are councilmen is intended to recall a theme introduced in Chapter 5. Community life in general, by which is meant both civic and business activities, appears to intersect government in many important respects. There is a meshing of persons and of activities, a meshing which makes positions in the government sphere, the civic sphere, and the business sphere practically interchangeable.[19] But, before commenting on this at length, we need to present the remainder

---

18 Eulau and Sprague, *Lawyers*, p. 132.

19 Our findings, therefore, support those social observers who contend that politics is not such a specialized career path as to prevent entry to any save those who devote a lifetime to mastering its intricacies. We differ, for example, from Suzanne Keller, who writes that "the available evidence suggests that it is becoming more and more difficult to move from one elite sphere to another," at least insofar as she applies this generalization to politics. For a general discussion of the "interchangeability of elites," see her *Beyond the Ruling Class* (New York: Random House, 1963), pp. 212–13.

of the data from Table 7–1, the kinds of previous skills viewed by councilmen as relevant to their official duties.

A large group of councilmen view their present role as an extension of previous community service or experiences. All told, about half the councilmen mention either service on a city commission, service in a civic post, a partisan role (by far the smallest group), attendance at council meetings, or general knowledge of local issues in explaining what from their previous experience has been of help to them in their work on the council. Quotations from the interview protocols indicate just how important these experiences were:

> The planning commission is the spawning ground. The planning commission is second to the council; it carries a lot of weight. Unless their decisions are appealed they are final. You can gain confidence on the planning commission, and know you're not looking foolish.

> My experience as president of the school board helped me to learn about the public—meeting the public and satisfying their demands, what the public is like and how to handle them.

> I guess the planning commission experience, because this is really your first taste. It's just like the guy they're throwing baseballs at in the carnival; you've gotta duck and roll with the punches. You've got to become ring-wise, learn what to say and what to do. Because no one problem is like any other.

> Being active in the other community affairs gives you good insight. I feel a councilman should work through various community affairs before running for the council.

> My work in the Chamber of Commerce. Any important decisions affecting the community are thrashed over in the Chamber of Commerce. They are closely allied with the work of the council. It has kept in close touch with matters of community interest.

This is just a sample from among the many concise responses which so clearly show a close relationship between preincumbency service to the community and transition to the role of councilman. There is found a convergence of civic roles and officeholding just as there is a convergence of occupational roles and officeholding.

We began this section by borrowing from organizational theory a working hypothesis: A councilman, in taking on his new role, faces situations which require that he develop a new self-image, new involvements, new values, and new accomplishments. However, the empirical evidence suggests a major modification of the working hypothesis. Certain experiences, roles, skills, and expectations from the preincumbency period prepare the aspirant for the new role and ease his transition into it. Generally, the new councilman does not come to his first meeting outfitted only with irrelevant skills, inaccurate information, and distorted expectations. His familiarity with municipal government, his view that civic, occupational, and council activities are the same enterprise, and, in many cases, his prior service on an official committee correct, or at least counteract, his misperceptions.

The Impact of Incumbency

A second perspective on the issue of continuity from noncouncil to council roles is provided by a direct question inquiring into the impact of incumbency. Councilmen were asked:

> As a result of your service, have you changed your opinion about any important aspects of the work of the council?

The responses were unexpected and, if we believe the organizational theorists, unusual. Three out of five councilmen said: "No, my views about council work have not changed in any important respect." Only about two-fifths (38 percent) reported changing their opinions as a result of officeholding. If a few councilmen knew what to expect, we could still be comfortable with the idea that "new roles equal new views." But if a sizable majority were well-informed prior to council service, we should dismiss that idea and seek a different one. We need an interpretation of the councilman's induction which fits our data and which is theoretically persuasive.

As we have said, there is an overlap between council duties and other community roles. An apprenticeship system, coupled with the perceived nexus between the business community and municipal government, provides most aspirants with firm views about council work. These views are but marginally affected by actual service on the council, partly because of anticipatory socialization and partly because lines between business, civic, and government activities are blurred, even obliterated, by an exchange of information and personnel. This argument is illustrated time and again by the actual responses of the councilmen. The 60 percent who did not change their views explained why; their explanations clearly support the interpretation we have introduced:

> I am more firmly convinced that running a city government is no different from running any other organization. Political overtones don't necessarily have to inject the problems you sometimes read about.

I had a good grasp of its functions and its operations prior to joining the council. I had come to a lot of meetings.

Nothing has happened to change my basic philosophy or thinking. I find that I'm correct, fundamentally. I look upon government as a business so it should be run as a business. Fundamentally, we are talking only about dollars—how to get money and how to spend money.

I had studied many of the major proposals. They stay about the same. They haven't influenced me one way or another.

I was pretty well versed in what a councilman's job was before I went on.

No, because of my great exposure to city affairs. I had been so much involved before. My eye-opener came long before joining the council.

I had had lots of experience with city government before I ran. I was VP of the Kiwanis when the chief of police was President, and the city attorney was VP when I was President.

It is an exaggeration to imply that no change in views took place, an exaggeration which would not serve our purposes. As we see in the next section, inductees did have things to learn when they became councilmen. Nevertheless, what the quotations should alert us to is the ease with which transition from the private to the public role occurs. Viewed from the perspective of the inductees (60 percent of them), there was no reason to change views just because they shifted from the planning commission or the Chamber of Commerce or the PTA or an executive's desk or whatever to a council seat. Problems are similar and previous expectations, for the most part, were correct.

What about the two out of five who did alter views as a result of council service? The views actually changed vary widely, from "I know more about limitations regarding state laws" to "The people are too apathetic. I thought people would be down to offer their opinions, but they just aren't interested." A few councilmen (nineteen) even admitted to becoming more liberal or more conservative because of their service. Another small group (eighteen) said that their changes were mainly in the area of new information. They are better informed about "council procedures" or about "how the city must work with county and state agencies."

For the most part, however, those whose views changed with service simply report that council work is harder than they expected, is more involved, and takes more time. Altogether, half of those whose views changed expressed themselves along the lines suggested by the following quotations:

> It takes longer than you think. You have to go through all the necessary steps.
>
> Except it is a tougher job than I thought it was, and more important.
>
> It's more important and time-consuming than I thought it would be.
>
> I thought I was going to set the world on fire. You find it just can't be done. I have been disillusioned.
>
> Things move much slower than I had anticipated. There are many more personal snags that tend to slow the progress down. I never foresaw this, and it really hinders the council.

Some councilmen certainly were not fully prepared for their council chores. They came to their council seat optimistic about what could be accomplished and ill-informed about how difficult it would be. Barber reports a similar syndrome among freshmen state legislators. During the initial recruitment stage, the general "lack of information means that the candidate's personal needs are rather free to affect his perceptions, enabling him to select a need-satisfying image of the legislature." Barber goes on to note that the recruiter, knowing of the candidate's inadequate information, "is relatively unrestrained in the type of appeal he can make. Favorable aspects of the legislator's job can be stressed and the negative side played down. For example, several legislators commented in the interviews that they were surprised at the time the work takes; they had been assured that only part of a few days a week would be required."[20]

What is interesting here is not that prior to election some city councilmen share with state legislators an overly optimistic view of their forthcoming duties; rather, it is the comparative infrequency of this response among local councilmen which merits interpretation. Whereas Barber leaves us with the impression that most state legislators are surprised (and dismayed) when they initially understand their legislative duties, we find that most city councilmen discover council duties to be much what they had expected of them.

It is the proximity of aspiring councilmen to municipal activities which explains this discrepancy between local and state politics. This proximity has at least two components. First, as has been shown now in several ways, there is convergence of pre-council roles and the council role. The civic, the semipublic, the community, and the occupational roles of councilmen are per-

---

20 Barber, *Lawmakers*, p. 24.

ceived as being similar to council roles. Second, there exists a geographic proximity in municipal politics which is generally absent at the state level. Interested citizens drop in to a council meeting in a way they never can to a state legislature. "I had lived in the city for almost ten years and had missed only five council meetings." If you are part of the attentive public, the chances of knowing a city councillor or a commission member are high, certainly higher than the odds of knowing a member of the state legislature. The smaller, local newspapers often carry more local news than state news; they certainly display it more prominently and dwell at greater length on the personalities in local politics.

The potentially traumatic impact of incumbency is lessened by the proximity to the council of likely recruits. The transition from a noncouncil to a council role is smoothed by the preparation most councilmen have for their tasks prior to election. This meshing of community life and council life is the result neither of a recruitment plan nor of formal criteria for candidacy. It is more the consequence of subtle self-selection and selection patterns operating among that strata of the population which provides citizens from whom leaders are selected. But, before discussing all the conclusions which might follow from these observations about the induction period, there are additional data to present.

How the Councilman Learns the Routines of Council Work and the Informal Norms of Council Life

We should not interpret the continuity between precouncil and council roles and the nontraumatic character of induction to mean that new councilmen have nothing to learn when they initially join the council. At a minimum, the neophyte must certainly instruct himself, or be instructed, about the routines and procedures of council work. In addition, we felt new councilmen would become acquainted during the induction stage with the informal rules of the game which are so influential in the life of small groups. In posing the following two questions to the councilmen we were most interested in the "how" of learning experiences during early incumbency.

> When you first became a councilman, do you remember how you learned about the job? I mean, how did you learn the routines of being a councilman?

> Now, in addition to learning the routines, were there any informal things that one had to learn in order to get things accomplished? How would you say you learned about these sorts of things?

It is the task of a different monograph in this series to explore the substantive answers to these, and related, questions. We should mention in passing, however, that 45 percent of the councilmen said there were no informal things to be learned. Of those who did list informal things (group norms, rules of the game, etc.) the answers fell into those categories which have been identified in other studies of legislative behavior: matters of personal behavior; matters of treatment of colleagues and staff; matters of political strategies—the acceptable and the unacceptable; matters of relationships with the public; and so forth.[21] For purposes of our analysis we coded the "how things were learned" jointly from the two questions.

The way in which new councilmen learned the council routines and the group norms is presented in Table 7–4.

Table 7–4

Percentage of Councilmen Indicating Various Methods by Which They Learned Council Routines or Group Norms (N = 431)*

Transferred knowledge from prior community service, prior attendance at council meetings, prior study of local issues, etc.	44%
Learned from fellow councilmen or from city staff members	38
Relied on source material such as booklets, council minutes, city budget, etc.	28
Learned as went along: general observation, trial and error, etc.	64

*Multiple responses allowed.

Two facts stand out clearly. First, nearly half the inductees (44 percent) relied at least in part on prior experiences for lessons about council work or group norms. This proportion is even greater than the number who learned from fellow councilmen or city staff. Second, there is much observational learning. In fact, one-fourth of the councilmen give "learning as I went along" as the *only* method by which they became acquainted with the routines and norms of council life. We will consider these two issues in turn.

---

21 See Donald Matthews, *U.S. Senators and Their World* (New York: Random House Vintage Books, 1960), especially Chapter 5; and John Wahlke, Heinz Eulau et al., *The Legislative System* (New York: John Wiley & Sons, 1962), especially Chapter 7.

The proportion saying they learned what they needed to know about council work by transferring previously acquired knowledge is much higher than we expected. Unlike the other questions about how preelection experiences smoothed the transition on to the council, the questions producing the data in Table 7–4 were deliberately worded to draw the respondent's attention to his council experiences. Nevertheless, nearly half the councillors insisted on citing prior lessons as relevant to their induction. As one put it, "It was from my previous experience. While I was serving on the commissions, we met with the council. I had appeared before them many times as a contractor. Also I learned a good deal from work in the Chamber of Commerce." This councillor appears to have touched every base—previous civic work, previous service on a city commission, and an occupation requiring appearances before the council—and to have learned what was relevant to council work well before his election. Another inductee "knew the councilmen personally, both past and present." He adds, "I knew the issues and how they voted. In fact, I knew more than some councilmen!" Many cited previous service on the planning commission or other official groups: "I had already attended council meetings before and was active in planning commission work and on the school board." Finally, one councillor who had attended numerous meetings simply said, "I did a lot of work to learn about the council prior to coming on." All told, 44 percent described their earliest learning about council duties along the lines suggested in these quotations.

More than three out of five councilmen (64 percent) felt that general observation, or a trial and error method, aided them in adjusting to their roles. Many of the responses falling into this category are little more than residual answers. One councillor, for instance, who "knew most of the routines from attending previous meetings" added, "Also, I just sat around and picked up minute details." Another remarked, "You learn to be a councilman by being one." In spite of the ease with which "observation," "exposure," "experience," or "trial and error" come to mind in describing how one goes about learning a new role, for many councilmen such methods did appear to be quite salient. Of councilmen who give only one response to the "How did you learn?" question, the overwhelming number cited observation.

What are we to make of this? The colorful words of one councilman provide a clue: "No one's going to take you under his arm. You just get kicked in the shins a couple of times, and you learn."

The induction of new members does not appear to be a high-priority task in city councils. The frequency with which new councilmen are left to their own devices—transferring previous knowledge, studying source materials, or just listening and watching—disallows the likelihood of much self-conscious instruction by senior members. Of course, there are lessons to be learned from longer-tenured colleagues and from the city staff. Nearly two out of five councilmen answered similarly to one who said, "I learned by asking the two already on the job and asking the city manager," or another who reported, "Everyone offered to show me. The departments showed me around and held conferences for me." But, in spite of answers such as these, only 5 percent of all councilmen interviewed felt they learned all they needed to know exclusively from colleagues or the staff.

Induction, in the minds both of the new councilmen and of the senior colleagues, clearly is not a period of in-role socialization. Problems of adapting to the new role are minimized by the frequency with which prior experiences provided opportunities for anticipatory socialization. As far as data reported in this chapter show, neither senior councillors nor city staff use the induction period to influence the thinking and behavior of new members. In concluding this chapter, we must, then, ask how induction fits into an understanding of leadership selection.

Conclusions

This chapter began with three research questions which were to be explored by studying the induction of new members into the council. One was the question of how new members adapt to their changed political status; a second was the question of how groups adapt to the frequent changeover in membership; the third was how induction is used, if it is, to influence the political values and office behavior of new councilmen.

Although providing fresh ways to look at these questions, the data proved not to be what we expected. In reviewing the central tendencies (and the reader should again be warned that we discuss the modal patterns, not the deviations, of which there are many) in the data, it is evident that we must greatly modify the working hypotheses stated early in our chapter.

First, councilmen are not learning new self-images, involvements, values, and accomplishments during the initial months of service. Becoming a councilman does not imply in any significant sense the "acquisition of a new role." There is found, instead, the gradual assimilation of norms, values, behaviors, and expectations, an assimilation beginning, in all likelihood, when the councilman-to-be first joins the politically active stratum. Occupational duties and civic roles are teachers every bit as effective as fellow councilmen. Perhaps they are even more effective because learning a role by holding an analogous one is instruction difficult to better. The new member is not the complete neophyte we expected him to be.

Second, our data tell us little about the way in which decision-making groups adapt to the frequent appearance of new members. They do tell us, however, what *does not* happen in city councils. Contrary to our expectations, the instruction of new members is largely left to chance. The new member either comes equipped with the skills and expectations proper to his duties or he acquires them on his own. Certainly, senior councilmen will answer questions, help the uninitiated along if he asks, and probably correct gross misperceptions, but the opportunity to substantially modify or shape views of the new recruit is apparently neglected. It is possible that older members, having themselves graduated from the apprenticeship system, realize that the important training has already taken place. There may be an implicit trust that the screening and sorting going on in the politically active stratum is guarantee enough that recruits will be prepared for the council.

This speculation leads directly to the third research question posed in this chapter: Is induction used to counter the "dangers" in open recruitment politics? Apparently not. Whether those who are victorious in the electoral politics of these municipalities have the appropriate traits or not, neither city staff nor senior councillors nor any other group take up the challenge of inducting them.

There are two explanations. Either those who could manage the induction period are indifferent to the possibilities, or, the open recruitment system does not produce such a heterogeneous collection of new recruits after all. The first explanation is unlikely. These are men with military, professional, and business experience; they hardly need reminding that, properly inducted, the recruit, the student, or the new employee will become an effective and committed member of the service, firm, or business. The second explanation is more likely, and it fits data reported in previous chapters. Unsuitable members or those who might choose unwise policies (the definition of unsuitable and unwise shifting from community to community) find the avenues to office closed. Leadership selection proceeds according to some minimal criteria, probably unrecognized and certainly not articulated, but criteria nevertheless. This greatly reduces any pressure to induct in a formal or heavy-handed manner.

Postscript: Chapter 8 as a Departure from the Paradigm

We have used a heuristic device, the Chinese Box Puzzle, to suggest some of the important processes through which a few men in a community come to govern the many. To clarify these processes we have concentrated on the modalities in the data, on the more or less pervasive patterns which reveal the workings of political recruitment and leadership selection. This analytic strategy has proven useful in our attempt to see leadership selection as a generic process in political communities; it is an analysis which self-consciously departs from the political career studies which form the base of most of the political recruitment literature. However, there has been a price to pay for choosing the approach we have. The paradigm has not permitted us to examine directly the links between leadership selection, on the one hand, and the functioning of representative democracy, on the other. Although such links were not intended as the central issue of the book, we are reluctant to pass over such an important issue completely. Thus, in Chapter 8, we take our analysis one additional step—to questions about career expectations and leadership turnover. The data to be analyzed in Chapter 8 do, of course, relate to the analysis in Chapters 2 through 7, for the processes by which leaders are selected must be related to the processes by which leaders are eliminated, or eliminate themselves, from office. But, more important, data on the termination of careers and movement out of office permit us to raise some initial and exploratory questions about the relationship between the selection of men for governing groups and the operation of those groups, especially questions relevant to democratic theorizing about the accountability of elected assemblies.

Chapter 8

Career Plans: An Issue
for Democratic Theory

Men, once elected to the council, will differ in their wish to stay there. For some councilmen, a term or two will be sufficient, and they gladly retire from public office. Other councilmen will find the job more attractive, will hope for a long tenure, and will compete for the office time and again. Yet others will be looking toward higher office; these are the politically ambitious who hope to use the council as a springboard into a state or federal post.

Office holders will differ as well in how effectively they can fulfill their wishes. Some councilmen, eager to retire, may submit to pressures of colleagues or constituents and consent to serve yet another term. Other councilmen who wish to remain in office will find they must exit involuntarily, their bid for reelection having ended in defeat. There will be councilmen ambitious for higher office but frustrated in their attempts, blocked by functionaries who control nominations or eliminated by the electorate itself.

The frequency with which councilmen intend to retire, intend to stay on the council, or intend to move to higher office raises important issues for city politics. Most obviously, the ambitions of councilmen, or lack of them, are related to the political problems of tenure and turnover. Is the council viewed as a springboard to higher office, thereby attracting persons ambitious for state and federal posts; or is it a terminus for political careers, thereby attracting citizens with primarily local commitments? Is the membership of the governing group frequently replenished with new recruits (and thereby new ideas) or is it unaltered from one election to the next (and therefore more experienced)? Is the opportunity for a council seat such that younger aspirants can expect steady progression toward public office or must they challenge incumbents if they ever hope to serve?

Career plans of incumbent politicians are related as well to several important issues raised by democratic theorists. It often is proposed that the officeholder is responsive to the voting public *because* the officeholder hopes to maintain his position. Those who govern guide their behavior in terms of calculations about potential voter response. But what if the officeholder has no desire to remain in office? Then, of course, he will not fear removal. And if he does not fear removal, what controls, if any, make him responsive to public preferences? This is an issue we can at least partly examine with data about the career ambitions of city councilmen.

The Career Plans of Councilmen: Withdrawal, Continued Tenure, and Political Ambitions

Councilmen were asked if they intended to stand for reelection and if they had any interest in higher office. From their responses to these two questions we placed them in three groups: those intending to retire from office, those intending to seek another term, those intending to seek higher office.[1] (A councilman who intends to seek another term but is also interested in higher office is placed in the third group.)

Table 8–1

Proportion of Councilmen Having Different Career Plans (N = 433)

Intend to Retire from Office	18%
Intend to Seek Another Term	53
Intend to Seek Higher Office	29
	100%

Table 8–1 presents the frequencies. It should be noted here, and kept in mind throughout this chapter, that the assignment of councilmen is biased in favor of the more ambitious career plans. This resulted from a decision to treat a "perhaps" or a "not sure" response as a "yes," the assumption being that politicians more often disguise an intent to run again or to seek another office with an ambiguous answer than disguise their plans to retire from

---

1 This classification is similar to one proposed by Joseph Schlesinger, *Ambition and Politics* (Chicago: Rand McNally & Co., 1966). He speaks of discrete, static, and progressive ambitions.

office. This means that the proportion coded as intending to run again or interested in higher office is inflated; these groups will include some who are in genuine doubt about their future plans.[2]

Councilmen Intending to Retire

For nearly one-fifth of the councillors, the present term is their final one. Their retirement is voluntary; they leave office neither because the electorate forces them out nor because they seek higher office. Why then do they retire? After years of observing politicians, a journalist wrote that though politicians may retire, "It is never in the least voluntary. . . . Every man who has held elective office wants to keep it or to get another better one."[3] Table 8–2 challenges this assertion. Councilmen offer many reasons for their voluntary retirement and only the most skeptical observer will doubt that most councillors mean what they say. (Some councilmen do not intend to seek another term because they will contest a different office; they do not appear in Table 8–2.)

In three cities, men have to retire because the city charter limits their tenure. Apart from this detail, however, Table 8–2 stimulates

Table 8–2

Reasons Given by Councilmen for Not Seeking Another Term (N = 77)*

PERSONAL REASONS		42%
Family, age, health, etc.	27%	
Business considerations	15	
DISSATISFACTION WITH COUNCIL JOB		13
Job is unrewarding	5	
Job is frustrating	5	
Job is too political	3	
RESPONSIBILITIES COMPLETED		56
On long enough	21	
Done his duty	17	
Turnover is necessary, need new faces	18	
CHARTER LIMITATIONS		9
NO REASON GIVEN		4

* Percentages total more than 100 because of multiple responses.

[2] For instance, if we shift the "don't know" and "perhaps" respondents into the less ambitious categories, Table 8–1 would read: Intend to Retire—24%; Intend to Seek Another Term—59%; Intend to Seek Higher Office—17%.

[3] Frank Kent, *The Great Game of Politics* (New York: Doubleday Doran, 1936), p. 217.

three general observations about tenure and turnover in the municipalities.

   1. The frequency with which personal matters or business pressures lead to retirement from the council underscores the voluntaristic nature of council service. These are men for whom the political role is a civic duty or possibly a hobby. When their council duties impinge on other interests, it is a simple matter to step aside. There is no career change involved, no seeking of a new job, no worry about the loss of a paycheck. The freedom with which they choose to run or not to run is clearly stated by a councilman from a middle-sized city in the East Bay.

> This is the end of my eighth year. Political power can become a way of life. I have children and a profession and although I enjoy politics, I don't want to make it a hobby. I have other interests. I want to spend time with my children.

Another councilman is retiring in response to family and economic pressures:

> The kids are growing up and they need college. I don't have enough time or money to raise kids, put them through college, and still work on the council.

These quotations are illustrative of a sentiment frequently expressed. A man serves on the council because he can afford the time away from family or business or other interests. When, for whatever reasons, the cost of continuing to serve becomes too high he simply drops out of elective politics.

   2. Newly elected councilmen, as noted in the previous chapter, come to their duties well-informed about what is expected of them. There is an overlap in perspectives and activities between the council job and other community roles; and councilmen are often prepared for their duties by having served an apprenticeship in a committee similar in form and responsibility to the council. Few councilmen are dismayed when they learn more about their official duties. The reasons given for retiring from the council provide additional support for this finding. A negligible number of councilmen say they are leaving because they found council work to be other than what they expected. There are a few who feel as does the incumbent from a city of seventy-five thousand who said, "I'll make no more effort. I'll never have to go through this agony again. I expect to seek no further positions. It's all been too much." (This councilman, by the way, had had no experience in community affairs prior to his election.)

There are others who refuse to run again because they find their present colleagues difficult to work with. One of the few female councillors indicates she is unsure about another term: "I don't know. If the struggle in the council becomes too spread—because the council is filled with out-of-state people who are bent on revolution of the city—I'm not interested in having a part of this development." And there are cases where general bad repute of the council is reason for withdrawing. "The council gets laughed at, and it gets a bad ride from the press—and that's hard when I'm not creating this, and I don't think I am. I think six years is enough to give your time. I'm overdue for a sabbatical."

For the most part, however, councilmen planning to retire depart from the council because of personal reasons or because of "having done their duty," and not because the council task is found unpleasant. These municipal officeholders knew what they were getting involved in; the council job turned out much as they anticipated.

3. The single most frequent reason for voluntary retirement is simply "I've done my duty" or "I've been on long enough." Very important to our analysis is the sentiment associated with this reason for departure. Following are typical responses from councillors intending to withdraw:

> No, I think this is the end. If I had my way, I'd limit it to two terms anyway. You get a lot of new blood that way. New ideas are needed and new councilmen can provide them. Give the next guy a chance.

> After a person has served eight years he goes stale; he loses his vigor and enthusiasm. A new man wants to get out and get eager. He is interested when he first comes in and he has new ideas and goals. This is healthier for the council than having an older man who is on the way down as far as interest and novelty on the council are concerned.

> I'm not particularly in favor of any councilman running for more than eight years, at least in a city the size of ours. If you are energetic and ambitious you use it up and should go elsewhere. You stagnate otherwise. You can really give something original and be enthusiastic to things like this for only four to eight years, I think.

Task groups, whether political or not and whether elected or not, require both "new blood" and "experienced hands."[4] There

---

[4] As Suzanne Keller writes, "Prevalent patterns of recruitment to the leading positions in politics, in science, in recreation, and in industry reflect the strains between two irreconcilable tendencies in social life—the need for order and the need for change." *Beyond the Ruling Class* (New York: Random House, 1963), p. 172.

is no simple organizational answer for finding the proper balance between admitting new recruits into the group and keeping those with experience around. Often an organization chooses a constitutional answer, forced retirement or statutory limits on how long one can serve. Although democratic government is sometimes drawn to a constitutional answer (the Twenty-Second Amendment, for instance), statutory limitations to political tenure contradict the logic of democracy. Equal access to office and free choice by voters are hindered by forced retirement laws.

The municipalities we are studying have solved the problem of "youth vs. experience" without resorting to constitutional devices. Approximately one-fifth of the councilmen intend to retire voluntarily.[5] Of their reasons for retiring, the most prominent one is the realization that "they have served long enough; it is time to step aside and let others have a chance." A high turnover ratio is thus guaranteed. For the councilmen discussed in this section, it is not fear of the electorate's wrath but their own sense of what is "appropriate" which guides their decision to run again or not. At any given time there is probably one in five incumbent councillors who intend neither to compete again for the council nor to seek other office. In retiring from elected office, they reason that since to serve is a voluntary duty, there is nothing to prevent them from voluntarily leaving. Besides, they say, it is time for some new blood.

Councilmen Who Intend to Seek Another Term

Slightly over half the councilmen intend to seek another term on the council but have no ambitions for higher office. Table 8–3 presents their reasons.

Many who intend to seek another term reason in a very personal, almost residual, manner. "I like the job"; "It is an interesting diversion"; "It is a hobby for me" are phrases used repeatedly. Whether in the colorful language of the long-term councilman who reports "I hate to give it up. If one doesn't play golf or other

5 As Hyneman concluded on the basis of his examination of legislative turnover: "The real task is to find why so many legislators, senators and representatives alike, choose not to run again." Charles S. Hyneman, "Tenure and Turnover of Legislative Personnel," *Annals of the American Academy of Political and Social Science* 195 (1938):30. In his analysis of eight states covering the period 1925–33 he found that more than 60 percent of the retirements from both lower houses and senates were due to failure to seek reelection. P. 26.

Table 8–3

Reasons Given for Seeking Another Term (N = 229)*

PERSONAL		26%
Likes being a councilman	13%	
A hobby, a diversion	6	
Social rewards (prestige, recognition, etc.)	4	
Miscellaneous	3	
CONTRIBUTES EXPERIENCE		50
Has valuable expertise	8	
Can continue to do a good job	12	
Wants to finish a project	30	
RESPONSIBILITY TO THE COMMUNITY OR TO CONSTITUENTS		12
WANTS TO KEEP OTHERS OUT OF OFFICE OR TO CHANGE CITY POLICIES		13
NO REASON GIVEN		34

* Percentages total more than 100 because of multiple responses.

things, this civic work gives you the kind of novelty and pleasure you need. I just feel like that. What is recreation I ask myself. Some guys get drunk, for me it is civic affairs"; or the more drab language of an aging businessman who said "My job with U.S. Steel is to be terminated in April. I will be retired. I will need something to do," the sentiment expressed is similar. The personal benefits of remaining on the council outweigh the sacrifices, at least for the present.

Beyond these personal reasons for seeking another term are reasons associated with duty, service, projects, or experience. Nearly all the councilmen who hope to continue justify extending their tenure in terms of a service orientation. The wish to contribute experience or expertise figures prominently:

> There is a lot of work left to do that the present council, which has some experience, can handle. We can do a better job than others because of our experience.

> I enjoy it and I can be of value to the community. I have been a commissioner of all the departments; anybody can come with a problem and I know where every pipe and everything is in the city. I am a great believer in experience.

> Certainly. I believe tremendous strides have been made since I have been on the council, though not necessarily because of me. Things are started and I believe I am an asset.

Other councilmen mention specific projects (a new civic center, a marina, urban renewal) which they helped initiate and which they hope to see through to completion.

There is considerable similarity between the reasoning of councilmen intending to seek another term and the reasoning of councilmen looking forward to voluntary retirement. As we saw, the major reasons for retirement are personal considerations and having done one's duty. The reasons for competing again also fall under the two headings of personal considerations and civic duty. Councilmen seeking another term differ from colleagues who are retiring because, for the former, (1) personal benefits still outweigh personal costs, and (2) the tour of duty is not yet completed.

This suggests a very important consideration for our analysis. Within a term or so, most of the councilmen who currently hope to continue in office will shift their views and will join those who voluntarily exit. One councilman states it well: He is seeking another term "because I feel that in the past four years a number of new programs have been initiated but not completed. With the knowledge I have gained in the last four years, I could be of value in the next four. The two others who are due to end their term aren't running and if I didn't, too, then there would be three new councilmen. I will only be on one more time though; eight years is enough."

Reflected in this comment is a theme appearing again and again in the protocols. A man is reluctant to deprive the community of his experience, hopes to see projects carried through, considers excessive turnover of personnel not a good thing, but recognizes that there is a limit to how long he will serve. Clearly any officeholder reasoning along such lines has placed self-imposed limits on his tenure. In this regard, the councilman quoted is representative of a modal pattern. Among the group planning to run again are many who actually do not have long-term career ambitions.

There is, then, a continually replenished group of incumbent councilmen who intend to exit from office voluntarily. At any given time, this group numbers from one-fifth to one-fourth of all officeholders. As one councilman steps down from office, another soon-to-retire councilman takes his place by declaring, "This will be my last term." One important implication is that aspirants for office need not always have to challenge incumbents. There almost always will be "openings." But even more important, as we shall see, the continuing, and sizable, proportion of voluntarily retiring councilmen holds implications for an understanding of democratic politics.

Councilmen with Political Ambitions

Less than a third (29 percent) of the councillors express some wish to move to a higher office. Two types of career lines are represented among them. For some, the council clearly is seen as a stepping stone to higher office. As one aspirant for Congress stated it, "I'll use the office as a stepping stone or I'll quit." And another who hopes someday to contest a seat on the County Board of Supervisors says, "I will run again, to stay in politics as a base to work from." But others seem not to have given much thought to a political career until they became councilmen. Serving on the council was itself the experience which whetted their interest in a political career. One councillor, for example, has become "intrigued with how much one liberal, idealistic person can accomplish in a community," and says he would be interested in "a Congressional spot someday, if a spot became open."[6]

Among the politically ambitious, then, are two types: Those who choose the council to pursue a political career, and those who become interested in a political career through council service. Although we cannot determine the exact proportions, we estimate that the latter outnumber the former by about two to one. This is not surprising. The data already presented overwhelmingly testify to the apoliticalness of most councilmen. Men serve as a civic responsibility or to pursue a business goal or to occupy leisure time. The selection processes at work in the eighty-seven municipalities studied simply do not recruit many councillors seriously intent on pursuing a political career. Whether he realizes it or not, the councilman who reasoned, "In the long view, once you go into public service, you go as far as your talents will take you," is very much in the minority among his colleagues. Although a few come to this awareness about themselves in the course of serving on the council, even fewer considered the council as an appropriate starting point for a political career.

Nevertheless, whenever the thought of higher office occurred to them, there are 127 councilmen who talk in terms of seeking a political office other than the council. Table 8–4 shows the offices mentioned.

---

6 Samuel J. Eldersveld reports similar occurrences in his study of Detroit party actives: "Party career aspiration is often merely a political manifestation, in a special context, of a socialized orientation. . . . Activity breeds more activity, and mobility triggers an aspiration for more mobility." *Political Parties: A Behavioral Analysis* (Chicago: Rand McNally & Co., 1964), p. 148.

Table 8-4

Offices Desired by Councilmen Who Have Progressive Ambitions (N = 127)

Local Office (such as school board, etc.)	5%
County Supervisor	43
State Legislative	18
Federal Legislative	11
Judicial	4
Miscellaneous	7
Not Specified	12
	100%

The reasons for seeking higher offices are much as we would expect from other studies of progressive ambitions.[7] A few councilmen express themselves in ways consistent with personality theories of *homo politicus*. A councillor contesting a state assembly seat at the time of his interview says, "The public service thing becomes increasingly significant to me. I'm probably a political type—extroverted and gregarious." Another councilman, probably revealing more than he intended, tells us, "There is something deep in me which says I have to seek the highest office." And a third reports, "Politics is a way through which individuals are able to express themselves. Some people do it through their work, some do it in sports or the arts. I do it in politics." This councilman, interestingly enough from a small residential community, is unclear about the office he might seek. "No specific one," he says, but he does want to seek other office. Responses which indicated that political ambitions were a way of satisfying personal needs were infrequent, however. Of course, the questionnaire was not designed to probe into personality needs and nothing should be concluded from the frequency or infrequency of such responses.

Most councilmen with political ambitions reason in ways similar to their colleagues content just to hold municipal office. The ambitious would like higher office "to be of more service," to "influence policies," or because "at a higher level" they could "do more good." Councilmen frequently explained their political ambitions in terms of changing policies at the state or federal level. One, who is "concerned at the socialistic trends of our federal government" would like to at least reach the state legislature so he

---

[7] See, for instance, John Wahlke, Heinz Eulau et al., *The Legislative System* (New York: John Wiley & Sons, 1962), Chapter 6. Also, Eldersveld, *Political Parties*, Chapter 7.

can "take part in deciding bills before the state of California." Other persons intend to contest offices because the present incumbents are undesirable. An aspirant for the state assembly thinks there are too many "carpetbagger attorneys from our area who don't know our problems." A businessman who intends to retire from the council to seek a school board position notes that "Medical doctors tend to dominate school boards everywhere. I don't think they are in a good position to manage the school systems as well as businessmen—so I might get active in that." A lawyer-councilman presently challenging the incumbent district attorney says, "He has been guilty of bad faith, deceit, incompetence, etc."

If it is difficult to sort out the motives which lead a man to seek a political career, it is even more difficult to attach weights to the motives identified and conclude that one motive (fulfilling personal needs) is "more important" than another (the wish to influence policy). About all we can conclude from data available to us is that ambitious councilmen have a mixture of personal and political and policy motives. We suspect, but can in no way demonstrate, that the mixture of motives among ambitious councilmen is similar to the mixture of the politically ambitious at other levels of American government.

Who Are the Politically Ambitious? Two Hypotheses

Statistically, councilmen who aspire to a higher office are behaving counter to the norm. How might we explain their ambitions? There are, of course, a great many things which affect such a complicated decision as whether to seek a higher office. We cannot review every useful hypothesis but have selected two—one organizational and one personal—which illustrate the kinds of considerations determining who are the politically ambitious.

An Organizational Hypothesis

The work of Schlesinger shows that political careers are affected by the opportunities for political mobility open to any given officeholder.[8] By describing in great detail the career lines from one political office to the next, Schlesinger is able to construct what he calls the "political opportunity structure of American

---

8 Schlesinger, *Ambition and Politics.*

politics." Although we cannot begin to duplicate Schlesinger's analysis at the municipal level, his approach does suggest a useful hypothesis: The more links a council has with other levels of government the more opportunities there will be for political ascent and the greater the number of politically ambitious councilmen.

To examine this theory, we compare councilmen in cities which are the centers of county government with councilmen in non-county-seat cities. Councilmen in county-seat communities are likely to find opportunities for informal contacts with politicians holding higher-level offices, opportunities less accessible to councilmen in other cities. Often the city offices and the county offices are housed in the same building. The organizational milieu and thus the perception of political opportunities should differ for councilmen in cities which are centers of political activity.

Table 8–5

Proportion of Councilmen from County-Seat
Cities with Political Ambitions Compared to
Proportion from Non-County-Seat Cities with
Political Ambitions

County-Seat Cities (N = 42)	Non-County-Seat Cities (N = 386)
64%	26%

As Table 8–5 shows, almost two-thirds of the councilmen who happen to serve in cities which are county seats have political ambitions, while only one-fourth of the councilmen in other cities think in terms of moving to higher-level office. To fully explicate this table, it is necessary to take a slight detour and draw together observations made in previous chapters about the differences in nonpartisan municipal politics and other arenas of American political life.

From a perspective of what is considered normal in organized political life, nonpartisan city councils are an anomaly. At least in a formal sense, councilmen have fewer links to other political units than is true of other officeholders. Compare, for instance, the local party precinct workers, the least influential members of the smallest party unit. Through an intricate and well-established network of organizational affiliations, the precinct worker is related to the national committee and through it to the highest elected officials. Connected in one organization are precincts, wards (divisions, areas, zones, sections, etc.), congressional districts, counties, states, and national conventions and committees. Although it is true that organizational units in the party often behave autonomously, it remains that they are linked, at least in an organization chart, to units above and below. The existence of a national party organization has the effect as well of maintaining certain organizational ties between partisan elected officials at different levels and between officials at the same level but in different locales (the Republican Governors Council, for example).

From all of this, however, nonpartisan city councilmen generally are excluded. Councils legally are responsible to the state, but they do not have formal organizational links; they simply conform to the municipal code. At best, formal organizational ties to other political units are approximated by a council of mayors, which includes neighboring cities, and the Association of Bay Area Governments, to which most cities belong. Membership in these connecting organizations is voluntary; neither group has much control over the cities. Cities will also be linked to counties, but this tie is often little more than a contract for services.

From the viewpoint of the councillor, the structural picture is one in which the council is the natural terminus for his career. In this regard a councilman is unlike elected officials in partisan positions. It is expected that the ward committeeman aspires for the opening on the district executive committee or that the state legislator dreams of Washington. The organized political world in which ward committeemen or state legislators live clearly points them to the next level of officialdom. Generally, the councilmen have no such clear lines to the next higher office; they are not on a career ladder for which the next rung is identified by an organization chart.

This is not to say that political careers follow a natural sequence of steps mapped out in an organizational chart. What we suggest is that in the absence of organizational links connecting offices at one level of government with offices at another level, politicians at the lower level will be less likely to cultivate political ambitions.

This helps us understand why so few councilmen aspire to higher office, and why councilmen in county-seat cities are more likely than other councilmen to express political ambitions. At least informal lines of communication are opened up in the county-seat cities; councilmen serving in such cities have more contact with county supervisors, the county party organizations, and prob-

ably even state and federal politicians. Because opportunities
are more in evidence, it is more realistic for councilmen in these
cities to think in terms of higher office. The career behavior of
councilmen, then, is affected by structural or organizational
conditions.

A Life-Circumstances Hypothesis

In addition to structural or organizational conditions, personal
life-circumstances are likely to affect a councilman's political am-
bitiousness. We have already shown in the descriptive material that
matters of health, family considerations, business pressures, and
so forth are given as reasons for not pursuing a political career.
To further indicate how individual life-circumstances affect political ambitions we present, in Table 8–6, the relationship between
age and ambitions.

Table 8–6

Proportion of Councilmen
of Different Age Groups
with Political Ambitions

Under 30 (4)	100%
31 to 35 (17)	53
36 to 40 (42)	43
41 to 45 (64)	41
46 to 50 (73)	23
51 to 55 (61)	13
56 to 60 (40)	10
Over 60 (59)	10

Clearly, where a man is in his life-cycle influences the way in
which he views opportunities in his political career.[9] An expectation reasonable for the forty-year-old may be very unreasonable
for the officeholder over sixty. Growing old has a dampening
effect on political ambitions. A councilman who sees his age as a
limitation reports, "I have toyed with the idea of seeking other
office, but I am sixty years old and that is too old to start something now." A younger, more ambitious man sees his age as an
asset: "I would love to run for the Assembly spot. The Assembly
is great for a man in his thirties, if you want to make a career of
politics."

[9] A very useful discussion of age and political ambitions can be found in
Schlesinger, *Ambition and Politics*, Chapter 9.

The obviousness of the pattern in Table 8–6 should not obscure the very important theoretical point to be made. It may be true, as Hughes writes, that the "career is the moving perspective in which a person sees his life as a whole and interprets . . . the things which happen to him."[10] But it is also the case that the perception of the career itself is filtered through the objective conditions of individual life-experiences. Thus, on the one hand, the career is a screen through which experiences are interpreted; on the other hand, experiences affect views of career possibilities and determine career choices.

For the volunteer councilman, a variety of things are happening to him independently of his political activities that affect his plans to retire, his intention to seek office again, or his aspirations to higher position. Growing old, matters of health, age of his children, increasing or decreasing occupational pressures, a change in residence, and so forth are conditions operating independently of political opportunities (a systemic variable) or of personal motivations (a personality variable). Such conditions should not, however, be ignored in any formula intending to explain the movement of men into and out of public office. It is unfortunate that in explanations of political recruitment these life-circumstances have been largely ignored or, at best, treated as residual, idiosyncratic variables.

Political Ambitions and Policy Views

There is a rich literature inquiring into the policy views of elected representatives. A central question in this literature is why officeholders adopt the policies they do. The many hypotheses advanced can be classified according to four general themes. Probably best known are the constituency theories: The legislator is a target in a field of forces, "forces" which bear such names as voters, interest groups, political party leaders, and legislative colleagues.[11] There are structural theories: The legislator is part of

---

[10] Everett C. Hughes, "Institutional Office and the Person," in *Men and Their Work* (Glencoe, Ill.: The Free Press, 1958), p. 63.

[11] The literature is sizable. For recent representative studies, see Warren E. Miller and Donald E. Stokes, "Constituency Influence in Congress," *American Political Science Review* 57 (1963):45–56; Lewis A. Froman, Jr., *Congressmen and Their Constituencies* (Chicago: Rand McNally & Co., 1963); Frank Sourauf, *Party and Representation* (New York: Atherton Press, 1962).

a complex role system; his perspectives reflect his location in the ongoing legislative system.[12] There are career theories: The policy views of the legislator are in some measure an extension of his prior political or occupational career.[13] Finally, there are personal trait theories: Policy choices can be traced to the legislator's personality or to his socioeconomic characteristics.[14]

To these hypotheses has now been added another, Schlesinger's ambition theory of politics. According to this notion, the politician responds to his future expectations or his aspirations; in Schlesinger's terms, to his "office goals." It is where the politician is going (would like to be going) which affects his behavior, not where he is or has been.[15] Ambition theory resembles reference group theory or anticipatory socialization hypotheses. Persons prepare themselves for the groups they hope to join or the positions they hope to hold long before they reach the aspired role. For example, while still in school, the medical student or law student takes on the characteristics of a doctor or lawyer. It is the anticipated role which provides behavioral cues. Merton outlines the reasons: "For the individual who adopts the values of a group to which he aspires but does not belong, this orientation may serve the twin functions of aiding his rise into that group and of easing his adjustment after he has become part of it."[16]

Ambition theory leads to the following hypothesis: The politician who aspires to a higher office will inform himself of its requirements and will adopt policy views consistent with anticipated incumbency in that office. More specifically, the person ambitious for a higher position is likely to support policies which expand the

---

[12] The most important empirical study following this approach is Wahlke, Eulau et al., *The Legislative System.*

[13] Again, the literature is sizable. The work of David Barber is illustrative. See his *The Lawmakers: Recruitment and Adaptation to Legislative Life* (New Haven: Yale University Press, paperback edition, 1965). In a study using some of the data reported on in this book it was found that political socialization experiences are unrelated to office behavior. Kenneth Prewitt, Heinz Eulau, and Betty H. Zisk, "Political Socialization and Political Roles," *Public Opinion Quarterly* 30 (Winter 1966–67):569–82.

[14] A particularly important article on personality theory is Lewis Edinger, "Political Science and Political Biography," *Journal of Politics* 26 (1964):423–39, 648–76. Other studies are reviewed in Kenneth Prewitt, "Political Socialization and Leadership Selection," *Annals of the American Academy of Political and Social Science* 361 (September 1965):96–111.

[15] Schlesinger, *Ambition and Politics*, especially pp. 3–6.

[16] Robert Merton, *Social Theory and Social Structure* (Glencoe, Ill.: The Free Press, 1957), p. 265

prerogatives of that office. It is the more specific hypothesis which Schlesinger emphasizes. For example, "because Congressmen can realistically aspire to the Senate, it is unlikely that the House of Representatives will ever seek to reduce the Senate's powers, as the British House of Commons reduced the power of the Lords in 1911. Similarly, as long as the states' governors see their hopes for advancement in the Senate, it is unlikely that attacks upon federal power will be directed at the Congress."[17]

Translated into terms relevant to our data, the ambitious councilman will view regional, state, and federal governments in ways different from his less aspiring colleagues. Those who will seek higher office should have policy views which favor the expansion of regional government and which support a more active role for state and federal authorities in municipal affairs. Table 8–7 shows this to be the case. More than half the councilmen with progressive ambitions adopt policy views consistent with expanding scope of regional, state, or federal participation in local affairs.[18] Councilmen with no ambitions are less inclined to support such policies.

The second implication of Table 8–7 takes us back to the previous discussion about the lack of organizational ties between city councils and other government units. The formal organizational vacuum in which councils operate is probably compensated for by the activities and contacts of councilmen who plan to seek other offices. It is likely that the ambitious councilmen informally link the councils with regional, state, and federal officeholders. They probably also help establish ties to the political party organization since support from the party is necessary if a partisan office is to be sought. If true that informal links are maintained in this way, it is apparent that some councils will have more connections than others. (As was clear in Table 8–5, the ambitious councilmen tend to be concentrated in certain cities.) For instance, on seventeen councils (20 percent) there are no incumbents who aspire to higher office; in contrast, on thirteen councils (14 percent) there are three or more members who have political ambitions.

---

[17] Schlesinger, *Ambition and Politics*, p. 200.

[18] Schlesinger writes: ". . . ambition theory makes us aware that men are unlikely to demean the object of their ambitions. If the best long-range career opportunities for American politicians are at the national level, it is unlikely that promising state officials will lead the fight to reduce the nation's powers." *Ibid.*, p. 201. A paper exploring this notion in more detail than is possible here is Kenneth Prewitt and William G. Nowlin, "Political Ambitions and the Behavior of Incumbent Politicians," *Western Political Quarterly* 22 (June 1969): 298–308.

Table 8–7

Relationship Between Career Plans and Policy Views Toward Expanding the Prerogatives of Regional, State, and Federal Governments

	Plan to Retire from Office (N = 77)	Intend to Seek Another Term (N = 229)	Have Political Ambitions (N = 127)
Favorable Views Toward Expansion*	36%	45%	52%
Unfavorable Views Toward Expansion	64	55	48
	100%	100%	100%

* The dependent variable in this table is based on an index score derived from responses to the following questions: "How, in your opinion, should the federal government take part in municipal or metropolitan problems?" "How do you feel about federal aid for urban renewal? Would you say you approve of it, or disapprove?" "Do you think the federal government should undertake a full-scale program of mass transportation in metropolitan areas?" "And how, in your opinion, should the state government participate in municipal or metropolitan problems?" "Would you be in favor of combining a few of the single-purpose special districts in the Bay Area with ABAG (Association of Bay Area Governments), thus giving ABAG increased responsibilities, or would you be opposed?"

Democratic Theory and Political Ambitions

Data about the political ambitions of city councilmen are related to some of the larger and more complicated issues in democratic theory. Scholars who consider the problems of American democratic government have struggled hard to discover just what—if anything—in a working democracy makes the officeholder responsive (and responsible) to the public. As a form of government, democracy presumably translates the preferences of the people into public policies and programs. One way of assuring that those who govern do so in accordance with the preferences of the general public is to provide the population with some means of sanctioning the governors.

In order to view the working of democracy from the perspective of political sanctions, it is useful to review quickly several approaches to the study of democratic controls on officeholders. The founding fathers, of course, wanted to guard against the excesses of popular control. They relied on constitutional engineering—checks and balances, separation of powers, federalism, and so forth—to place limits on officeholders, but they were not too concerned with instituting public control.

Subsequent reformers, not satisfied with the extant electoral machinery, initiated changes designed to extend the control of the public over the elected officeholder. Democracy is preserved, they reasoned, by universal suffrage; equal weight to all votes; direct primaries and direct elections; referendum, recall, and initiative procedures; and the secret ballot. But following Bryan's campaign of 1896 and the eventual establishment of electoral reforms, more careful observers recognized that democracy was not easily safeguarded by institutional tinkering alone. (Lippmann persuaded most students of democracy that electoral reforms falsely assumed that the public was interested and informed about political matters. By rejecting the assumption, Lippmann was able to question the presumed consequences of electoral reform[19]).

Democratic theorists then began to discover party competition. Democracy is preserved less by constitutional engineering and institutional reform than it is by the struggle between men for political power. Schumpeter, an early and influential proponent of this theory, wrote, "The democratic method is that institutional arrangement for arriving at political decisions in which individuals acquire the power to decide by means of a competitive struggle for the people's vote."[20] This idea was subsequently expanded on by Janowitz and Marvick and by Dahl and Lindblom.[21] Competitive elections became the keystone in the analysis of democracy. In the words of a recent empirical study:

> The existence of competitive electoral opportunities for citizens to select public officials or decisional outcomes is a sufficient condition for the existence of Developed Democracy.[22]

The theory of "competitive democracy" is probably the most prevalent interpretation of American politics available in the writings of scholars today. The view persists in spite of growing

---

19 Lippmann wrote in 1925: "The ideal of the omnicompetent, sovereign citizen is, in my opinion, a false ideal. . . . The individual man does not have opinions on all public affairs. He does not know how to direct public affairs. He does not know what is happening, why it is happening, what ought to happen." *The Phantom Public* (New York: Macmillan Co., 1925), p. 39.

20 Joseph A. Schumpeter, *Capitalism, Socialism, and Democracy* (New York: Harper & Row, 1947), p. 269.

21 Morris Janowitz and Dwaine Marvick, *Competitive Pressures and Democratic Consent* (Ann Arbor: Michigan Governmental Studies, University of Michigan Publication Distribution Service, 1956). Robert A. Dahl and Charles E. Lindblom, *Politics, Economics and Welfare* (New York: Harper & Row, 1953).

22 Robert E. Agger, Daniel Goldrich, and Bert E. Swanson, *The Rulers and the Ruled* (New York: John Wiley & Sons, 1964), p. 652.

evidence that competition is not characteristic of many elections in the United States. For instance, in 1955,

> . . . three out of every four state legislative bodies or congressional delega-tions were so completely dominated by a single political party that that party controlled more than 66 percent of the members of the group. Ex-cluding the 15 Border and Southern states, fully half of the remaining 33 state legislatures were controlled by one party holding at least two out of every three seats; in only six states was the controlling margin below 55 per-cent. Within the same group of non-Border, non-Southern states, 25 of the 33 congressional delegations were dominated by one party controlling two-thirds or more of the delegation members; only four delegations were so evenly divided as to give the majority party less than 55 percent of the mem-bers. . . . Over three-fourths of all congressional districts can be classified as relatively safe districts.[23]

Ranney classified states between 1946 and 1963 according to their competitiveness and found only half of them could even be called two-party.[24] Dahl writes that the smaller the political unit, the less competition there is: "The frequency of two-party competi-tion, in fact, is roughly correlated with the size of the political unit: it declines from the national arena to statewide contests for U.S. Senator, governor and other statewide elective offices, and declines again from statewide elections to contests in smaller units —congressional districts, cities, and towns."[25] It is probably not necessary to add that this observation is particularly damning when one considers the actual numbers of political units of differ-ent sizes; for instance, whereas there are 50 states, there are more than 35,000 municipalities and towns.

Approaches to democratic politics emphasizing constitutional reform or party competition make an assumption which is closely related to data about political ambitions: As a system of govern-ment, democracy depends on a supply of men intent on gaining and then holding political office. This view is strongly urged by Schlesinger: "Ambition lies at the heart of politics."[26] He reasons, with particular relevance to democratic theory, that:

> To slight the role of ambition in politics, then, or to treat it as a human fail-ing to be suppressed, is to miss the central function of ambition in political

23 Warren E. Miller, "One-Party Politics and the Voter," *American Political Science Review* 50 (1956):707.

24 Austin Ranney, "Parties in State Politics," in Herbert Jacob and Kenneth N. Vines (eds.), *Politics in the American States* (Boston: Little, Brown & Co., 1965), p. 65.

25 Robert A. Dahl, *Pluralist Democracy in the United States* (Chicago: Rand McNally & Co., 1967), p. 190.

26 Schlesinger, *Ambition and Politics*, p. 1.

systems. A political system unable to kindle ambitions for office is as much in danger of breaking down as one unable to restrain ambitions. Representative government, above all, depends on a supply of men so driven; the desire for election and, more important, for reelection becomes the electorate's restraint upon its public officials. No more irresponsible government is imaginable than one of high-minded men unconcerned for their political futures.[27]

The logic of Schlesinger's hypothesis (and the assumption made by electoral reformers as well as by theorists who stress party competition) can be simply put. Men in office want to stay there; they choose policies therefore, which match their understanding of the electorate's preferences.

This logic is either implicit or explicit in a great deal of contemporary scholarship about American democracy. Downs, for instance, has such sentences as, "Voting itself is a device to influence the future policies of government . . . because the government's action was conditioned by how it thought men would vote."[28] Dahl has employed similar reasoning: "The effective political elites, then, operate within limits often vague and broad, although occasionally narrow and well defined, set by their expectations as to the reactions of the group of politically active citizens who go to the polls."[29] After observing closely democratic politics as it operated in New Haven, Dahl feels his theoretical assumption is justified. Mayor Lee, to some degree anyway, measures policies and programs in terms of a calculus that very much includes his estimate of voter response at the next election. Lee is a professional at the game of politics; he is also ambitious in our sense of the term. He can hardly afford indifference to the shifting preferences of the voting citizens.[30] Lindblom, in a book which differs considerably from rational-man models of democracy, nevertheless observes that although citizens do not actually choose on election day, "the fact that they could choose compels choices and commitments responsive to their preferences to be made earlier by party leaders."[31] Or, to cite again the clearly stated passage from

---

[27] *Ibid.*, p. 2.

[28] Anthony Downs, *An Economic Theory of Democracy* (New York: Harper & Row, 1957), p. 238.

[29] Robert A. Dahl, *A Preface to Democratic Theory* (Chicago: University of Chicago Press, 1956), p. 72.

[30] Robert A. Dahl, *Who Governs?* (New Haven: Yale University Press, 1961), *passim.*

[31] Charles E. Lindblom, *The Intelligence of Democracy* (Berkeley and Los Angeles: University of California Press, 1967), p. 98.

Schlesinger, "The desire for election and, more important, for reelection becomes the electorate's restraint upon its public officials."[32]

The various ways in which this point is stated in the literature should not obscure the basic similarity of the arguments. Elected officials are responsive to public preferences because officials are accountable; they are accountable because they want to remain in public office and because they recognize that the voting public determines whether they will or not. The role of the electorate is to give or to withhold consent about who should govern; this power is one of holding political leaders accountable at periodic elections.

Pitkin has taken the notion of "accountability" and used it to interpret the theory of representative government. She writes that periodic accountability of elected leaders is a device or a means to a more important purpose. "The point of holding him to account after he acts is to make him act in a certain way—look after his constituents, or do what they want."[33] It is, therefore, through the ideas of "accountability" and "representation" that the connection is made between political ambitions and democratic politics.

There are two questions to be raised about the hypothesis linking political ambitions to democratic controls: First, do the ambitious politicians differ in theoretically meaningful ways from their unambitious colleagues? Second, what is the distribution of the trait "ambition" among elected officeholders?

Comparing Ambitious and Nonambitious Councilmen

If it is correct to assume that officeholders are sensitive to public preferences because they, the officeholders, want to keep their positions, then those aspiring to higher office should differ in several important respects from colleagues intending to retire. In particular, ambitious councilmen should differ in their views of campaigning, elections, public preferences, and their representational role.

Prior to comparing such views, we should eliminate one consideration. We asked councilmen to estimate the degree of citizen

---

32 Schlesinger, *Ambition and Politics*, p. 2.
33 Hanna F. Pitkin, *The Concept of Representation* (Berkeley and Los Angeles: University of California Press, 1967), p. 57.

Table 8–8

Relationship Between Career Plans and Evaluations of Citizen Interest in Political Matters

| | CAREER PLANS | | | |
	Intend to Retire (N = 77)	Intend to Seek Another Term (N = 229)	Intend to Seek Higher Office (N = 127)	Index of Difference*
PROPORTION OF COUNCILMEN BELIEVING THAT:				
Not many citizens are interested in council matters	43	41	39	—4
Citizens are not much concerned about local elections	28	25	25	—3

* The "index of difference" used in this and the following tables is presented simply to indicate the percentage difference between the two extreme categories in the career typology; it is the difference between the proportion among those intending to retire and the proportion among those with career ambitions who respond "yes" to items used in the table.

interest and activity in local politics. Table 8–8 shows that councilmen with very different career plans are in agreement about the activity level of the public. It is unlikely, therefore, that relationships between the career typology and views of the electorate are attributable to the different electoral milieu in which the councilmen live. Put differently, a politically active citizenry might require officeholders to adopt certain views quite independently of their personal career plans. Conversely, an inactive or uninterested populace can be ignored by the ambitious as well as the unambitious.

Campaign Activity

For several reasons, the ambitious councilmen should differ from their less ambitious colleagues in their attitudes toward campaigning and in their campaign activity. The man aspiring to a higher office will have to prove to interested onlookers that he has "voter appeal." Party functionaries who control the routes to state and federal offices will have to be impressed if the councilman intends to contest a partisan seat. Or, if the interest is in another nonpartisan post (usually that of county supervisor), the aspirant still needs to prove that he can handle himself in the competition of an electoral battle.

Further, the ambitious councilman probably will be more willing than his colleagues to pay the cost of intensive campaigning. Personal energies, funds, and time are investments more likely to be committed to a campaign by the ambitious than by the councilman ready to retire in a term or two, anyway. In addition, the ambitious councilman will probably receive more psychological gratification from campaign activity than will his less politically ambitious colleagues. The man hopeful of moving to a higher post has found in politics sufficient reward to merit making even greater investment.

Table 8–9 presents relevant data. In greater numbers than their colleagues, the ambitious were more intent on winning their last election, worked harder to that end, and received pleasure from campaigning for office.

Table 8–9

Relationship Between Career Plans and Campaign Activity

| | CAREER PLANS | | | |
	Intend to Retire (N = 77)	Intend to Seek Another Term (N = 229)	Intend to Seek Higher Office (N = 127)	Index of Difference
PROPORTION OF COUNCILMEN WHO:				
Like campaigning for office	26	29	44	+18
Campaigned hard in last election	25	29	41	+16
Strong desire to win in last election	33	38	61	+28

Views of the Electorate

Democratic theory stressing accountability of the officeholder to the electorate makes an implicit assumption: Men in public office who want to stay there will be more sensitive to the electorate than will officeholders unconcerned about retaining their positions. This assumption has been left implicit in empirical work largely because theorists have not considered the possibility that public offices, even elected ones, might be filled by persons totally indifferent or even antagonistic to a long-term political career.

Our data suggest the importance of making explicit any hypothesis about the relationship of career ambitions and attitudes toward the electorate. And, however inadequately, it is necessary to test the hypothesis as well as simply stating it explicitly.

Table 8–10 presents relevant findings. The pattern supports the implicit assumption in democratic theory that officeholders wishing to retain their positions will be more concerned about the electorate than will officeholders unconcerned about their political future. The differences are not great; however, they are consistent and in the hypothesized direction.

Table 8–10

Relationship Between Career Plans and Views About the Electorate

| | CAREER PLANS | | |
	Intend to Retire (N = 77)	Intend to Seek Another Term (N = 229)	Intend to Seek Higher Office (N = 127)	Index of Difference
PROPORTION OF COUNCIL-MEN WHO:				
Think that elections hold councilmen responsible	66	75	81	+15
Think group conflict helps council to know what the people want	40	49	55	+15
Respect the intelligence of the average citizen	26	32	37	+11
Believe citizens can think in terms of what is best for entire city	29	40	40	+11
Rarely or never vote against the majority of the people	52	73	67	+15
Often run errands for constituents	25	34	41	+16

In greater proportions than their colleagues, the councilmen thinking in terms of higher office believe that elections help the public control their leaders, recognize that differences within the electorate help make clearer the preferences of the people, and feel that the average citizen is to be respected. Further, the ambitious councilmen are more hesitant about voting against the (perceived) views of the majority, and they more often serve their constituents in their capacity as errand-runner.

Tables 8–9 and 8–10 provide support for the specific hypothesis —derived from general democratic theory—that men wanting to stay in office treat campaigning, the electorate, and voter preferences with more respect than do men intending to leave office. However, it remains to be discussed whether the more inclusive theory suggested about elections and democratic controls is sound. It is to the general theory rather than the specific hypothesis that we next turn our attention.

Desire for Reelection: How Widely Distributed?

If periodic elections make democracy a workable form of government by holding the officeholder accountable to the public, then it is indeed very important to determine how many officeholders plan on standing for reelection. The burden of the chapter thus far is that the city councilman in the San Francisco area who expects or hopes for long political tenure is in the minority. A clear one-fifth already are serving their last term; among the majority who will run again for the council but do not have ambitions for a higher post are many who anticipate voluntary retirement from office within a term or so. *If* political ambition or the desire for reelection is the key element serving as a restraint upon public officials, then the voters in our municipalities frequently are being denied the means of democratic control. A few choice, but not atypical, quotations will illustrate the view widespread among the councilmen:

From a councilman who is not sure if he will stand for reelection or not,

> I won't know until my time is up. I don't think a councilman can do a good job if he is concerned about counting votes. If something is best for the city, you have to go against some groups. And you don't want to have to worry that these groups may not vote for you in the next election if you vote wrong.

And another doubtful candidate,

> I promised myself I wouldn't decide ahead of time whether to run or not. I don't want to do things to collect votes.

Three councilmen who feel it is easy to go against majority preferences,

> I am an independent type of individual. I don't feel the weight of voter responsibility. I am not all fired up for a political career.

> You don't always follow the majority; you shouldn't give a damn whether you get elected or not. Don't be afraid to be defeated.

> Because I don't really care if I get elected or not.

Finally, a councilman who finds it easy to ignore the pressures which mount from community influentials,

> I doubt if the City Council would consider preferentially the opinion of such a person. This City Council doesn't give a damn if it is reelected.

It is no exaggeration to contend that half or more of the city councilmen neither plan to stand for reelection nor look upon electoral defeat as a threat to their future. These are not office-holders who in deciding policy issues make calculations about voter response. Therefore, *insofar* as the desire for reelection is necessary before the voters can sanction elected officials, it appears that public accountability is severely hampered in the municipalities studied.

How atypical are Bay Area city councilmen? It is important to determine how widely spread in American politics is an indifference to reelection characteristic of many of our councilmen. Though the data for doing so systematically are not available, a few tutored estimates can be made. First, the rate of voluntary retirement probably is inversely related to the level of government and thus the stakes involved, local officials being the most indifferent to reelection and federal officials being the least. Second, among local officials, those from nonpartisan, reform cities probably have a higher rate of voluntary retirement than do those in partisan municipalities. We suggest, then, that the rate of indifference to reelection (in the neighborhood of 50 percent) is higher in the communities studied here than in other parts of the United States and for other levels of government.

However, though proportionately fewer, there are found officials spread throughout the American political system who are indifferent to reelection. Hyneman, in his major study of twenty-five state chambers between 1925 and 1935, found that only about 30 percent of the retirements from state office were due to defeat in elections or primaries. After his exhaustive study of turnover, he commented, "The real task is to find why so many legislators, senators and representatives alike, choose not to run again."[34] Eulau, writing about state legislators some twenty years after the Hyneman study, reports similar figures. The proportion of legislators

---

34 Hyneman, "Tenure and Turnover," p. 30.

in each of four states who either intend not to stand for reelection or are doubtful about it is as follows: Tennessee—66 percent; Ohio—40 percent; California—34 percent; and New Jersey—24 percent.[35] Barber's study of the Connecticut state legislators provides additional support. In Connecticut, "election defeat accounted for less than 26 percent of retirements from the House in the seven elections between 1946 and 1958. *Thus by far the largest proportion of retirements may be classified as pre-election turnover.*"[36] Among the first-term representatives interviewed by Barber, 35 percent report that they definitely or probably would not be willing to serve more than two or three terms.[37]

Similar data are not available for federal officeholders. It is likely that Schlesinger's conclusion about the relationship between ambitions and level of office is the correct one. He writes:

> We can infer, therefore, that the impact of ambitions upon the behavior of public officials will be greater on those in high than in low office, greater upon congressmen than upon state legislators, greater upon United States Senators than upon United States representatives. Such an arrangement is surely felicitous in a democracy, for it provides progressive controls over public officials as their power to do good or evil increases.[38]

Though what Schlesinger writes is probably the case, it should not obscure two important observations we can make in concluding this chapter. First, with respect to the substance of the question about ambitions and democratic controls, it appears that of the ninety thousand or so governmental units in the United States, the overwhelming majority will be filled with persons a sizable percentage of whom are indifferent to reelection. This is not the place to evaluate the relative importance of city councils and state legislatures in the American political system. But even the layman's knowledge of contemporary politics is sufficient to suggest that decisions affecting the very real issues of domestic tension and social unrest are every day being made at the municipal and state levels. Power to do small "evils" or small "goods" in municipal councils or state houses is additive and, thus, cumulative. The absence of democratic controls at the local level is no less relevant because these controls are relatively more salient at the national level.

---

35 Wahlke, Eulau et al., *The Legislative System*, p. 122. Figures reported here were computed from Table 6.1 in *The Legislative System*.
36 Barber, *Lawmakers*, p. 8. (Italics added.)
37 *Ibid.*, p. 20.
38 Schlesinger, *Ambition and Politics*, p. 193.

Second, our data question the accuracy of a hidden assumption in certain schools of democratic theorizing. Irrespective of the distribution of a trait we might call "indifference to reelection," it is a variable which should be considered in theories which treat elections as the key to democratic control. There is a relationship between desire for reelection and greater sensitivity to the electorate and, presumably, its preferences. Because there is such a relationship, it is necessary for purposes of theory construction to consider the implications of "indifference to reelection." The reasons for this have been clearly stated by the councilmen themselves:

I am an independent type of individual. I don't feel the weight of voter responsibility. I am not all fired up for a political career.

You don't always follow the majority; you shouldn't give a damn whether you get elected or not. Don't be afraid to be defeated.

I am free to do as I feel. In general it is easy to vote against the majority because I don't have any political ambitions.

Chapter 9

Conclusions: Leadership
Selection and Representative
Democracy

At the beginning of this study we introduced a paradigm—the Chinese Box Puzzle. This paradigm has been used to direct attention to the series of individual experiences and social processes that successively narrow the very many citizens in the public at large to the very few citizens who hold formal governmental powers. Analysis of data about councilmen in eighty-seven Bay Area cities from the perspective of the paradigm has proved very useful for interpreting the manner in which a handful of men come to govern these communities.

Although not presuming to offer a theory of leadership selection as it affects city government under the rules of representative democracy, we can review the various findings reported in this book and present a summary statement. This statement is best phrased in the language of problematics, using that term in the sense suggested by Dewey. There are problem areas in political life which can be formulated as theoretical problems for political analysis. The problem toward which we direct our remarks in this concluding chapter is one which weaves in and out of an ancient, yet eminently current, discussion: How is the working of democracy affected by the processes of leadership selection?

Political Leaders and Political Followers:
Some Important Differences

Theorists interested in the working of democracy spend considerable energy on the complex paradox of how public leaders can be both "different" and yet "representative," different in the sense that they are unlike the populace from which they are chosen and yet representative in the sense that they somehow act in accordance with the preferences of that populace. Although this is too large an issue for fully adequate treatment here, we can present certain observations from the veiwpoint of what this study has revealed.

Perhaps the most useful beginning point is to consider an important way in which the councilmen appear *not to be different* from the citizens they are expected to represent. Based on data from the present and other studies, we concluded that those holding council office today did not undergo general political socialization experiences in ways markedly different from those of citizens who never will hold office. With the exception that some of the councilmen were introduced as youths to the possibility of a political or parapolitical career, the politician-to-be did not receive special training or preparation. Nor was he inducted into the general political culture in ways different from his age peers of the same social and economic background. Although possibly fascinated by political matters at an early age, the youth who later comes to hold office appears to have learned the norms of democratic politics from roughly the same agents and in approximately the same manner as any youth of his social status. In an earlier chapter, where this notion is more fully developed, we concluded that in this environment no specialized elite political culture is set off against the more general mass political culture. An important nondifference, then, between the few who govern and the many who are governed is the manner of induction into the general polity.

In other respects, however, the men who govern the eighty-seven cities studied are unlike the populaces they represent. In the first place, the officeholders clearly differ from the general population with respect to certain social and economic characteristics. Men who hold office overwhelmingly are chosen from the upper two-fifths of the communities they govern. This difference is clear from the data, is consistent with many other studies of political leadership, and presents no surprises.

Social class difference between governors and governed is perhaps the most obvious or at least the most frequently remarked upon difference, but it certainly is not the only one. The analysis presented here reveals another important characteristic that differentiates councilmen from the citizens they represent. The former differ from the general population in terms of their familiarity with and lengthy exposure to the workings of politics. The men who hold office have graduated from the active stratum in the community, what Mosca calls "the second stratum of the ruling class." This observation may, at first glance, appear to be only a statement of the obvious. Certainly, the men who govern will be selected from among those citizens who tend to have a long-standing interest in managing public affairs. However, this need not be the case. It takes little imagination to conceive of a political system in which the active stratum is not the source of officeholders. Any arrangement in which there is selection by lot from among all citizens would assure that offices were filled by persons with very different types of political backgrounds, including persons with no prior political interest. Or, a heavy reliance on patronage appointments can select candidates with whatever backgrounds are seen as desirable by the political boss.

To find, as we have, that a large number of councilmen have had long years of experience in the politically active stratum prior to their election or appointment to office is not surprising, but it is not so obvious as to be passed over without comment. By virtue of their activities, contacts, experiences, and perspectives the councilmen are "unlike" the populations they govern. Time after time the councilmen bemoaned the lack of interest in local affairs among the citizens. Time after time they implied, or said outright, that the ill-informed citizen possibly did not really deserve to speak out on all matters. The councilmen, therefore, see themselves as different if in no other respect than that they know more than others about how the community is managed. This immediately poses an interesting problem for theories of leadership selection and representative democracy. Might not the leaders, since they know so much more about *how* the community is managed and so much more about its problems, come to believe that they know more about how it *should be* governed? A simple difference in information level between governors and governed, a difference which is a clear product of the leadership selection patterns, can create a subtle but critical problem for representative democracy.

There is yet another important way in which officeholders differ from the general population. It is a particularly interesting difference for, unlike the two just mentioned, it is built into the political system. We speak here of the unavoidable *status* difference between the few who are chosen and the many who choose. This is Eulau's point, and his own language outlines the argument clearly:

It is an error, I think, to assume that the "chosen"—whether elected or selected—are or can ever be "like" their choosers. The very fact of their having been elected or selected—having been "elevated" through some mechanism of choice from one position into another—makes the "chosen" fundamentally different from their choosers. Having been chosen, the representative has at least one attribute that differentiates him from the represented, no matter how similar, socially or psychologically, he may be in all other respects. Status differentiation, then, is a crucial property of any representational relationship.[1]

Eulau's argument is a telling one. Even if we had discovered no systematic socioeconomic bias in the selection processes and no tendency for councilmen to be selected from among the distinct group of political actives, we would still confront the issue of "difference" between leaders and led, between the few who govern and the many who are governed.

The Chosen Few and the Problem of Accountability

To observe that the governors are different from the governed immediately presents a problem. If the governors are unlike the governed, how does representative democracy work? We cannot here present any extended treatment of representation, a topic which, in any case, is analyzed in another volume of the series, but we can match our findings with some of the broad hypotheses most frequently found in theories of representative democracy as it is presumed to work in the United States.

We begin by reformulating the problem: Elected officials are unlike the people they must govern. In their social and economic characteristics, in their long and intimate attention to political matters, and in their superior status as the chosen, the councilmen are elevated above the remainder of the populace. Given their superior position and their responsibility for managing the affairs of the community, how are the officeholders to be restrained? More particularly, what is the guarantee that they will govern in accordance with the preferences of the citizens?

The word which most frequently appears in answers to this question is "accountability." If only the leaders, however superior they may be in some respects, can be held accountable for their actions, then some minimal though necessary attention of public leaders to average citizens will be assured.

---

1 Heinz Eulau, "Changing Views of Representation," in Ithiel de Sola Pool (ed.), *Contemporary Political Science* (New York: McGraw-Hill Book Co., 1967), p. 80.

The many hypotheses on the topic of accountability in representative democracy can be classified into three general but serviceable categories. The oldest of these in reference to American political theory is, of course, the constitutional hypothesis. This hypothesis stresses institutional checks and balances; men in office are restrained by a formal system of separation of powers or some other constitutional arrangement. The second general hypothesis, and certainly the one most widely pursued in contemporary writing, stresses mass electorates and their power to sanction officeholders; men in office are accountable to the voters and therefore restrained by their calculations of possible voter disapproval. The third hypothesis emphasizes the way in which the leaders police themselves: Men in office have so accepted the democratic norms that they are self-restrained. We can briefly consider these hypotheses from the viewpoint of findings generated by the "Chinese Box Puzzle" approach to leadership selection.

Institutional Checks and Accountability

Madison, the constitutional architect *par excellence*, proposed an intricate system of checks on men holding office in order to protect the community from an arbitrary exercise of power. He put little store in mass elections because, of course, he was as fearful of the tyranny of the majority as the tyranny of the minority. Similarly, his view of human nature led him to disallow the possibility that the conscience of the leadership would be sufficient to inhibit impulses to tyranny. If there is to be accountability, it will be because power is somehow shared among competing groups of political leaders, each with authority in its own sphere but each in part dependent upon others for the initiation and execution of policy.

Our attention to the processes of leadership selection provides no data that bear on Madison's thesis. We shall bypass this hypothesis, but note one thing. City councils are interesting anomalies in a nation priding itself on its "separation of powers" system. As primarily legislative bodies, councils are not pitted against either an executive or a judicial branch. Councils hire the chief executive in the person of the city manager and the chief legal authority in the person of the city attorney. Both offices report to the council and, in law at least, have no independent base of power.

Of course, councils are very much limited by their legal status in relation to state and federal authority. The federal system imposes important constraints. However, if we consider the city itself as the unit of analysis, councils operate with a certain political autonomy. Within the constraints established by federal and state laws, councils operate the city government unburdened by numerous internal checks in the form of other governmental units with which power is to be shared. But it is the task of a separate monograph to explore just what this political-legal status may mean for representative democracy in the local community. All that we can do at this point is observe that the Madisonian hypothesis may require adjustment to fit the realities of city government.

Electoral Sanctions and Accountability

In his *Preface to Democratic Theory*, Dahl outlines as clearly as perhaps any contemporary theorist the thesis that accountability of public leaders is guaranteed by competitive elections. For instance, he writes, "I am inclined to think that it is in this characteristic of elections—not minority rule but minorities rule—that we must look for some of the essential differences between dictatorships and democracies." The logic pursued by Dahl is familiar to any student of democratic theory. The politicians being subject to elections must operate within limits set by "their expectations about what policies they can adopt and still be reelected." Elections, then, "are crucial processes for insuring that political leaders will be somewhat responsive to the preferences of some ordinary citizens."[2]

At first glance, the thesis that elections assure accountability of the governors to governed is a persuasive one. It does, however, rest upon the two assumptions we noted earlier: (1) Elections are the route to political office, and (2) men once in office will wish to remain there. But our analysis has uncovered at least a half-dozen reasons for doubting that elections are the critical device for insuring accountability in the communities studied.

In the first place, nearly one-quarter of the councilmen begin their careers in office by being appointed. For them, the route to office requires no appeal for voter support. This fact, when combined with our knowledge of the very high incumbent win ratio (four out of five incumbents who stand for reelection are success-

---

2 Robert A. Dahl, *Preface to Democratic Theory* (Chicago: University of Chicago Press, 1956), pp. 131–32.

ful) should caution us against the easy assumption that account-ability is assured by the simple occurrence of periodic elections.

Not only do councilmen frequently gain office with no atten-tion to elections, but they leave office for reasons other than elec-tion defeat. There is a high rate of voluntary retirement from office, as councilmen have set self-imposed limits on their tenure. Nearly one-fifth plan definitely to retire at the end of the present term; another third or so of the incumbents appear to be planning for only one more term. A high and persistent rate of voluntary departure from office suggests the need for a major qualification to the thesis that elections assure accountability of officeholders. For if the elected official plans to exit from office in any case, why should he fear voter disapproval? And if he has no need to fear voter disapproval, what is the guarantee that he will feel "ac-countable"?

Yet another finding underlines the point. Incumbents not only retire voluntarily, but those who choose not to retire seldom are forced from office by an election defeat. In as many as twenty-one cities no incumbent failed to be reelected if he so wished. In fewer than a half-dozen cities did as many as even half the incumbents fail to stay in office if they stood for reelection. If it is so atypical for the general election to eliminate incumbents, it is difficult to believe that the councilmen are restrained by "their expectations about what policies they can adopt and still be reelected."[3]

Findings showing the relatively weak impact of elections in de-termining who stays and who leaves the councils are only part of the story. The interview data suggest another qualification to the thesis that elections can assure accountability. In any political system the pathways to office tend to be characterized by certain modal patterns. These patterns or common experiences become part of the political life and, hence, of the political folklore of the community. This folklore, in turn, influences the thinking of the men who spend many hours in close contact with political matters. An important pattern noted in the cities studied is the apparent emphasis on service in voluntary, civic roles as part of the approach to office. This pattern appears to be reflected in the thinking of the councilmen as an ethic of volunteerism.

Combined, then, with the de facto nonpaid and part-time vol-unteer status of the councilmen are leadership selection processes which repeatedly underscore this status. As observed earlier, the

---

3 *Ibid.*, p. 132.

elected council post is often little more than an extension of a community role formed by and spelled out in the numerous voluntary organizations that dominate civic life in the Bay Area cities. The community leaders first learn about managing the city in their duties either as volunteer civic workers or as businessmen. The civic and business roles which usher men into the elected positions are very unlike the role of political representative as explicated in the theoretical literature on democracy. There is no voting constituency which periodically reviews the actions and polices the behavior of men who serve in these voluntary positions.

Thus there is structured into city politics in these nonpartisan communities an ethic of volunteerism. This ethic can serve to undermine an already weakened election system. The volunteer in office, especially if he is relatively indifferent about staying there, may be a devoted public servant as he defines that role but he is unlikely to be constantly sensitive to voter preferences. His political thinking has been formed by a series of experiences which minimize for him the importance of mass electorates.[4]

Perhaps the case has been put too strongly. Certainly, city politics would not function just as they presently do if elections were suddenly to vanish. At the very least, elections serve as a reminder even for the volunteer councilman that he is supposed to consider voter preferences. Nevertheless, the findings indicate that the student of politics who would base his theory of representative democracy on the power of elections to enforce accountability would be making untenable empirical assumptions about the Bay Area cities.

Democratic Norms, Self-Restraint, and Accountability

There is a third broad hypothesis which attempts to explain accountability in representative democracy. Some students of politics propose that public officials hold themselves accountable, or, perhaps more accurately, that public officials measure their behavior against some normative standard or code of political ethics. It is this code, internalized by the leadership, which makes representative democracy work. Various authors have elaborated on this thesis but probably none so eloquently as V. O. Key.

---

[4] It is interesti g to consider Schlesinger's previously cited observation in the light of this stress on volunteerism in the recruitment of councilmen: "No more irresponsible government is imaginable than one of high-minded men unconcerned for their political futures." *Ambition and Politics* (Chicago: Rand McNally & Co., 1966), p. 2.

He begins, as do most observers of politics, with the axiom that, however democratic a system is, there still must be a division of labor. This division of labor implies in turn a political hierarchy in which citizens exercise unequal political influence. Once this axiom is accepted, Key writes, "the comprehension of democratic practices requires a search for the peculiar characteristics of the political influentials in such an order, for the special conditions under which they work, and for the means by which the people keep them in check."[5] Key is raising the question of representative democracy: How can a few have most of the political influence yet still be kept in check by the people? He answers:

> The longer one frets with the puzzle of how democratic regimes manage to function, the more plausible it appears that a substantial part of the explanation is to be found in the motives that actuate the leadership echelon, the values that it holds, in the rules of the political game to which it adheres, in the expectations which it entertains about its own status in society, and perhaps in some of the objective circumstances, both material, and institutional, in which it functions.[6]

These motives, values, rules, and expectations include, according to Key, a fundamental regard for the opinions of the people. The elected leaders are solicitous of the views of the masses not because the elected fear voter sanctions; rather, the governors remain sensitive to shifts of public sentiment because that is what men holding office *are supposed to do.*

Why do public officials think this way? Key uses socialization theory to comment about why the leaders behave and feel as they do.

> That theory amounts to the proposition that these political actors constitute in effect a subculture with its own peculiar set of norms of behavior, motives, and approved standards. Processes of indoctrination internalize such norms among those who are born to or climb to positions of power and leadership; they serve as standards of action, which are reinforced by a social discipline among the political activists. . . . Beliefs generally accepted among these persons tend to establish habits and patterns of behavior with considerable power of self-maintenance or persistence through time.[7]

Key has stated the argument with force. His is a proposition about democratic governance that, along with an emphasis on competitive elections and on the formal machinery of government, relies heavily on the values that leaders have come to hold. Leaders

5 V. O. Key, *Public Opinion and American Democracy* (New York: Alfred A. Knopf, 1964), p. 542.
6 *Ibid.,* p. 537.
7 *Ibid.,* pp. 537–38.

police themselves. We can consider how the data presented in this study might relate to Key's set of ideas.

There is, first of all, a clear indication that men governing the Bay Area cities were socialized into the general democratic culture of the United States. Insofar as this socialization includes instruction in the importance of limited power, of tolerance toward opposition, of civil liberties, and of minority rights, then these public officials are likely to have beliefs consonant with democratic practices. Insofar as their socialization into the subculture of political actives includes exposure to and acceptance of the norm that leaders should be sensitive to the public's wishes, the councilmen undoubtedly have retained a sensitivity to the preferences of the people.

Thus, in one sense, the general thesis put forth by Key appears to be sound. Councilmen have learned the political norms characteristic of the middle- and upper-middle-class citizens in the United States. Further, as members of the politically active stratum, they are repeatedly reminded of the virtues of the democratic form of government. However, some of the patterns revealed in the data lead us to be less sanguine than Key. It is not clear that internalized restraints are sufficient to guarantee a leadership accountable to the public.

Key makes a critical assumption: The code of political ethics presumably internalized by the leadership bids them to be sensitive to the less influential members of the community. Of interest to the theorist, then, is the way in which the leadership defines the "members of the community." Insofar as the experiences of the leader limit his vision, he will be unable adequately to see the full range of needs and pressures which are characteristic of his community. To use a cliché, "he will be out of touch." With this issue in mind, we can review two findings from our study of leadership selection.

The Politics of Replaceability. There are two general types of turnover in political leadership. One type, made famous by Pareto's phrase "the circulation of elites," results not only in a change of personnel but also in a change of policy. In Pareto's analysis, the circulation of elites is synonymous with social and political change. The second type of turnover is more aptly described by the phrase "interchangeability of elites," or, to use a phrase more descriptive of what we have found, "recruitment by replaceability." Under conditions of replaceability, there is leadership turnover but the new officials are nearly always chosen from those same circles which produced their predecessors. This pattern of replaceability, or substitutability, is consistent with the motivating impetus behind nonpartisan politics just as circulation of elites is probably consistent with competitive party politics. The politics of replaceability assure leadership turnover but need not lead to major changes in policy or program.

In applying gross typologies to the empirical case, one nearly always finds that the actual situation is mixed. Although leadership turnover in the Bay Area cities is both circulation and replaceability, it does appear that much more of the latter than the former occurs. This is not to say that councilmen handpick their successors. It is to say that the processes which elevate a few to positions of formal authority tend time and again to find recruits who think along lines similar to those who preceded them in office.

There is, then, structured into leadership selection a parochial quality to the experiences which put men into office. Although the active stratum itself may be formed by men of diverse backgrounds, the intramural recruitment processes which nominate and elect (or appoint) candidates to office appear to reward a set of modal characteristics. One officeholder, upon deciding to retire, is replaced by another with a roughly similar background.

The Restricted Constituency. There is to be found another pattern in the data which might be relevant to Key's thesis about the internalization of the democratic norm. The "constituency" which forces itself on the attention of the councilmen tends to be rather narrow. The intraelection period in the political life of the cities is dominated by civic and business leaders. The proportion of the population active in council matters expands somewhat during the campaign and election period, but even then the actives constitute a relatively narrow segment. This suggests that the constituency salient to the officeholders—if we assume that the more active citizens are the most likely to be seen—will represent a restricted part of the total population.

Why do these two patterns—one indicating a politics of replaceability and one indicating the presence of a restricted constituency—lead us to be less optimistic than Key about the self-restraint of leaders and the working of democracy? The Key thesis, it will be recalled, stresses that the norms which guide the public leader include the value of self-imposed responsiveness. But Key does not consider a critical question: What happens when the public which is seen by the councilman and with which he comes into frequent contact constitutes some political and social subset of the total community? The leadership can be responsive to those they consider the appropriate spokesmen for the community and yet representative democracy, defined as Key has done so, will not be working.

The Unresolved Paradox

The study of leadership selection in eighty-seven American cities begins with a puzzle and ends with a puzzle. In exploring data about the first puzzle—how do the few who govern come to be selected from the many who are governed?—we uncover the second one. The leadership selection processes help create and sustain a political system in which the governors are unlike the governed; how, then, does representative democracy work?

Two traditional answers to this question can be challenged on the basis of the data presented. First, it does not appear that the hovering presence of electoral sanctions serves to guarantee that the councilmen will be constantly solicitous of public preferences. Second, there are reasons to doubt that a set of normative restraints are sufficient to assure leadership sensitivity to the full range of possible public preferences.

Since the working of representative democracy is one of those things the student of political recruitment hopes to understand, these findings help us in our theoretical endeavors. At the least, the data fail to confirm some important hypotheses; interpreted in stronger language, the data falsify some widely held hypotheses. Still, having said this, we must conclude that the study has not been able to answer the question of what makes representative democracy work in the face of "unrepresentative governors." It is perhaps in data other than those devoted to leadership selection that we must seek the answer.

Appendix: The Research Project and the Data

This Appendix provides a brief *description* of the *context* for the analyses and interpretations reported in this and the other monographs of *The Urban Governors* series. These analyses and interpretations are grounded in or inspired by data collected at a specific "point" in time—actually over a period of some eighteen months, from January 1966 to June 1967—in a particular region of the United States. The data are "representative," therefore, in only a very limited sense. Although none of the writers of each monograph would claim greater universality for his interpretations than the data warrant, the temptation on a reader's part to forget or ignore the limitations of a clearly bounded space-time manifold is always present. The reader is entitled, therefore, to information about the setting of each study, if only for comparison with settings which are more familiar to him and which serve as his own frames of reference.

Needless to say, we cannot describe here the San Francisco Bay metropolitan region, its cities and its people, in their full richness and diversity. Clearly, only certain aspects of the environment are relevant, and this relevance must be determined by the objectives of the particular research project in which we were engaged. Before presenting the relevant context, therefore, the research project itself will be described in brief outline.

The City Council Research Project

As mentioned already in the Preface, the Project was a research and training program with as many as twelve participants working together at one time. Because the Project was intended, from the beginning, to maximize the independent research creativity of each participant, the research design had to be sufficiently flexible to permit the collection of data which would satisfy each Project member's research concerns. The monographs in this series reflect the heterogeneity of the research interests which found their way into the Project. At the same time, each researcher was necessarily limited by the Project's overall objective, which was, throughout, to gather data which would shed light on the city council as a small political decision-making group.

Our interest in the city council as a decision-making group stemmed from prior research on governance through democratic legislative processes. Political scientists have been traditionally concerned with the variety of "influences," external to the legislative body as well as internal, that shape both the legislative process and the legislative product. It was an assumption of the research that these influences could be studied more intensively in the case of small bodies than in the case of larger ones, like state legislatures or Congress, that already have been widely investigated. In particular, it was assumed that a decision-making body is both the sum of its parts and greater than the sum of its parts. Therefore, both the council as a collective unit and the councilman as an individual unit could be selected for the purposes of analysis. In the major book of this series, by Heinz Eulau and Kenneth Prewitt, the council as such serves as the unit of analysis. In the accompanying monographs, individual councilmen primarily serve as the units.

Convenience apart, the choice of the universe to be studied was dictated by the research objective. On the one hand, we needed a sufficiently large number of decision-making groups to permit systematic, quantitative, and genuinely comparative analyses at the group level. On the other hand, we needed a universe in which "influences" on the individual decision-maker and the decision-making group could be studied in a relatively uniform context. In particular, we sought a universe which provided a basic environmental, political, and legal uniformity against which city-by-city differences could be appraised. We therefore decided on a single metropolitan region in a single state in which we could assume certain constants to be present—such as *relative* economic growth, similar institutional arrangements and political patterns, identical state statutory requirements, and so on.

The price paid for this research design should be obvious. The San Francisco Bay metropolitan region is quite unlike any other metropolitan region, including even the Los Angeles metropolitan area, and it differs significantly from the Chicago, Boston, or New

York metropolitan complexes. Undoubtedly, metropolitan regions, despite internal differences, can be compared as ecological units in their own right. But as our units of analysis are individual or collective decision-makers in the cities of a particular, and in many respects internally unique region, the parameters imposed on our data by the choice of the San Francisco Bay metropolitan area recommend the greatest caution in extending, whether by analogy or inference, our findings to councils or councilmen in other metropolitan regions of other states.

All of this is not to say that particular analyses enlightened by theoretical concerns of a general nature cannot be absorbed into the growing body of political science knowledge. The City Council Research Project consciously built on previous research in other settings, seeking to identify and measure influences that have an impact on legislative processes and legislative products. The effect of the role orientations of councilmen with regard to their constituents, interest groups, or administrative officials may be compared with the effect of parallel orientations in larger legislative bodies. Their socialization and recruitment experiences, their differing styles of representational behavior, or their political strategies are probably influences not unlike those found elsewhere. Similarly, the relationships among individuals in a small group and the norms guiding their conduct may be compared with equivalent patterns in larger legislative bodies. Perceptions of the wider metropolitan environment and its problems, on the one hand, and of the city environment and its problems, on the other hand, and how these perceptions affect council behavior and outputs are of general theoretical interest. In terms of the developing theory of legislative behavior and processes, therefore, the data collected by the Project and utilized in the monographs of this series have an import that transcends the boundaries of the particular metropolitan region in which they were collected.

The Research Context

San Francisco and its neighboring eight counties have experienced an extraordinary population growth rate since the end of World War II. Many of the wartime production workers and military personnel who traveled to or through this region decided to settle here permanently in the postwar years; they and thousands of others were attracted by moderate climate year around, several outstanding universities, closeness to the Pacific Ocean and its related harbors, headquarters for hundreds of West Coast branches of national firms and, of course, the delightful charm of San Francisco itself. Other resources and assets exist in abundance: Inviting ski resorts and redwood parks are within short driving distance; hundreds of miles of ocean lie to the immediate west; mile after mile of grape vineyards landscape the nearby Livermore and Napa valleys. All of these, linked by the vast San Francisco Bay and its famous bridges, make this one of the nation's most distinctive and popular metropolitan regions.

Larger than the state of Connecticut and almost as large as New Jersey and Massachusetts combined, this nine-county region now houses four million people; about six million more are expected by 1980. At the time of the study, ninety cities and at least five hundred special districts served its residents.

As has been pointed out already, no claim can be made that the San Francisco Bay region is typical of other metropolitan areas; indeed, it differs considerably on a number of indicators. Unlike most of the other sizable metropolitan regions, the Bay region has experienced its major sustained population boom in the 1950's and 1960's. This metropolitan area is also atypical in that it has not one major central city but three—namely San Francisco, Oakland, and San Jose. And while San Francisco continues to be the "hub" and the region's dominant city, Oakland and San Jose are rival economic and civic centers. San Jose, moreover, anticipates that its population will triple to nearly a million people in the next twenty years. Of additional interest is the fact that this region has pioneered in the creation of one of the nation's prototypes of federated urban governmental structures. Its Association of Bay Area Governments, organized in 1961, has won national attention as one of the first metropolitan councils of local governments.

Although in many respects unlike other metropolitan regions, the San Francisco Bay region resembles some in the great diversity among its cities. Omitting San Francisco proper, 1965 city populations ranged from 310 to 385,700. Population densities in 1965 ranged from 71 to 12,262 persons per square mile. The rate of population growth between 1960 and 1965 ranged from zero to 204 percent. Median family incomes ranged from $3,582 to $23,300, and percent nonwhite from 0.1 to 26.4.

Institutionally, the governments of the cities in the San Francisco Bay region are predominantly of the council-manager or council-administrator form, although some of the very small cities may

Map A–1
Bay Area Place Names

rely on the chief engineer rather than on a manager or administrator. Cities may be either of the "charter" or "general law" type. Charter cities differ from general law cities in having greater control over election laws, the size of their councils, the pay of municipal officers, and tax rate limitations. General law cities have five councilmen, while charter cities may have more than this number. Among the cities included in the research, the number of councilmen per city ranged from five to thirteen.

All local officials in California, including, of course, those interviewed in the City Council Research Project, are elected under a nonpartisan system. With a few exceptions, councilmen run at large and against the entire field of candidates. In five cities there is a modified district election plan in which candidates stand in a particular district but all voters cast ballots for any candidate. Ten cities elect the mayor separately; in the remaining cities the mayor is either the candidate receiving the highest number of votes or is selected by vote of the council.

Council candidates must have been residents of the community for at least one year prior to their election. For the most part they are elected to serve two-year terms, though charter cities may vary this. Only three cities have tenure limitations. The great majority of councilmen receive no compensation for their services or, if any, only a token compensation to cover expenses. For most, the council is a part-time activity.

The powers of the city councilmen may be exercised only as a group; that is, individual councilmen have no power to act alone. The council may meet only at duly convened public meetings and at a place designated by ordinance. Council meetings must be regularly scheduled and held no less than once a month, but when council action is required between regularly scheduled meetings, the statutes allow procedures for calling special meetings. The "Brown Act," passed in 1953 and in effect during the time our interviewing took place, requires all council meetings to be public and publicized, except for executive sessions on personnel matters.

The Data Bases

Five sets of data were generated or systematized by the Project. First, data from the U.S. Census of Population for 1960 and estimates for 1965 served a variety of analytical purposes. Because the data included in the census and its categories are well known, we need not say more about this data set. Specific uses made of census data and the rationale for such uses are explained in each monograph wherever appropriate. All members of the research team were involved in readying the census data for analysis.

Second, data concerning city income, resources, and expenditures were available in the State Controller's *Annual Report of Financial Transactions Concerning Cities of California.* These reports include breakdowns which are suitable for comparative analysis of Bay region cities for the year 1958–59 through 1965–66. How the measures derived from this data set were handled is described in appropriate places of the monograph series where the data are used. Robert Eyestone was largely responsible for preparing this data set.

Third, local election data over a ten-year period, 1956 through 1966, were collected by Gordon Black, with the collaboration of Willis D. Hawley at the Institute of Governmental Studies, University of California, Berkeley. These data were obtained directly from the various cities, and they include the voting returns for each of five elections in each city, the registration figures for the city at each election period, and a variety of facts about individual candidates. These facts include incumbency, partisan affiliation, length of time in office, and the manner in which the incumbents gained office, whether by appointment or by election. A number of measures were constructed from these data, including measures of competition, partisan composition, voluntary retirement, forced turnover, and so forth. Descriptions of these measures can be found in the monographs which employ them.

Fourth and fifth, the core of the data on which the analyses are based came from interviews with city councilmen or from self-administered questionnaires filled out by councilmen. These two data sets need more detailed exposition.

1. *Interview data.* With the exception of a city incorporated while the field work was under way (Yountville) and the city of San Francisco itself, interviews were sought with 488 city councilmen holding office in all the other eighty-nine cities of the San Francisco Bay area. Although interviews were held with some members of the board of supervisors of the city-county of San Francisco, these interviews are not used in this and the other monographs, owing to the city's unique governmental structure and the highly professionalized nature of its legislative body.

In two of the eighty-nine cities (Millbrae and Emeryville), all councilmen refused to be interviewed. In the remaining eighty-seven cities, 435 incumbent councilmen were interviewed. This constitutes 89 percent of the total population or 91 percent of the councilmen from the eighty-seven cities which cooperated in the study. The interviews were conducted by members of the research team or by professional interviewers. Most of the respondents were interviewed in their homes, places of business, or city hall offices. All of them had been invited to visit the Stanford campus, and a small number accepted the invitation and were interviewed there.

Although the bulk of the interviewing was done between January and April 1966, some councilmen were interviewed as late as June 1967. The interview schedule was an extensive one. It included some 165 major open-end questions and additional probes, ranging over a wide variety of topics. Every effort was made to record verbatim the comments which most councilmen supplied in abundance. The interviews lasted from two to five hours or longer and averaged about three hours. Parts of the interview schedule were pretested as early as 1962 and as late as 1965, with councilmen in the metropolitan region itself and with councilmen in a neighboring county.

The interview data were coded by members of the research team responsible for particular analyses. The coded data were recorded on seventeen machine readable storage cards. They will be made available for secondary analysis on tape in due time, upon completion of all studies in *The Urban Governors* series.

2. *Questionnaire.* In addition to the interview, each respondent was asked to fill out a questionnaire made up of closed questions. These included a set of thirty-five check-list items, two pages of biographical items, and a set of fifty-eight agree-disagree attitude items. The strategy of self-administered questionnaires was dictated by the length of the interview, for, in spite of its length, the data needs of the team members could not be satisfied by the interview instrument alone. The questionnaires were left with each respondent by the interviewer. If at all possible, interviewers were instructed to have the questionnaires filled out by the respondent immediately upon completion of the interview, but the length of the interview often did not permit this, and respondents were then asked to return the questionnaires by mail. As a result, there was some loss of potential data because councilmen neglected to return the completed forms. Nevertheless, of the 435 councilmen who were interviewed, 365, or 84 percent, completed the question-

naires. Perhaps the greatest strategic mistake in this procedure was our failure to administer the biographical and demographic background items as part of the interview.

The Sample: A Brief Profile

Although individual demographic data for all 435 councilmen who were interviewed are not available, our sample of 365 for which the data are at hand is probably representative. We shall present, therefore, a brief profile of these respondents.

On the average, San Francisco Bay region councilmen are well educated and have comfortable incomes (see Figure A–1). They are engaged in either business or professional activities. Table A–1 shows the principal lines of work of those council members who are not retired or housewives.

Table A–1

Principal Employment of City Councilmen
(Of Employed Councilmen) (N = 351)

Manufacturing, Utilities	22%
Banking, Insurance, Accountancy	21
Business, Commerce, Real Estate	13
Lawyer	10
Construction, Trucking	16
Civil Servant, Public Administration	14
Agriculture	4
	100%

Councilmen in the Bay region are predominantly middle-aged, usually coming to the council while in their forties or around fifty years of age. The turnover rate of city councilman positions is relatively high, with only a few members staying in office for more than three or four terms. The data in Figure A–1 show that close to 70 percent of the councilmen came into office for the first time within the previous five years. In open-end conversations with councilmen, many responded that they looked upon the job as a community service, as something that should be rotated among the local activists like themselves.

Fifty-six percent of the Bay region councilmen who are currently employed work in their home community, the community on whose city council they serve. This is not too surprising, for it is customary for local "home town" businessmen and lawyers to

Figure A–1

Background Profile of San Francisco Bay Region
City Councilmen

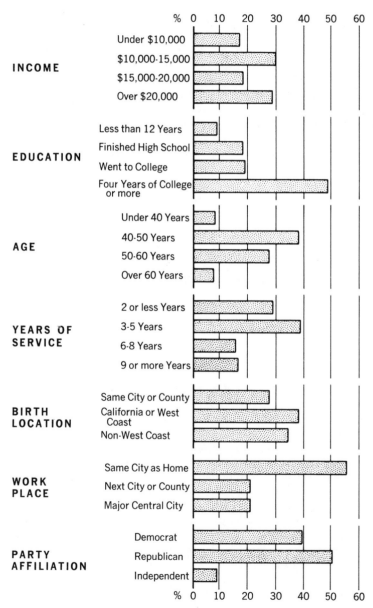

be involved in community service and civic undertakings, which often constitute the chief recruitment vehicle for the identification of city political leadership. While a majority of the councilmen are employed in their local communities, it is instructive to note that most of the councilmen are not natives of their present city or county. Most, however, are California or West Coast natives. Approximately a third moved to the Bay region from other parts of the United States, with about a dozen having been born in some other country.

The background profile data also indicate that Republicans outnumber the Democrats by an 11 percent margin in the Bay region's nonpartisan city council posts, although during recent years the party registration rates for the general electorate have favored the Democratic party in approximately a three-to-two ratio. Nine percent of the councilmen identify themselves as Independents.

Bibliography

Excellent bibliographies on political recruitment, political elites, and political leadership are readily available. Thus, rather than append a lengthy list of titles here, I will simply indicate, in a three-part bibliographic note, the writings which have most influenced the preparation of this study of city councilmen. First, for bibliographic sources I found the bibliographies as well as the cited studies in the following works to be particularly useful: *Public Leadership* by Wendell Bell, Richard Hill, and Charles R. Wright (San Francisco: Chandler Publishing Co., 1961) is an exhaustive though noncritical review of works published prior to 1960; an annotated bibliography prepared by George T. Force and Jack R. Van Der Slik, *Theory and Research in the Study of Political Leadership* (Public Affairs Research Bureau, Southern Illinois University, 1969), can be used with profit to update Bell et al., as well as other earlier bibliographies. Less ambitious bibliographic efforts though for some purposes of broader scope can be found in T. B. Bottomore, *Elites and Society* (London: C. A. Watts, 1964); Suzanne Keller, *Beyond the Ruling Class* (New York: Random House, 1963); and Dwaine Marvick (ed.), *Political Decision-Makers* (New York: The Free Press of Glencoe, 1961). A useful interdisciplinary bibliography is one compiled by Lewis J. Edinger and Donald Searing, included in Edinger (ed.), *Political Leadership in Industrialized Societies* (New York: John Wiley & Sons, 1967).

Second, general theoretical writings of several political scholars were referred to often during the design of the study and during the writing stage. These include: David Easton, *A Systems Analysis of Political Life* (New York: John Wiley & Sons, 1965); Suzanne Keller, *Beyond the Ruling Class* (New York: Random House,

1963); Harold Lasswell, *Politics, Who Gets What, When, and How* (New York: McGraw-Hill Book Co., 1936); Lasswell and Daniel Lerner (eds.), *World Revolutionary Elites* (Cambridge: M.I.T. Press, 1966); and Lasswell's essay "The Selective Effect of Personality on Political Participation," in R. Christie and M. Jahoda (eds.), *Studies in the Scope and Method of "The Authoritarian Personality"* (Glencoe, Ill.: The Free Press, 1954); Gaetano Mosca, *The Ruling Class* (New York: McGraw-Hill Book Co., 1939); and Max Weber's writings, see Hans H. Gerth and C. Wright Mills (eds.), *From Max Weber: Essays in Sociology* (New York: Oxford University Press, 1946).

Finally, the book-length empirical studies, or collections of studies, which were a constant source of ideas as well as providing data against which to measure findings from the study of city councilmen include: David Barber, *The Lawmakers: Recruitment and Adaptation to Legislative Life* (New Haven: Yale University Press, 1965); Robert A. Dahl, *Who Governs?* (New Haven: Yale University Press, 1961); Samuel J. Eldersveld, *Political Parties: A Behavioral Analysis* (Chicago: Rand McNally & Co., 1964); Heinz Eulau and John Sprague, *Lawyers in Politics* (Indianapolis: Bobbs-Merrill Co., 1964); Eugene Lee, *The Politics of Non-partisanship* (Berkeley and Los Angeles: The University of California Press, 1960); Dwaine Marvick (ed.), *Political Decision-Makers* (New York: The Free Press of Glencoe, 1961); Donald Matthews, *The Social Background of Political Decision-Makers* (Garden City, N.Y.: Doubleday & Co., 1954) and *U.S. Senators and Their World* (New York: Random House Vintage Books, 1960); C. Wright Mills, *The Power Elite* (New York: Oxford University Press, 1956); Joseph Schlesinger, *Ambition and Politics* (Chicago: Rand McNally & Co., 1966); John Wahlke, Heinz Eulau, William Buchanan, and LeRoy C. Ferguson, *The Legislative System: Explorations in Legislative Behavior* (New York: John Wiley & Sons, 1962).

Index

Accountability, 209
   and constitutional checks, 209–210
   and democratic norms, 212–214
   and electoral sanctions, 210–212
Achievement traits, 23, 65
Active stratum, 9–10, 53–56
   formation of, 59–62, 76–77, 91, 104–106
Adrian, Charles R., 140, 143n, 146
Age
   and political ambitions, 188–189
   and political socialization, 63–64, 83
Agger, Robert E., 193n
Almond, Gabriel, 85n
Altbach, Philip G., 70n
Ambitions, 11, 19, 175–176
   and age, 188–189
   and political opportunity, 185–188
   and views of the electorate, 198–200
Anticipatory socialization, 120, 156, 166, 190
Apoliticalness, 102–103, 136, 183
Appointment to office, 5, 27
   as co-optation, 135
   numbers, 131
   as sponsorship, 133–135
   success of, 137
Apprenticeship, 5, 10, 12, 27, 112–113, 119
Ascriptive traits, 23, 65
Association of Bay Area Governments, 187, 220
Auxiliary government, 132, 139

Banfield, Edward C., 101n
Barber, James David, 28n, 30n, 66n, 91n, 119–120, 151–152, 168, 190n, 202
Bell, Wendell, 24n, 25n, 43n, 98n
Bendix, Reinhard, 162n
Black, Gordon, 130n
Blacks, 42, 44, 143
Browning, Rufus P., 66n, 96n
Bryce, James, 4
Buchanan, William, 20n, 66n, 170n
Businessmen, 29, 40
   in politics, 89–90, 124, 157–159

Campaigns, 139, 149, 197–198
Campbell, Angus, 54n, 75n
Candidates, 7, 13, 53, 109, 118
Caplow, Theodore, 156n
Career choice, 111
Careers, political, 20, 57
   and elections, 117–118
   and sponsorship, 5, 18
Chinese Box Puzzle, 6–8, 22, 36, 55, 174, 205
City commissions, 112, 166–167
City Council Research Project, vii, 217, 219, 222
Civic associations
   and leadership selection, 84–86, 143, 161
   and volunteerism, 211–212
Class, social. See Socioeconomic bias
Cole, G. D. H., 125

231